"If you can't explain it simply, you don't understand it well enough."
-Albert Einstein

Copyright, Use, and Resale Prohibitions
All content in this book is copyrighted under the U.S. Copyright laws, and NEVER LIMITED PUBLISHING owns the copyright and the Book itself. Other than as stated in this Single Use License Agreement, you may not copy, print, modify, remove, delete, augment, add to, publish, transmit, sell, resell, create derivative works from, or in any way exploit any of the book's content, in whole or in part, and you may not aid or permit others to do so. The unauthorized use or distribution of copyrighted or other proprietary content is illegal and could subject the purchaser to substantial money damages. Purchaser will be liable for any damage resulting from any violation of this License Agreement, including any infringement of copyrights or proprietary rights.

PMI-ACP, PMI-RMP, PMP, PMI-SP, PgMP, CAPM, PMBOK, and PMI are registered marks of the Project Management Institute, Inc. All other products or services mentioned in this book are trademarks of their respective companies or organizations.

Author: Al Smith, Jr. PMI-ACP, Lean/Six Sigma Black Belt, CRISC, SCJP, CFT
Co-Author: Vanina Mangano, PMP, PMI-RMP, PMI-SP, ITIL, Project+
The PM Instructors™

A Never Limited Publishing Book
ISBN 978-1469964188

Ver 3.8-8-12

Printed in the United States of America.

All rights reserved.
Copyright © 2012 by The PM Instructors™

First Printing 2012
Never Limited Publishing books may be purchased for educational, business, or sales promotional use.
For more information contact 888-687-6629.

# Table of Contents

## Course Introduction ........... 11
### Learning Objectives ........... 12
### The Project Management Institute ........... 13
### PMI's Code of Ethics and Professional Conduct ........... 15
### Exam Costs ........... 16
#### Eligibility Window ........... 16
#### CCR ........... 16
### Exam Requirements ........... 17
#### Education Background ........... 17
#### Education Background ........... 17
#### Training Providers ........... 17
### Application Process ........... 19
### Exam Format ........... 20
### Exam Blueprint ........... 21
### Using the Course Materials ........... 26
### Using the Course Materials ........... 27
#### Record to Memory ........... 27
### Sample Question ........... 28
### Exam Question Characteristics & Components ........... 30
#### ormat of Questions ........... 30
#### The Challenge ........... 30
### Brain Dump ........... 31
### Study Tips ........... 32
### Preparing for Exam Day ........... 33
### Summary ........... 34

## Introduction to Agile ........... 35
### Agile Introduction ........... 36
### Terminology Lesson ........... 37
### History ........... 39
### Manifesto Values and Principles ........... 41
#### Twelve Principles ........... 42
### The Agile Framework ........... 45
#### Software Development Lifecycle ........... 45
### Variations in Agile Methods and Approaches ........... 46
#### Agile Software Development Methods ........... 46
### Framework Comparison ........... 47
### Incremental Development ........... 48
#### Agile Software Development ........... 48
### Assessing Suitability ........... 49
### Agile Modeling ........... 50
### Applying New Agile Practices ........... 51
### Principles of Systems Thinking ........... 52
#### Process Engineering ........... 52
#### Defined Process Control ........... 53
### Process Engineering ........... 54
#### Empirical Process Control Model ........... 54
### Control Limits for Agile Projects ........... 56

| Waterfall Methodology | 58 |
|---|---|
| Agile vs. XP vs. Scrum Terminology | 59 |
| Pulling It All Together | 60 |
| Reinforcement Training | 62 |
| Agile Self-Assessment | 63 |
| Summary | 66 |

## Module 1: Value Drive Delivery ............................................................................ 67

| Module 1 Objectives | 68 |
|---|---|
| **Quality Control Process** | **69** |
| Verification and Validation | 69 |
| **Maximizing Values and Minimizing Waste** | **70** |
| Thinking Lean Centers on 5 Basic Principles | 70 |
| **Chartering** | **71** |
| **Value-Based Analysis** | **73** |
| Value-Driven Planning | 74 |
| **Value-Driving Planning** | **75** |
| Product and Innovation Development | 76 |
| **How to Identify Value** | **77** |
| **Increase Value through Quality** | **81** |
| Quality, Six Sigma, Lean | 81 |
| Drivers of Quality | 82 |
| **Customer Value Prioritization** | **83** |
| Applying Lean to Build-in Quality | 83 |
| **Anti-Value** | **84** |
| Risk Erodes Value | 84 |
| **Anti-Value Planning** | **86** |
| **Early Value** | **87** |
| Incremental Delivery | 87 |
| **Release Early, Release Often** | **89** |
| **Positive Value** | **90** |
| Incorporating Customer Feedback Loops, Conditions of Customer Satisfaction | 90 |
| Collecting the Voice of the Customer | 91 |
| Conditions of Customer Satisfaction Categories | 92 |
| The Kano Model of Customer Satisfaction | 94 |
| **Customer Feedback Techniques** | **95** |
| Collecting the Voice of the Customer (VOC) | 95 |
| **Value Stream Analysis** | **96** |
| Value Chain, Value Stream | 96 |
| Make the System "Fast-Flexible-Flow" | 98 |
| Value Stream Mapping | 100 |
| **Optimizing the Value Stream** | **101** |
| Value Stream Diagram | 101 |
| Takt Time/Cycle Time | 102 |
| Emergent Design | 103 |
| Acceptance Testing | 105 |
| **Operating as a Lean/Agile Organization** | **106** |
| Know the Health of your Project | 106 |
| Enterprise Risk Management | 108 |
| Just in Time (JIT) | 110 |

- Kanban ........................................................................................................................ 111
  - Kanban Board ........................................................................................................ 112
  - Incremental Delivery ............................................................................................. 113
  - Minimal Marketable Feature ................................................................................. 115
- **Value-Based Prioritization** ....................................................................................... 116
  - Customer-Value Prioritization .............................................................................. 117
  - Net Present Value (NPV) ....................................................................................... 118
  - Return On Investment (ROI) ................................................................................. 119
- **Calculating Financial Operational Efficiency** ........................................................ 120
  - Payback Period ...................................................................................................... 120
  - Discounted Payback Period .................................................................................. 122
- **Reinforcement Training** ............................................................................................. 123
- **Exercise 1** ...................................................................................................................... 124
- **Module 1 Quiz** ............................................................................................................. 125
- **Summary** ...................................................................................................................... 131

# Module 2: Stakeholder Engagement ............................................................................ 132
- **Module 2 Objectives** .................................................................................................... 133
- **Managing Stakeholder** ................................................................................................ 134
  - Identifying Stakeholders ....................................................................................... 134
- **Empowering Stakeholders** ......................................................................................... 135
  - Stakeholder Management vs. Engagement ......................................................... 135
  - Make Issues Highly Visible and Readily Available ........................................... 136
- **Commitment Required from Stakeholders** ............................................................. 138
  - Stakeholder Engagement Differs from Stakeholder Management .................. 138
- **User the Value Stream to Ensure User Knowledge** ................................................ 139
  - Multiple Stakeholders Who Will Derive Value from Your Product ............... 139
- **Promoting Collaboration and Participation** ............................................................ 140
  - Improving the Stakeholder Engagement Value Stream .................................... 140
- **Who are the Stakeholders** .......................................................................................... 141
  - The Key Stakeholders Found in 5 Categories ..................................................... 141
- **Who Has What at Stake?** ............................................................................................ 142
  - The Business ........................................................................................................... 142
  - The Customers ........................................................................................................ 145
  - Domain Experts ...................................................................................................... 148
  - Developers .............................................................................................................. 150
  - End Users ................................................................................................................ 152
- **Continuous Improvement** .......................................................................................... 154
  - Managing Stakeholder Expectations .................................................................... 154
  - Both Lean and Agile Can Help Us ........................................................................ 156
  - Seven Principles of Stakeholder Engagement .................................................... 157
- **Agile Business Case Development** ........................................................................... 158
  - Making Your Business Case .................................................................................. 158
- **Elements of an Agile Project Charter** ....................................................................... 159
  - Capturing the Values of Stakeholders ................................................................. 159
  - Product Overview Documents .............................................................................. 160
- **Meeting the Business Objectives** .............................................................................. 161
  - Participatory Decision-Making (PDM) ................................................................ 161
- **Progress Reports** .......................................................................................................... 162
  - Information Radiators ........................................................................................... 162
- **Managerial Reports** ..................................................................................................... 165

- Reports to Stay Away From ..................................................................................................... 166
- Reinforcement Training .......................................................................................................... 167
- Exercise 2 ................................................................................................................................ 168
- Module 2 Quiz ......................................................................................................................... 169
- Summary ................................................................................................................................. 174

# Module 3: Boosting Team Performance Practices ............................................... 175
## Module 3 Objectives ............................................................................................................. 176
## Characteristics of a High-Performance Team ...................................................................... 177
- High-Performance Teams Are the Special Forces of an Agile Organization ....................... 177
- Clearly Defined Vision .......................................................................................................... 178
- Established Levels of Competence ...................................................................................... 179
- Empowered to Solve Problems ............................................................................................ 180

## Traditional Team Roles and Responsibilities ........................................................................ 181
- The Team Defines When It's Done ....................................................................................... 181
- Types of Teams ..................................................................................................................... 182
- Advantages and Disadvantages of Teams ............................................................................ 187

## Factors that Increase Success .............................................................................................. 188
- Team Space/ Osmotic Communication ................................................................................ 188
- Falling Short of Success ........................................................................................................ 189

## Why Teams Fall Short of Success ......................................................................................... 190
- Environmental Influences .................................................................................................... 190
- Goals ..................................................................................................................................... 191
- Roles ..................................................................................................................................... 192
- Relationships ........................................................................................................................ 193
- Processes .............................................................................................................................. 194

## Increasing Team Success Rates ............................................................................................ 195
- Team Contracts .................................................................................................................... 195

## Connecting with Your Team ................................................................................................. 199
- Emotional Intelligence/Servant Leadership ......................................................................... 199

## Expanding your Emotional Intelligence ............................................................................... 200
- Parker Team Player Survey (PTPS) ....................................................................................... 200

## Players on the Team ............................................................................................................. 201
- The Contributor ................................................................................................................... 201
- The Communicator/The Challenger .................................................................................... 202
- The Collaborator .................................................................................................................. 203

## Team Dynamics .................................................................................................................... 204
- Balancing between Contributor and Collaborator .............................................................. 204

## Interpersonal Growth Within Team Growth ....................................................................... 205
- Self-Assessment ................................................................................................................... 205
- Extend your Repertoire by Incorporating More the Strengths of other Styles .................. 206

## Team Growth ....................................................................................................................... 207
- Building Team Trust Through Commitments ...................................................................... 207
- Protecting your Team .......................................................................................................... 209

## Coaching and Mentoring Teams .......................................................................................... 210
- The Stages of Team Development ...................................................................................... 210

## Team Development ............................................................................................................. 211
## High Performance Teams .................................................................................................... 215
- Forming a High-Performance Team .................................................................................... 215

## Conflict Resolution .............................................................................................................. 216
## Roles and Responsibilities ................................................................................................... 218

  Roles and Responsibilities ............................................................................................ 218
**Makeup of an Agile Team** ........................................................................................................ **219**
**Building an Agile Project Team** ................................................................................................. **220**
  Agile Team Member Qualities .................................................................................... 220
  project manager vs. Agile Coach................................................................................. 221
**Team Inspiration** ....................................................................................................................... **222**
  Adaptive Leadership .................................................................................................... 222
**Establishing Agile Team Values** ............................................................................................... **223**
  Agile Team Values ....................................................................................................... 223
  Agile Team Principles/Agile Team Practices .............................................................. 224
  How to Motivate a Team ............................................................................................. 225
  Creating a Value-Driven Agile Team Environment/Service Leadership ..................... 226
**The Art of Faciiltation** .............................................................................................................. **227**
  Facilitating Cross-Functional Teams ........................................................................... 227
  Facilitating Distributed Teams .................................................................................... 228
**Creating a Safe Team Environment** ......................................................................................... **230**
  Team Dynamic and Hierarchy ..................................................................................... 230
**Team Collaboration** .................................................................................................................. **232**
  Cooperation vs. Collaboration ..................................................................................... 232
**Close Communication** .............................................................................................................. **234**
  Agile Customer Communication ................................................................................. 234
  Communication Stratagems ........................................................................................ 235
  Release Planning Meeting ........................................................................................... 236
  Iteration Planning Meeting ......................................................................................... 238
  Daily Stand-Up Meeting .............................................................................................. 239
  Review Meeting .......................................................................................................... 241
  Retrospective Meeting ................................................................................................ 242
  Communication Creates Commitment ....................................................................... 243
  What Does It Mean to Be Left Alone? ........................................................................ 244
**Leadership Techniques** ............................................................................................................ **245**
  Moving from Innocence to Mastery ........................................................................... 245
**Work Practices to Keep the Team Together** .......................................................................... **247**
**Team Maintenance** .................................................................................................................. **248**
  Building and Maintaining High-Performance Is One of the Principles of Agile Organizations ................. 248
  Gratuitously Offer Genuine Positive Feedback .......................................................... 249
  Insist on Excellence but Understand that Employees are Human ............................. 250
**Reinforcement Training** ........................................................................................................... **251**
**Exercise 3** .................................................................................................................................. **252**
**Module 3 Quiz** .......................................................................................................................... **253**
**Summary** ................................................................................................................................... **258**

**Module 4: Adaptive Planning** ................................................................................................... **259**
**Module 4 Objectives** ................................................................................................................. **260**
**Adaptive Planning in Action** ..................................................................................................... **261**
  Agile Software Development ...................................................................................... 261
  Just Enough Planning .................................................................................................. 263
  Adapting Planning Helps Provide Better Visibility to Stakeholders ........................... 264
  Making the Commitment to Deliver at the Beginning of Each Iteration ................... 265
  Trust, Commitment, and Collaboration ..................................................................... 266
  Trust Requires Commitment and Collaboration ........................................................ 268
**Why Discipline is Required** ...................................................................................................... **269**

    Sustainable Adaptive Planning Requires an Organization the Respects Change ........... 271

## Planning at Multiple Levels .......... 273
    Planning at the Last Responsible Moment .......... 273
    Planning Horizons .......... 274
    Rolling Wave Planning .......... 275
    Progressive Elaboration .......... 276
    Comparing Planning Techniques .......... 278

## Project Decomposition .......... 279
    Feasibility Study Projects .......... 279

## Planning Strategy .......... 280
    Basic Execution Sequence .......... 280

## Levels of Planning .......... 282
    5 Levels of Agile Planning .......... 282
    Vision and Roadmap/Strategy .......... 283
    Release Planning/Iteration Planning .......... 284
    Daily Planning .......... 285

## Planning Techniques .......... 286
    The 3 Most Common Levels of Planning .......... 286
    Release Planning .......... 287
    Iteration Planning .......... 288
    Daily Planning .......... 290
    Planning Diagram .......... 292
    Portfolio Planning .......... 293

## Estimating Tools and Techniques .......... 294
    Release Burndown .......... 294

## Estimating Tools and Techniques .......... 295
    Release Burndown Chart Example .......... 295
    Velocity .......... 296
    Tracking Velocity on a Burndown Chart .......... 297
    Estimating Velocity/Team Capacity .......... 298

## Estimating Tools and Techniques .......... 299
    Velocity Burndown Chart Example .......... 299

## Estimating Tools and Techniques .......... 300
    Calculating Velocity Scenario .......... 301
    Relative Sizing .......... 302
    Point to Scale .......... 303
    Affinity Estimates .......... 304
    Top-Down Estimating .......... 305
    Bottom-Up Estimating .......... 306
    Wideband Delphi .......... 308
    Planning Poker .......... 309
    Release Backlog/Backlog Item .......... 310
    Release Burndown Chart .......... 311

## Iteration Planning Concepts .......... 312
    Iteration .......... 312
    Scope Verification .......... 313

## Daily Planning Concepts .......... 314
    Feature/Task/WIP Queue .......... 314
    WIP Limits/Impediments .......... 315

## Reinforcement Training .......... 316

## Exercise 4 .......... 317

| | |
|---|---|
| Module 4 Quiz | 318 |
| Summary | 323 |

## Module 5: Problem Detection Resolution .................................................. 324

| | |
|---|---|
| Module 5 Objectives | 325 |
| Resolve Impediments | 326 |
|     The Average Employee Is Trying to Do a Good Job | 326 |
| Creating an Open and Safe Environment | 327 |
|     Dealing with On the Job Conflicts | 327 |
| Engage Risk and Mitigation Strategies | 328 |
|     Risk Management is a Team Responsibility | 328 |
|     It Takes Discipline to Make Work Visible and Open to Adaption | 329 |
|     5 Core Risk Areas Common to All Projects | 331 |
| 5 Core Risk Areas Common to All Projects | 332 |
| Risk Management Planning | 336 |
|     What is Risk Management | 336 |
|     Informal Risk Management | 337 |
| Risk Management Techniques & Terminology | 338 |
|     Risk Burn-Down Graphs/Risk-Adjusted Backlog | 338 |
|     Constraints/ /Risk-Based Spike | 339 |
| Agile Correlation to PMI Risk Management | 340 |
|     Plan Risk Management/Identify Risks | 340 |
|     Perform Qualitative Risk Analysis/Perform Quantitative Risk Analysis | 341 |
|     Plan Risk Responses | 342 |
|     Monitor and Control Risks | 343 |
| Communicate Status of Risk and Impediments | 344 |
|     Seven Cardinal Rules For the Practice of Risk Communication | 345 |
| Reinforcement Training | 346 |
| Exercise 5 | 347 |
| Module 5 Quiz | 348 |
| Summary | 353 |

## Module 6: Continuous Improvement .................................................. 354

| | |
|---|---|
| Module 6 Objectives | 355 |
| Lean | 356 |
|     History | 356 |
| Quality Improvement | 358 |
|     Six Sigma | 358 |
| Lean/Six-Sigma (LSS) | 359 |
| The Liker Pyramid | 360 |
| Incorporating Lean into Your Organization | 362 |
|     Building a Lean Organization | 362 |
| 3 Key Concepts of Lean | 366 |
|     Waste | 366 |
|     Complexity | 367 |
|     Variation | 368 |
| Variance and Trend Analysis | 369 |
|     Types of Variation | 369 |
| Identifying Opportunities | 371 |
|     Continuous Improvement | 371 |
| Systemic Improvements | 372 |

    Key Elements of a Lean Organizations ................................................................................ 372
    Kaizen ................................................................................................................................... 374

**Kaizen Events** ............................................................................................................................. 377

**Method Tailoring** ....................................................................................................................... 380

    Theory vs. Practice ............................................................................................................... 381

    Agile Adoption Strategies ..................................................................................................... 383

**Incorporating Feedback** ............................................................................................................ 385

    Understanding the Process and your Project ...................................................................... 385

    Kano Questionnaire ............................................................................................................. 386

**Identifying the Minimal Marketable Feature** ............................................................................ 388

**Reinforcement Training** ............................................................................................................ 389

**Exercise 6** .................................................................................................................................. 390

**Module 6 Quiz** ........................................................................................................................... 391

**Summary** ................................................................................................................................... 396

**Full Length Practice Exam Questions** .......................................................................... 397

**Exercise Answers** ............................................................................................................ 428

## Introduction
- PMI-ACP Exam Preparation Course

The PM Instructors
A Technical Training & Consulting Company

www.ThePM-Instructors.com

© 2012 The PM Instructors™

The accompanying audio portion of this self-study courseware is located at:
www.pmiacptraining.com/book/self-study_audio.htm

# Learning Objectives

- Introduction to PMI
- Application Process
- PMI-ACP Exam Requirements, Format, Blueprint, Costs
- About Exam Day

# The Project Management Institute

- Snapshot of background
    - Founded in 1969
    - Not-for-Profit member based organization
    - Over 350,000+ members worldwide, in 170+ countries
    - www.PMI.org

PMI offers a variety of credentials. Credential aspirants may pursue one or earn multiple credentials throughout their career. As with the PMI-ACP℠ credential, the PMP®, PMI-RMP®, PMI-SP® and PgMP® credentials have application requirements that must be met, such as a minimum number of hands-on experience in the topic related to the credential. The CAPM® is considered to be an entry-level credential into the project management profession, and is meant for those that do not yet have sufficient experience to pursue the PMP® credential.

# The Project Management Institute

- A Guide to the Project Management Body of Knowledge (*PMBOK*® Guide)

- The "de facto global standard" for the project management profession

- Certification exams largely based on its contents
    - The Program Management Professional (PgMP)®
    - The Project Management Professional (PMP)®
    - The Certified Associate in Project Management (CAPM)®
    - PMI Risk Management Professional (PMI-RMP)®
    - PMI Scheduling Professional (PMI-SP)®
    - PMI Agile Certified Practitioner (PMI-ACP)®

# PMI's Code of Ethics and Professional Conduct

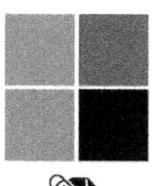

2.10

"As practitioners of project management, we are committed to doing what is right and honorable. We set high standards for ourselves and we aspire to meet these standards in all aspects of our lives—at work, at home, and in service to our profession.

This Code of Ethics and Professional Conduct describes the expectations that we have of ourselves and our fellow practitioners in the global project management community. It articulates the ideals to which we aspire as well as the behaviors that are mandatory in our professional and volunteer roles.

The purpose of this Code is to instill confidence in the project management profession and to help an individual become a better practitioner. We do this by establishing a profession-wide understanding of appropriate behavior. We believe that the credibility and reputation of the project management profession is shaped by the collective conduct of individual practitioners."

PMI.org. 2012. Project Management Institute. 31 Jan. 2012 Inc.http://www.pmi.org/en/About-Us/Ethics/Code-of-Ethics.aspx

The PM Instructors
A Technical Training & Consulting Company

www.ThePM-Instructors.com

© 2012 The PM Instructors™

---

PMI and its members are expected to adhere to PMI's Code of Ethics and Professional Conduct, when dealing with team conflicts, project sponsor challenges, vendor negotiations, cultural differences and government regulations. The excerpt above is taken from the Code to explain its vision and purpose.

The full PMI Code of Ethics and Professional Conduct and be found at:
http://www.pmi.org/en/About-Us/Ethics/~/media/PDF/Ethics/ap_pmicodeofethics.ashx

# PMI-ACP Exam Costs

|  | Member | Non-Member |
|---|---|---|
| Computer-Based Testing | $435 | $495 |
| Paper-Based Testing | $385 | $445 |
| Computer-Based Re-examination | $335 | $395 |
| Paper-Based Re-examination | $285 | $345 |
| CCR Credential Renewal | $90 | $130 |

The exam may be taken in computer-based format and paper-based format.

And as of 2012, the fees range $435 to $495, based on your membership status and the format you select.

An applicant has a one-year window to take the certification exam once their application has been approved by PMI. If an applicant fails, they may re-take the exam up to two times within the one-year eligibility window.

After achieving a credential, credential holders must meet Continuing Credential Requirements (CCR). Every three years, credential holders must earn a specified number of Professional Development Units (PDUs) in order to maintain their credential status as active.

# PMI-ACP Exam Requirements

| Educational Background | General PM Experience | Agile PM Experience | Agile PM Education |
|---|---|---|---|
| **Secondary Degree**<br><br>• High School Diploma<br>• Associate's Degree<br>• Global Equivalent | **2000 hours**<br>(12 Months) working on a project<br><br>Experience must have been accrued in the last 5 years. | **1500 hours**<br>(8 Months) working on a project team using Agile methodologies<br><br>Experience must have been accrued in the last 2 years.<br><br>Hours are in addition to the 2000 general PM hours | **21 Contact Hours**<br>Hours accrued must be directly related to Agile project management topics |

**Overlapping Hours/Projects Are Counted as Individual Hours**

A high school diploma or associate's degree or the global equivalent requires a minimum of 12 months of hands-on project management experience totaling 2,000+ hours, and 21 educational "contact" hours earned in the area of project management.

Project management work experience refers only to hours spent working on project management related activities within the past 5 <u>consecutive</u> years; education "contact" hours refers specifically to project related training / education. Note: there is no specific timeframe that contact hours must have been earned.

Training providers may include Registered Education Providers (REP), PMI component organizations, training companies or consultants, company sponsored-programs, distance learning companies that include an end of course assessment, and university/college courses.

# PMI- ACP Exam Requirements
## CALCULATING TOTAL MONTHS

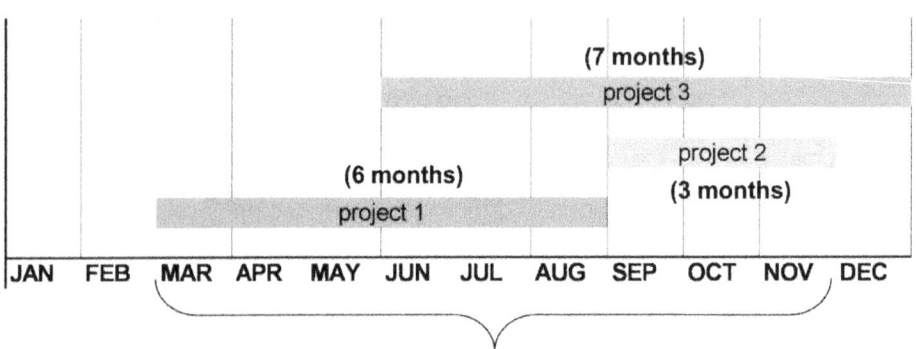

So what does Overlapping Hours, or Projects, Are Counted as Individual Hours mean, you ask?

Well, in this example, even though an individual worked on project 1, for 6 months, and project 3, for 7 months, June, July and August can only be counted once; not twice, even if the person was working on two separate projects. The same holds true for September, October and November where an overlap takes place between project 2 and project 3.

# PMI-ACP Application Process

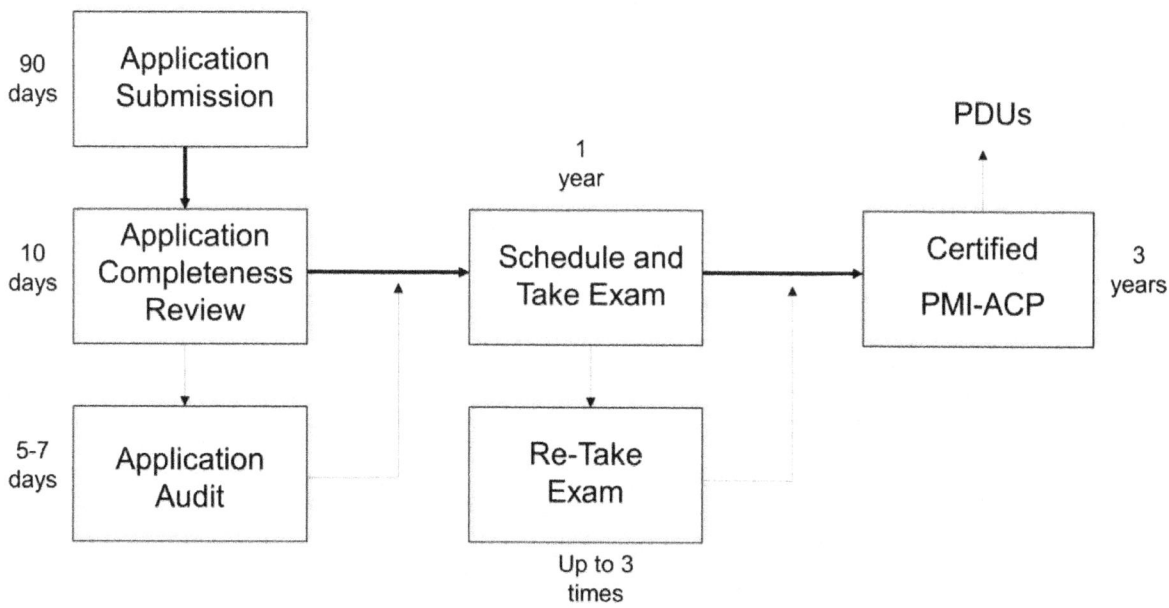

1. After submitting the credential application to PMI, the application will be checked to make sure it is complete. The application will be processed within 3-5 business days. Once an applicant begins an application, they will have up to 90 days to submit it. If the application is found to be complete, applicant will be asked to submit payment.

2. (If audited only) Applications are selected to participate in the audit process at random, although PMI reserves the right to audit applications at any time. Approximately 12% of applications are selected for a random audit. If an application is selected, the applicant will be required to show documented proof of meeting eligibility requirements. If audited, applicants have up to 90 days to complete the audit process.

3. After payment (or passing the audit), the applicant may schedule and take the exam. The eligibility window of 1 year begins on the day that the application (or audit) is approved. Applicants may take the exam up to three times within the eligibility window. Computer-based exam results are provided immediately.

4. The CCR cycle is every 3 years on the anniversary of passing the exam. Requirements for PMI-ACP credential holders include 30 Agile project management related PDUs. PDUs are not applicable to CAPM credential holders, since this credential does not renew.

# PMI-ACP Exam Format

- 120 multiple choice questions
  - 100 scored, 20 pre-test
  - Pass / Fail exam
    - *Proficient*
    - *Moderately Proficient*
    - *Below Proficient*
- 3 hour exam + 15 minute tutorial
- Computer-based testing (CBT) vs. paper-based testing (PBT)

**Exam Scoring**

- 100 scored questions
- 20 pre-test questions. Pre-test questions are *anonymously* mixed in with the scored questions. Pre-test questions allow PMI to first analyze questions before deciding on whether to absorb them as part of the official database of scored questions.

This is a pass or fail exam. Those taking a computer-based exam will receive an immediate score. Applicants do not see the total number of correct / incorrect questions. Instead, each exam domain receives the following result:

- **Proficient:** *above average level of knowledge*
- **Moderately proficient:** *average level of knowledge*
- **Below proficient:** *below average level of knowledge*

  PMI does not publish a passing / failing percentage.

Computer-based testing is the primary method of taking the exam. In order to qualify to take a paper-based test, applicants must reside 186.5+ miles from the nearest computer-based testing center. Paper-based testing may be administered by an employer who has a minimum of 10 employees taking the exam (distance is not a factor in this case).

# PMI-ACP Exam Blueprint

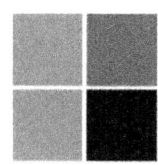

| | |
|---|---|
| Tools and Techniques | 50% of Exam |
| Knowledge and Skills | 50% of Exam |
| Level I | 33% |
| Level II | 12% |
| Level III | 5% |

50% of the exam will cover the Tools and Techniques as described in the PMI-ACP Examination Content Outline.

The other 50% will cover the Knowledge and Skills section, which is further broken down into three levels, where level 1 is 33% of the exam, level 2 is 12% of the exam and level 3 is 5% of the exam.

# PMI-ACP Exam Blueprint (continued)

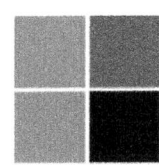

### 50% Tools and Techniques

**10 Categories**

1. Communications
2. Planning, Monitoring, and Adapting
3. Agile Estimation
4. Agile Analysis and Design
5. Product Quality
6. Soft Skills Negotiation
7. Value-Based Prioritization
8. Risk Management
9. Metrics
10. Value stream analysis

**Note:** The official *PMI-ACP Examination Content Outline* uses bullets to indicate the topics but we have replaced them with numbers for studying purposes.

# PMI-ACP Exam Blueprint (continued)

## 50% Knowledge and Skills

**Level** (33% of Exam)
1. Active listening
2. Agile manifesto values and principles
3. Assessing and incorporating community and stakeholder values
4. Brainstorming techniques
5. Building empowered teams
6. Coaching and mentoring within teams
7. Communications management
8. Feedback techniques for product
9. Incremental delivery
10. Knowledge sharing
11. Leadership tools and techniques
12. Prioritization
13. Problem solving strategies, tools, and techniques
14. Project and quality standards for agile projects
15. Stakeholder management
16. Team motivation
17. Time, budget and cost estimation
18. Value based decomposition and prioritization

# PMI-ACP Exam Blueprint (continued)

## 50% Knowledge and Skills (continued)

**Level II** (12 % of Exam)
1. Agile frameworks and terminology
2. Building high performance teams
3. Business case development
4. Collocation / Distributed teams
5. Continuous improvement processes
6. Elements of a project charter for an agile project
7. Facilitation methods
8. Participatory decision models
9. PMI's code of ethics and professional conduct
10. Process analysis techniques
11. Self assessment
12. Value based analysis

# PMI-ACP Exam Blueprint (continued)

## 50% Knowledge and Skills (continued)

**Level III** (5 % of Exam)
1. Agile contracting methods
2. Agile project accounting principles
3. Applying new agile practices
4. Compliance
5. Control limits for agile projects
6. Failure modes and alternatives
7. Globalization, culture, and team diversity
8. Agile games
9. Principles of systems thinking
10. Regulatory compliance
11. Variance and trend analysis
12. Variations in agile methods and approaches
13. Vendor management

# Using the Course Materials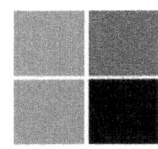

 Tool and Technique           Record to memory!

 Knowledge and Skills         Discussion Point

 Domain

This courseware has been designed to map as close as possible to the 2011-2012 PMI-ACP Examination Content Outline. However, because many of the exam topics address several areas of Agile, and in multiple contexts, a direct 1-to-1 mapping is not viable. Instead, the following icons have been placed on pages that attempt to address a specific exam topic:

Indicates the courseware topic is specifically mentioned in **Tools & Technique**

Indicates the courseware topic is specifically mentioned in **Knowledge and Skills**

Indicates the courseware topic is specifically mentioned in a **Domain**

Additionally, the icon will also include a reference number that maps back to the PMI-ACP Examination Content Outline. For example:

Maps to **Level I** . **Bullet** 6
**1.6**

**Note:** Our hope was to assist readers by enabling them to quickly associate what they are currently studying back to the outline, please remember that PMI states that the topic outline should only be used as a starting point for your study preparation. The exam is likely to include an array of related Agile topics not explicitly stated in the outline, therefore consider the non-iconized pages important for addressing the broader areas of Agile.

# Using the Course Materials (continued)

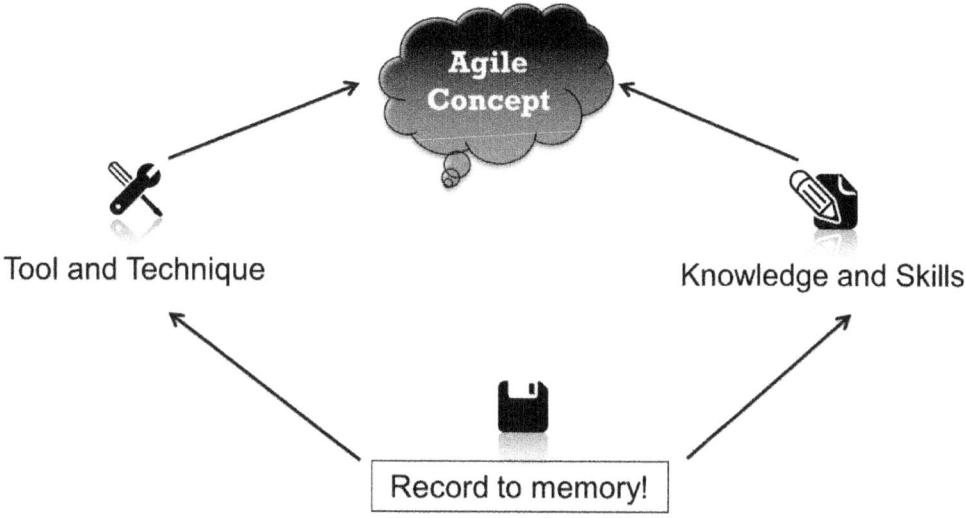

As Enterprise Architects and project managers, the authors of this course are staunch believers in the benefits of reuse. In everything we do we strive to make our efforts always serve multiple purposes. In doing so not only does this allow us to learn things faster, we waste less time doing repetitive tasks. The benefit of this philosophy is that it fits nicely with Agile and Lean--and why we realized we were Agile/Lean people long before we knew about the certifications. We've also applied that philosophy to the way we successfully prepared for the exam and went on to create this book. While creating our studying strategy we noticed that the PMI-ACP Examination Content Outline has a lot of overlap in different areas, sending our reuse bells into a flurry of excitement. Specifically, many of the topics are designed to address the [core] Agile concepts or problem domains, but from various contexts. And upon identifying those patterns one can quickly learn how to apply Agile and more importantly, easily pass the exam. To facilitate this learning experience we have marked and duplicated several passages in this book as **Record to memory!** The purpose of that isn't to memorize the section verbatim, but rather, to cue you in that what you're reading is going to be used as solutions in several upcoming problem domains, and that if you take the time to digest the content now it will save you time down the road.

**What this Material is Not:** This courseware is not meant to provide exhaustive explanations of Scrum, XP, Lean or any of the other Agile practices. There are numerous books currently available to provide that level of detail, many of which we based this courseware on, and are listed in the reference section. The purpose of this courseware is to provide you with JUST ENOUGH information to ensure you pass the PMI-ACP exam and introduced you to thinking *Agile*.

# Sample Question

1. All of the following are characteristics of a project EXCEPT:

    A. Repetitive and ongoing

    B. Temporary

    C. Have a definite beginning and end

    D. Result in a unique product or result

The question above shows a common question format that uses the key word "EXCEPT". All questions will contain four potential options: A, B, C, or D. There is only one correct answer.

# Sample Question (continued)

1. All of the following are characteristics of a project EXCEPT:

    → A. Repetitive and ongoing

    B. Temporary

    C. Have a definite beginning and end

    D. Result in a unique product or result

The correct answer for the question above is A.

# Exam Question Characteristics & Components

- Noise
- Common Terminology
- Too Much Information
- Select the BEST answer
- NOT / EXCEPT
- Situational
- Calculation

All questions will be delivered in multiple-choice format with one correct answer. However, there are many formats within the scope of a multiple-choice question that one can see on the exam. The bullets above describe the various ways that a question may be asked.

What makes PMI exams challenging is that there may be more than one right answer. You must select the BEST answer from a PMI perspective. This means that during the preparation process, you will need to train yourself to answer questions from a PMI standpoint, and not your own. Many organizations follow different processes and use various terms differently. This is not only what makes the exam challenging, but what also presents a benefit, as it promotes a common agreement of terms and processes.

# Brain Dump

- What is a "brain dump" list?

    - You must return ALL scratch paper to the test center representative after your exam, including your brain dump sheet.

    - Examples: all formulas, process names, name of theorists and theories, types of power, conflict management techniques, etc...

> What you write down on the scratch sheet of paper provided the moment you sit down at your test station.
>
> Maximum time: 15 min.

As soon as you take your seat at the exam station, we recommend that you utilize the note pad provided, and write down as many formulas, process names, names of theorists and theories, types of power, conflict management techniques, etc., that immediately come to mind. Doing this will allow you to recall everything, from both your long-term and short-term memory. The best time to do this is during the free 15 minute exam introduction.

# Study Tips

- Think like PMI
- Answer all questions
- Read full question and options
- Look for key words
- Pace yourself
- Use process of elimination
- Be prepared and confident before taking exam
- Create a brain dump list

Think like PMI: remember, the way you may have seen a situation being resolved in the real-world, may not be the way you should respond to PMI question.

Answer all questions: you will not lose points for incorrect questions, but you will lose points for unanswered questions.

Read full question and options: because of the noise, too much information questions and negation questions, it is important to read the entire question, because what may sound true toward the beginning of a question, may not be true by the end of the question.

Look for key words: identify words to help narrow down what the question is asking.

Pace yourself: do not spend too much time on one question, but make sure you allocate enough time to read each question carefully, and still complete the exam.

Use process of elimination: if you are not sure what the correct answer is, start by eliminating the least likely response to narrow down you choices. There is usually always one option that is completely wrong and can be eliminated immediately.

Be prepared and confident before taking exam: know your terminology and take practice exams before taking the real exam. However, look for quality practice exam questions, not just a quantity of them.

Create a brain dump list: the previous pages describe this.

# Exam Day

- ☐ Schedule your exam strategically
    - ✓ Alert
    - ✓ Rested
    - ✓ Prepared

- ☐ Arrive up to 1 hour early

- ☐ Bring all required items to the test center
    - ✓ 2 forms of ID
    - ✓ Eligibility letter

- ☐ Bring all recommended items to the test center
    - ✓ Dress in layers
    - ✓ Bring a snack
    - ✓ Brain dump list for pre-test review

Use this checklist to prepare yourself on the day of the exam.

Schedule your exam strategically so that you can show up: Alert, Rested and prepared

Arrive up to 1 hour early, so you do not show up frazzle. Some exam centers will let you take the exam early if space is available and you request it.

Bring all required items to the test center:

2 forms of ID, and your eligibility letter

Bring all recommended items to the test center

Dress in layers, so that you can take off clothes if you get cold instead of having to take the exam while shivering

Bring a snack in case you get hungry during the exam.

And, create your Brain dump list for pre-test review

If you take aspirin, you may consider taking one before the exam, because you will likely get a stress headache during the test.

# Summary

- Introduced to PMI
- Reviewed the Application Process
- Examined PMI-ACP Exam Requirements, Format, Blueprint, Costs
- Discussed How to Prepare for Exam Day

# Agile Introduction
- PMI-ACP Exam Preparation Course

# Agile Introduction
## Objectives

- ✓ Describe Agile Terminology
- ✓ Examine History
- ✓ Relate the Manifesto Values and Principles to Everyday Work
- ✓ Explain the Agile Framework
- ✓ Discuss Incremental Development
- ✓ Asses the Principles of Systems Thinking
- ✓ Compare Agile vs. XP vs. Scrum

# Terminology Lesson

- **Customer** – Works to ensure the team focuses on delivering stories that generate the highest business value possible
- **Customer Proxy** – Assists the customer by making himself/herself available to the team when the customer is not available
- **Team Lead** – Guides the direction of development to make sure the team delivers now and in the future
- **Project Manager** – Guides direction of the project to make sure the team delivers now and in the future
  - *Scrum equivalent of the Product Owner*
  - *XP equivalent of a Product Manager*
- **Business Analyst** – Helps the customer reveal his/her needs and goals to deliver the right product

Huge debates are currently taking place in the Agile project management and IT industries between the definitions and roles of an Agile project manager, product manager and product owner. This is primarily the result of the cross-functional traditional management/Agile non-management hats the individual is required to wear during a project. This course isn't attempting to provide an answer to that debate, or take sides. As a result, you may see the term project manager or product manager used in this material interchangeably because of the context within which it is being used, but keep in mind it is referring to the description of the role described above.

To keep the roles closely mapped to real world scenarios, this material will position the Customer as the individual having the greatest stake in the outcome of the product being developed. For example, if Ziggly Wiggle Repair shop hires The PM Instructors to manage a project, Ziggly Wiggle Repair shop is the Customer. As such, they can designate a resource from their company to represent them as the Customer, or if they do not have a free resource they can delegate the responsibilities of being the Customer to a product manager that works for The PM Instructors. So now, the product manager is responsible for their own tasks, as well as those of the Customer.

Note: To make things even more confusing, a product owner may also be referred to as a Customer. This courseware will avoid doing that whenever possible.

# Terminology Lesson (continued)

- **Team Member** – Encompasses everyone on the Agile Team, but can be specified into:
  - *User Experience (UX) Designer* – Helps the Agile customer discover usability needs, helps the team meet these needs, and verifies they have been met.
  - *Developer* – Implements stories with high business value using good techniques and practices.
  - *Architect* – Ensures the team implements good techniques and practices.
  - *Tester* – Provides information on the state of the project.
- **Facilitator** – Assists the team with Agile skills, removing impediments and implementing conflict resolution.
  - *Scrum equivalent of the Scrum Master*
  - *XP equivalent of the Agile Coach*

An important concept to understand about an Agile team is that no one has a "single source of power". While everyone on the team has a specific role, because of the value placed on being adaptable, responsibilities assigned to a particular role may change in order to achieve the project goal. Additionally, Agile teams are designed and encouraged to be self-empowered and self-managed. As such, no one is allowed to function as a manager over other members, but rather, to operate in an open environment made up of collaborative peers, facilitators and coaches.

# History

- **Agile Manifesto**
  - Published February 2001 by a group of 17 software developers
    - Many of the authors formed the Agile Alliance to promote software development according to the manifesto's principles

- **Original Signatories and Agile Contributions**
  - Mike Beedle – Agile Enterprise (XBreed)
  - Arie van Bennekum – DSDM
  - Alistair Cockburn – Crystal, Adaptive Software Development
  - Ward Cunningham – Extreme Programming, CRC
  - Martin Fowler – authored *Analysis Patterns, UML Distilled, Refactoring, and Planning Extreme Programming*
  - Jim Highsmith – Adaptive Software Development, Crystal
  - Andrew Hunt – co-authored *The Pragmatic Programmer*

Many of the books used to create this courseware and included as additional references in the back were authored by the original signatories and Agile Contributors.

# History (continued)

- **Original Signatories and Agile Contributions** (continued)
  - Ron Jeffries – Extreme Programming
  - Jon Kern – Feature Driven Development
  - Brian Marick – Agile Testing
  - Robert C. Martin – Extreme Programming
  - Ken Schwaber – Scrum
  - Jeff Sutherland – Scrum
  - Dave Thomas – co-authored *The Pragmatic Programmer*

# Manifesto Values and Principles

## The Agile Manifesto States:

- We are uncovering better ways of developing software by doing it and helping others do it. Through this work we have come to value:

**Individuals and interactions** over processes and tools
**Working software** over comprehensive documentation
**Customer collaboration** over contract negotiation
**Responding to change** over following a plan

*That is, while there is value in the items on the right, we value the items on the left more.*

Understanding these values is important not only for the exam, but also for understanding the core of Agile. In short, these Agile principles are stating that good working software is the result of individuals willing to collaborate together in order to adjust to the inherent need for change during the SDLC.

# Manifesto Values and Principles (continued)

- **Twelve Principles**
  - *We follow these principles:*
    1. Our highest priority is to satisfy the customer through early and continuous delivery of valuable software.
    2. Welcome changing requirements, even late in development. Agile processes harness change for the customer's competitive advantage.
    3. Deliver working software frequently, from a couple of weeks to a couple of months, with a preference toward the shorter timescale.
    4. Business people and developers must work together daily throughout the project.

Another driving theme behind Agile development is the commitment to deliver QUALITY software, ON TIME. When these objectives are achieved we increase the VALUE of the product and end up with SATISFIED CUSTOMERS.

# Manifesto Values and Principles (continued)

## Twelve Principles (continued)

5. Build projects around motivated individuals. Give them the environment and support they need, and trust them to get the job done.
6. The most efficient and effective method of conveying information to and within a development team is face-to-face conversation.
7. Working software is the primary measure of progress.
8. Agile processes promote sustainable development. The sponsors, developers, and users should be able to maintain a constant pace indefinitely.
9. Continuous attention to technical excellence and good design enhances agility.

# Manifesto Values and Principles (continued)

- **Twelve Principles** (continued)
    10. Simplicity—the art of maximizing the amount of work not done—is essential.
    11. The best architectures, requirements, and designs emerge from self-organizing teams.
    12. At regular intervals, the team reflects on how to become more effective, then tunes and adjusts its behavior accordingly.

Simplicity is truly a cornerstone in the Agile development methodology. By focusing our efforts on SIMPLICITY instead of needless complexity and wasteful practices, we can achieve a value in a shorter amount of time.

# The Agile Framework

- **Software Development Lifecycle (SDLC)**
  - Agile methods are focused on different aspects of the software development lifecycle
    - **Practices**: Extreme Programming(XP), Pragmatic Programming, Agile Modeling
    - **Managing the software project:** Scrum
    - **Full SDLC**: DSDM, RUP
  - Dynamic Systems Development Method (DSDM) and Rational Unified Process (RUP)
    - Don't need complementing approaches to support software development; the others do to a varying degree

---

Agile can be used in several areas of the SDLC. For example, Extreme and Pragmatic programming are Agile software development practices that can be leveraged by developers; Scrum provides a means to manage projects using Agile techniques; whereas DSDM and RUP provide a means to execute Agile through all phases of the SDLC (see Framework Comparison).

In other words, where XP and Scrum would require complementing approaches to satisfy all phases of an Agile SDLC, DSDM and RUP are complete Agile SDLC processes in themselves.

# Variations in Agile Methods and Approaches

- **Agile Software Development Methods Include:**
  - Extreme Programming (XP)
  - Scrum
  - Crystal
  - Feature Driven Development (FDD)
  - Open Unified Process (OpenUP)
  - Agile Modeling
  - Rational Unified Process (RUP)
  - Agile Unified Process (AUP)
  - Dynamic Systems Development Method (DSDM)
  - Essential Unified Process (EssUP)
  - Velocity Tracking

3.12

Each of the software develop methods have their own set of strengths and weaknesses (further indicated on the Framework Comparison page). How would you compare your experiences with the various methods and suitability for the project you were working on?

# Framework Comparison

☺ = Project Management  ☐ = Process  ⬛ = Practices

| Framework | Concept Creation | Requirements Specification | Design | Code | Unit Test | Integrate Test | System Test | Acceptance Test | System In Use |
|---|---|---|---|---|---|---|---|---|---|
| Adaptive Software Dev. | | ☺☐ | ☺☐ | ☺☐ | ☺☐ | ☺☐ | ☺☐ | ☺☐ | ☺☐ |
| Agile Modeling | | ⬛ | | ⬛ | ⬛ | | | | |
| Crystal | | | ☺☐ | ☺☐ | ☺☐ | ☺☐ | ☺☐ | | |
| DSDM | ☺☐⬛ | ☺☐⬛ | ☺☐⬛ | ☺☐⬛ | ☺☐⬛ | ☺☐⬛ | ☺☐⬛ | ☺☐⬛ | ☺☐⬛ |
| XP | | ☐⬛ | ☐⬛ | ☐⬛ | ☐⬛ | ☐⬛ | ☐⬛ | | |
| Feature Driven Dev. | | ☺☐⬛ | ☺☐⬛ | ☺☐⬛ | ☺☐⬛ | ☺☐⬛ | ☺☐⬛ | | |
| Open Source | | ☺ ⬛ | ☺ ⬛ | ☺ | ☺ | ☺ ⬛ | ☺ ⬛ | ☺ ⬛ | |
| Pragmatic Programming | | ⬛ | ⬛ | ⬛ | ⬛ | ⬛ | ⬛ | | |
| RUP | ☺☐⬛ | ☺☐⬛ | ☺☐⬛ | ☺☐⬛ | ☺☐⬛ | ☺☐⬛ | ☺☐⬛ | ☺☐⬛ | ☺☐⬛ |
| Scrum | | ☺☐⬛ | ☺☐⬛ | ☺ | ☺ | ☺☐⬛ | ☺☐⬛ | | |

For organizations that would prefer to use Agile for their full SDLC, approaches like the Dynamic Systems Development Method or the Rational Unified Process can be used. In other words, the Dynamic Systems Development Method (DSDM) and Rational Unified Process (RUP) do not need complementing approaches to support software development. Conversely, all of the other approaches like, Scrum, XP and Crystal, need complementing approaches to a varying degree.

# Incremental Development

## Agile Software Development

- A group of software development methodologies based on iterative and incremental development
  - Requirements and solutions evolve through collaboration between self-organizing, cross-functional teams.
- A conceptual framework that promotes foreseen interactions throughout the development cycle
  - Promotes adaptive planning, evolutionary development and delivery
    - A time-boxed iterative approach: *time-box iteration*
    - Encourages rapid and flexible response to change
- Agile management methods can also be applied in development projects other than software development.

---

The first thing that should come to mind when you think of Agile is that it's based on iterative and incremental development, which means the development work is divided into small manageable pieces. As a result, the requirements and solutions evolve through collaboration among team members as more information is acquired about the problem domain.

Second, because of this increased flexibility, Agile teams have the freedom to evolve their solutions in response to customer changes. However, even though Agile provides this level of flexibility, specific amounts of time are allotted to complete the work within time-boxes. So a common term you may encounter here is time-boxed iteration.

Because the focus of Agile is on, completing units of work in a disciplined manner, it is industry agnostic, and as a result, it can be used on projects other than software development.

# Assessing Suitability

- **Agile Development Can Be Suitable for Certain Types of Environments…**
  - Including small teams of experts
  - Some things that may negatively impact the success of an Agile project are:
    - Large-scale development efforts (>20 developers)
    - Distributed development efforts (non-collocated teams)
    - Mission-critical systems where failure is not an option at any cost (e.g., software for surgical procedures)

*Handwritten notes: Assess Suitability; constraints — Time, Cost, Scope*

# Agile Modeling

- **Agile Modeling (AM) is a Practice-Based Methodology for Effective Modeling and Documenting of Software-Systems**
  - A collection of values, principles, and practices for modeling software
    - Can be applied on a software development project in an effective and light-weight manner
    - Meant to be tailored into other, full-fledged methodologies such as XP or RUP, enabling you to develop a software process which truly meets your needs

Sec. 4

Where traditional software practices may use the Unified Modeling Language (UML) to create artifacts and document software, Agile teams would look toward Agile Modeling (AM). Like Agile, AM is meant to provide a simplified means of collecting *just enough* information required to complete the current amount of design an Agile team is currently working on; producing more documentation than is needed results in *wasted* effort.

# Applying New Agile Practices

- Agile techniques and software processes can be tailored into your own software development process.

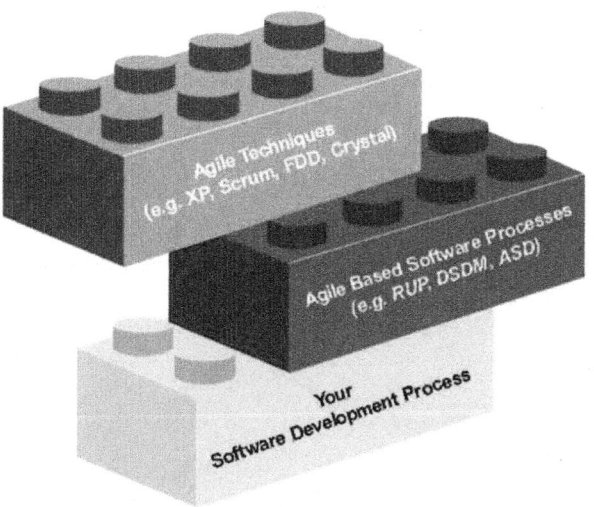

Using Agile doesn't tie you to a specific development solution. Just as it can accommodate a combination of different practices, management techniques, and development processes, it can also be tailored to the different flavors of an organization's development processes. Building an Agile project in this manner is like having the freedom to build your own application from a collection of software Legos.

Note: The caveat to doing this is that a team/organization should be highly experienced and familiar with the principles of Agile so that their expertise carries over into their new SDLC. Not having the necessary experience when using this approach can lead to new, and undocumented complexities, beyond the capabilities of the team/organization.

# Principles of Systems Thinking

- **Process Engineering**
  - Focuses on the design operation, control, and optimization of processes
    - **Defined Process Control Model (Theoretical)**
    - **Empirical Process Control Model**

Process engineering, also known as systems engineering, focuses on the design, control, and optimization of operational processes. These processes can span the range of chemical and physical processes all the way down to biological processes. A process is typically managed through the systematic use of computer-based methods. Process engineering encompasses a vast range of industries, such as petrochemical, mineral processing, advanced material, food, pharmaceutical, and biotechnological industries.

The two types of process controls you'll need to understand for the exam are the Defined Process Control Model and the Empirical Process Control Model.

# Principles of Systems Thinking (continued)

- **Defined Process Control**
  - Process control assumes that a process is well enough understood to be automated and to produce quality results

    "It is typical to adopt the defined (theoretical) modeling approach when the underlying mechanisms by which the process operates are reasonably well understood". Ogunnaike (1992)

    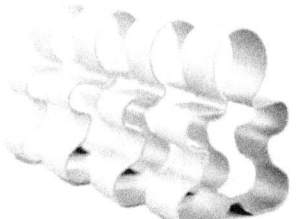

  - Quality improvement initiatives such as Six Sigma strive to improve the quality of process outputs by identifying and removing the causes of defects (errors)
    - When this is accomplished, variability in manufacturing and business processes is minimized

When every piece of work in a process can be completely understood, the Defined Process Control Model can be used. In other words, when a well-defined set of inputs are provided and the same outputs are generated every time, the process can be defined and controlled to repeatedly produce the expected results. For example, a business that manufactures cookies would expect to have a defined process that controls how their cookies are created in mass production.

# Process Engineering

- **Empirical Process Control Model**
    - Control process implies information gained by means of observation or experimentation

3.9

- **Three Requirements to Support Empirical Process Control**
    - Visibility
    - Inspection
    - Adaptation

Conversely, the Empirical Process Control Model provides control through frequent **visible inspection** of and **adaptations** to the process. In other words, because the process is assumed to be imperfectly defined and likely to produce unpredictable and unrepeatable outputs, the engineer maintains control through observation. For example, when building software, the initial design requirements may be defined up front, but midway through the project the requirements may change, and as a result, the development process must also be changed.

For the exam, you must be able to identify and explain the three requirements of the Empirical Process Control Model.

# Process Engineering (continued)

- **Empirical Process Control**
  - **Visibility**
    - To control the aspects of the process that affect outcome, and such aspects must remain visible throughout the process
  - **Inspection**
    - To ensure that unacceptable variations are detected early, and the aspects of the process that affect outcome may be inspected frequently
  - **Adaptation**
    - If the current outcomes are observed to be outside the acceptable limit, the inspector of the process must be able to adjust the process being used

> Agile encourages frequent inspection and adaptation by using a leadership philosophy that encourages teamwork, self-organization, and accountability.

# Control Limits for Agile Projects

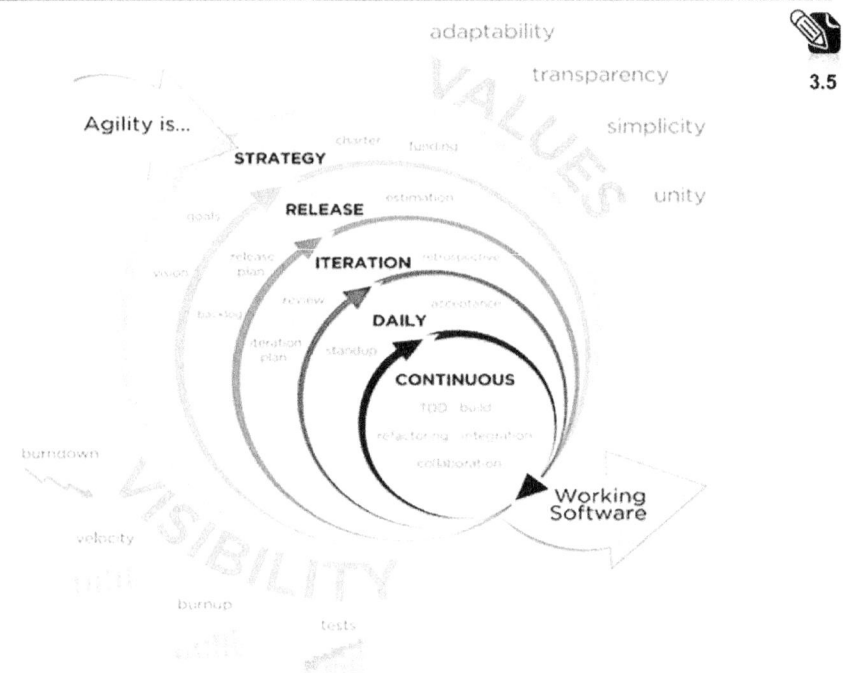

Requirements gathering, varying technology, and human interaction create complexity that must be addressed in software development.

Agile attempts to address and set control limits on these issues by treating the development process like constantly curving lines that need to be viewed, inspected, and adapted. As information is gathered the needs of the project can be refined through progressive elaboration.

Each of these cycles will be explained later in the course.


Image provided by: VersionOne, Inc.

From Wikipedia, the free encyclopedia

Source: http://commons.wikimedia.org/wiki/File:Agile-Software-Development-Poster-En.pdf

# Control Limits for Agile Projects (continued)

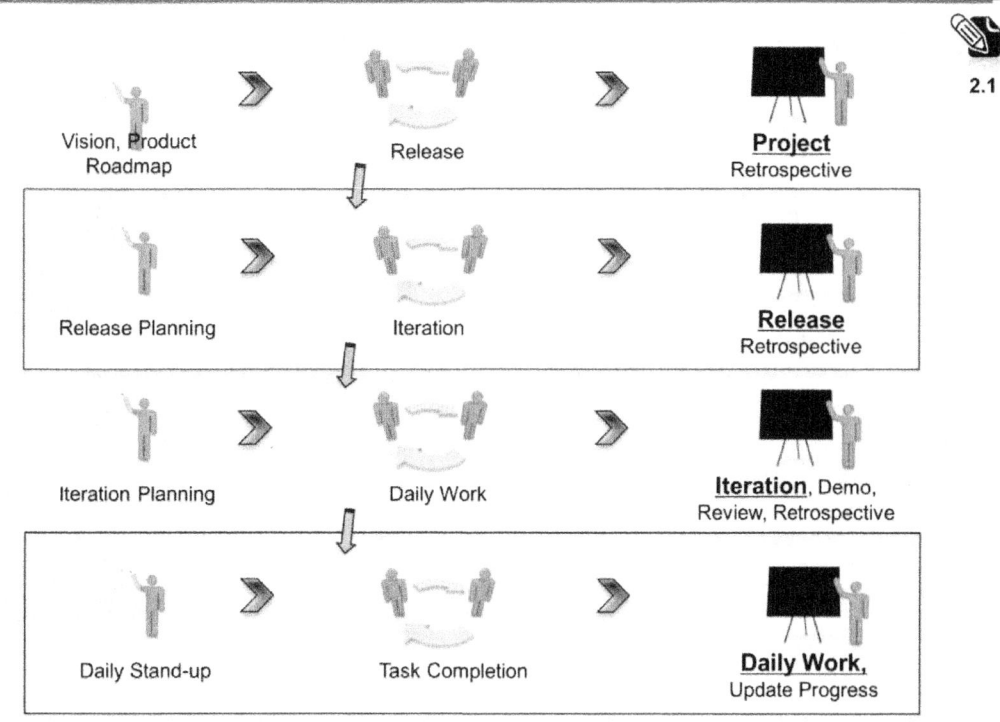

Agile methodologies are adaptive rather than prescriptive or defined. By incorporating frequent feedback from stakeholders and team members using retrospectives, the methodologies encourage modification and/or incorporation of new practices while discarding practices that are not beneficial.

**Establishing a Product Vision -** A high-level description of the desired outcome is captured in the product vision. It is used to explain why the project was being undertaken and the value it would bring to the company. The Product Roadmap can be considered a more detailed version of the Vision.

**Release Planning** - Planning occurs when stories from the product backlog are taken on by the team during an iteration(s) for completion and contribute toward the release of a version of the product. Release planning is conducted at the beginning of a release.

**Iteration Planning -** A list of prioritized features are converted into actual work to perform during the iteration planning meeting. This meeting can be divided into two parts:

1. During the first part, the team determines what features should be worked on during the iteration.
2. The second involves determining which tasks are required to realize completion of the features.

**Daily Stand-up -** Team members give daily reports on what they completed yesterday, what they plan to work on today, and what issues may be impeding their progress during the daily stand-up meeting. This meeting is time-boxed into 15 minutes and is conducted while all team members are standing.

# The Agile Antithesis

**Waterfall Methodology**
An approach to project management named by the discrete gate handoffs from one project stage to the next.

**Big Design Up Front (BDUF)**
BDUF follows a sequential design process in which progress is steadily flowing in a straight line or downwards like a waterfall, through the distinct phases of completion.

> For example, traditional stages flow through discrete stages of requirements gathering, analysis & design, implementation, testing, deployment and change management.

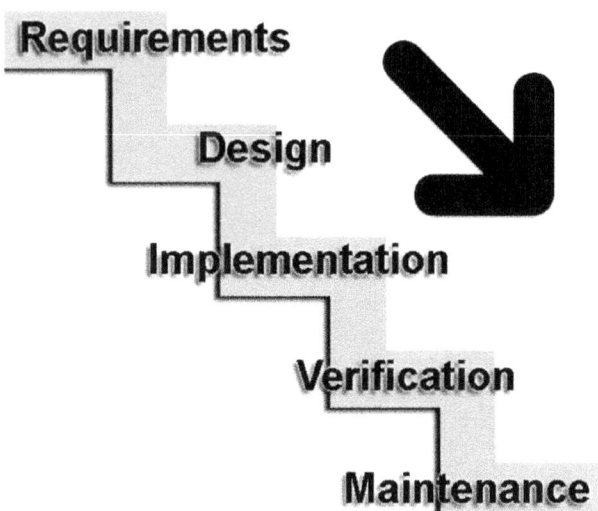

It can be said that the Antithesis of the Agile methodology is the Waterfall Methodology.

Waterfall is an approach to project management named by the discrete gate handoffs from one project stage to the next.

Similarly, project can fall victim to Big Design Up Front (BDUF). BDUF follows a sequential design process in which progress is steadily flowing in a straight line or downwards like a waterfall, through the distinct phases of completion. For example, traditional stages flow through discrete stages of requirements gathering, analysis & design, implementation, testing, deployment and change management.

What do you think, are these methodologies more similar to the Design Control Process or the Empirical Control Process?

# Agile vs. XP vs. Scrum Terminology

| Agile | XP | Scrum |
|---|---|---|
| Release Planning | Release Planning | Product Backlog |
| Iteration Planning | Iteration Planning | Sprint |
| Iteration Demo | Iteration Demo | Sprint Review |
| Stories | Stories | Backlog Items |
| Stand-Up Meetings | Stand-Up Meetings | Daily Scrum |
| Agile Facilitator | Coach | ScrumMaster |
| Agile Project Manager* | Product Manager | Product Owner |

**For the Exam:** With the different Agile methodologies also come different terminologies. While the table above is not an exhaustive list of all of the variations in terminology they are the most relevant for the exam.

The PMI-ACP exam is written to be "practice neutral". In other words, you won't be tested on the specific terms or variations of Agile, but rather, the tools and techniques used to manage Agile projects. Hence, the purpose of the exam is to test your knowledge on the driving principles and practices of Agile, instead of the implementations. With that in mind, however, the exam tends to use more XP references than Scrum.

*Discussed in more detail in upcoming slides.

# Pulling It All Together

## Synopsis

- Agile is based on embracing change as you are working
  - Requirements change over time
  - Recognize that incremental change of your system over time enables agility
- Strive to obtain rapid feedback on your work
  - Ensure that it accurately reflects the needs of your project stakeholders
  - If you don't know why you are working on something or you don't know what the audience requires, then you shouldn't be working on it

---

Let's go through a quick synopsis of what we have learned about Agile so far.

First, Agile is based on embracing change as you are working. Why is this important? Well, because requirements are likely to change over time.

Therefore, by recognizing and embracing the fact that incremental change will occur to your system over time, enables agility. And upon embracing that change you can strive to obtain rapid feedback on your work to ensure that what you're developing accurately reflects the needs of your project stakeholders. Also, always remember, if you don't know why you are working on something, or what the audience requires, then you shouldn't be working on it.

## Pulling It All Together (continued)

- You need multiple models in your intellectual toolkit to be effective
  - Travel light by discarding unused models once they have fulfilled their purpose
    - Models are not necessarily documents
- Open and honest communication is often the best policy to ensure effective teamwork
- Focus on quality work
  - Adapt AM to meet the precise needs of your environment

As an Agile practitioner, you will need multiple models in your intellectual toolkit to be effective.

However, remember to travel light by discarding unused models once they have fulfilled their purpose.

And, keep in mind that models are not necessarily documents. They can be prototypes that were created to prove out a concept or as risk based spike solutions.

Most important of all, maintain open and honest communication as it is often the best policy to ensure effective teamwork.

This in turn will allow the team to focus on delivering quality work.

Lastly, adapt Agile Modeling to meet the precise needs of your environment, remember, Agile is about striving to deliver, high quality products that are, *Just Good Enough*.

# ✚ Reinforcement Training

## Questions & Exercises

### ■ Time to Test your New Knowledge!
Take the Agile Self-Assessment.

 One of the concepts we'll be addressing later in the course is referred to as *Fail Fast*. How do you think this relates to what you just learned about Agile?

# Agile Self-Assessment

## Exam Practice Questions

1. Lean has just been used to optimize the workflow at a company. Which of the following BEST describes what would come next?
   A. Six Sigma quality improvement implementation
   B. Higher quality and lower production
   C. Three Sigma waste reduction plan
   D. Creation of a new organizational chart

2. A project manager on a construction project is in the process of conducting risk management activities. While preparing for a planning meeting to address a possible slip in the schedule, he asks a team member to track down a crucial piece of information that would help him mitigate the risk by helping him to more accurately readjust the schedule. Which of the following pieces of information should the Agile project manager reference?
   A. Velocity history
   B. WBS
   C. Project plan
   D. Risk register

3. Which of the following planning events can be identified as the starting point where the team begins identifying the features they wish to deliver in the project during the Stand-Up meeting?
   A. Priority planning
   B. Daily planning
   C. Feature planning
   D. Adaptive planning

4. Which of the following BEST describes an important characteristic of a High-Performance Agile Team?
   A. Self-organizing
   B. Fast
   C. Technical
   D. IT specialist

5. A project manager has requested an increase to her project budget based on a confident belief that developers will be needed to assist the Help Desk with technical support calls once the project has been released. Based on the complexity of the new application and the current experience of the existing Help Desk staff, she believes the project's success will be at risk due to poor customer satisfaction. The project stakeholders have denied her request because they believe her concern falls outside the scope of the project. All of the following are benefits of engaging stakeholders during a project, EXCEPT:
   A. Stakeholder engagement decreases the probability of the project veering off course.
   B. Stakeholders may have influence over the project budget.
   C. Stakeholder engagement encourages collaboration with the development team.
   D. Stakeholders are responsible for providing technical details to the development team.

6. A good project manager understands that:
   A. Change is inevitable
   B. A well-constructed schedule requires no changes
   C. The baseline is fixed
   D. Many projects are alike

7. The project has been going well until you recently discover a member of your development team has wasted 6 days working to complete his favorite feature of the project, even though that feature only has to be 50% implemented for the business to release it after the first iteration. This discovery comes as a shock to the entire team. How could this situation have BEST been avoided on an Agile project?
   A. By managing and monitoring the team closer
   B. By helping the customer understand that the completed feature will save time in the long run
   C. By making sure everyone on the team understands the charter of the project
   D. By making the developer check in their code at the end of the night

8. This team model consists of a group of people who have a traditional boss but who also share some of his/her responsibility and authority.
   A. Team Spirit Model
   B. Traditional Model
   C. Task Force Model
   D. Distributed Model

9. Which of the following is a specific type of Lean waste?
   A. Breakdown
   B. Complexity
   C. Rejects
   D. Error Handling

10. Top-Down estimating can BEST be described as:
    A. Using the WBS to approximate the size (duration and cost) and risk of a project (or phase)
    B. Using experience from previous project data to draw accurate estimates for new "analogous" projects
    C. Writing points on the bottoms of plastic cups, turning them upside, and assigning stories to them
    D. Writing points on the bottoms of index cards, turning them upside, and assigning stories to them

# Agile Self-Assessment Answers

1. Answer: A

   Explanation: Answer A is the most logical one because after a company has used Lean to improve its business processes, the next step would be to improve the quality of its output. In other words, it wouldn't make much sense to improve the speed at which you are delivering low quality. Three Sigma reduction plan is a fabricated option. Creating a new organizational chart could happen as a result of the new Lean, but there is no indication that the creation of a new organizational chart is required. Therefore, the next logical step would be to move into the quality improvement phase.

2. Answer: A

   Explanation: The velocity history can be used as a means of mitigating the risk of schedule slippage by helping create a more accurate release plan.

3. Answer: B

   Explanation: As features are completed within each iteration, they must be accepted and reviewed by both the team and the product owner as Done-Done. This aim is achieved through daily planning.

4. Answer: A

   Explanation: Although a high-performance team can be all of these things, the best answer in relation to Agile is self-organizing.

5. Answer: D

   Explanation: A stakeholder can be anyone who can be affected by or who affects the Agile team but *may* not participate in the work directly. So although there may be stakeholders who can contribute technical expertise to the project, they are not responsible for providing technical implementation details to the development team. Stakeholders assist best by ensuring the project stays on track and maintains value. The technical implementation required to deliver that value is the responsibility of the development team.

6. Answer: A

   Explanation: The Agile Manifesto states that there is more value in responding to change than there is in following a plan. It is impossible to plan out a project to perfection. There are too many moving parts and factors, regardless of the similarity a project may have to others managed in the past. A good Agile project manager understands that change is inevitable, which is why visibility, inspection, and adaptation are so important on projects. That's not to say that this tendency should be an excuse for poor planning. All other statements made within the remaining options are false.

7. Answer: C

   Explanation: Since Agile methods are often used on projects where uncertainty around requirements and high rates of change exist, there is typically less certainty around scope. To avoid this tendency, it is important that everyone understands the project charter. Answer A is incorrect because Agile teams are expected to be self-empowered and self-organizing with no need for direct management. Answer B is incorrect because it is not the role of the Agile project manager to tell the customer what his values should be. Answer D is incorrect because simply checking in the code every night would not have prevented this problem either.

8. Answer: A

9. Answer: B

   Explanation: Complexity is the only formal type of waste specifically called out in Lean.

10. Answer: B

# Agile Introduction
## Summary

- ✓ Described Agile Terminology
- ✓ Examined History
- ✓ Related the Manifesto Values and Principles to Everyday Work
- ✓ Explained the Agile Framework
- ✓ Discussed Incremental Development
- ✓ Assessed the Principles of Systems Thinking
- ✓ Compared Agile vs. XP vs. Scrum
- ✓ Took an Agile Self-Assessment

# Value-Driven Delivery

## Module 1
- PMI-ACP Exam Preparation Course

# Module 1
## Objectives

- Asses Ways to Maximize Value and Minimize Waste
- Discuss How to Increase Value through Quality
- Explain Customer Valued Prioritization
- Compare Value to Anti-Value
- Interpret Release Early, Release Often
- Describe Value Stream Analysis
- Optimize the Value Stream
- Demonstrate Value-Based Prioritization
- Illustrate Financial Operational Efficiency

# Quality Control Processes

- **Verification**
  - A quality control process that is used to evaluate whether a product, service, or system complies with regulations, specifications, or conditions imposed at the start of a development phase
    - Verification can take place in development, scale-up, or production. It is often an internal process

- **Validation**
  - A quality assurance process of establishing a high degree of evidence that a product, service, or system accomplishes its intended requirements
    - It often involves acceptance of fitness for purpose with end users and other product stakeholders

---

Let's begin by taking a look at Verification.

Verification is a quality control process that is used to evaluate whether a product, service, or system complies with regulations, specifications, or conditions imposed at the start of a development phase; it can also take place during development, scale-up, or production. It is often an internal process.

Then we have Validation.

Validation is a quality assurance process use to establish a high degree of evidence that a product, service, or system accomplishes its intended requirements.

It often involves acceptance of fitness for purpose with end users and other product stakeholders.

Note: In the real world, the Verification and Validation processes may also be referred to as, V & V.

# Maximizing Value and Minimizing Waste

- **Thinking Lean Centers on 5 Basic Principles:**

    1. Identify value from the standpoint of the end customer.
    2. Identify the sequence of steps in the value stream for each product and eliminate steps that do not create value.
    3. Isolate and tighten each value-creating step that occurs in the sequence to achieve a continuously smooth flow of product toward the customer.
    4. Develop a pull system to allow customers to pull value from upstream activity.
    5. Continuously improve the process by:
        - Actively removing waste and defects until perfect value is created with no waste—and perfection is achieved.

The purpose of Lean is to create more value for customers with fewer resources. Every action one takes during a process should be focused on maximizing customer value while minimizing waste.

Providing a perfect stream of value to the customer through the creation of processes that have zero waste is the ultimate goal. Organizations that strive to understand the needs of their customers and that focus on continuously increasing value to them are the epitome of a Lean organization.

# Chartering

- **Synchronizes the Project Team and Customer at a High Level on the Project's Value and Goals**
  Sec. 6
  - Gain agreement into the W5+
    - What
    - Why
    - Who
    - When
    - Where
    - How
      - … defines attributes of the project and give authority to proceed.

Chartering happens prior to release planning. It provides an opportunity to address any special needs or considerations that may need to be accounted for and monitored during the project.

The customer, product owner, or business sponsors begin the chartering session by explaining in a few statements (elevator pitch) what the product is and why it is valuable. The purpose is to gain the support of the stakeholders and team members in understanding What, Why, Who, When, Where, and How the product is going to be delivered.

- What is the value?
- Why does it add value?
- Who it is for?
- When does it need to be completed?
- Where are we going to look for information to get it completed?
- How will we know when it's done and if it was a success?

Answering these questions invokes a higher level of engagement for the team members and establishes a deeper level of commitment for all involved.

# Chartering (continued)

- **Synchronizes the Project Team and Customer at a High Level on the Project's Value and Goals** (continued)
  - Since Agile methods are often used on projects where uncertainty around requirements and high rates of change exist, there is typically less certainty around scope
    - In general, Agile charters have less detail
    - Elements of Agile change should be clearly outlined in the charter

Since Agile methods are often used on projects where uncertainty around requirements and high rates of change exist, there is typically less certainty around scope.

In other words, Agile charters have less detail, and elements of Agile change should be clearly outlined in the charter.

To avoid confusion, it is important that everyone understands the project charter.

Keep in mind that a charter can also be used to provide structure to something as basic as a small research initiative assigned to a team member. The purpose of creating a charter for smaller initiatives is to keep members focused on the objective of what they have been tasked to accomplish, just as the project charter is used to keep everyone on the project focused.

# Value-Based Analysis

## What is it?

- In Agile, it is the systematic analysis that identifies and selects the best value alternatives for:

  - Process designs
  - Processes
  - Systems

- It flows by repeatedly asking…
  - "Can the cost of this item or step be reduced or eliminated without diminishing the effectiveness, required quality, or customer satisfaction?"

---

Value-Based Analysis (VBA) is a decision process that relates the needs of the customer with the specific resources available in the marketplace. It asks a set of Critical to Quality (CTQ) questions to determine what the customer needs and what resources are available to meet those needs.

In Agile, it is the systematic analysis that identifies and selects the best value alternatives for:

Process designs
Processes
Systems

In short, it is accomplished by repeatedly asking, "Can the cost of this item or step be reduced or eliminated without diminishing the effectiveness, required quality, or customer satisfaction?"

# Value-Based Analysis (continued)

## ■ Value-Driven Planning

1.13

- A plan to do the most valuable things with your resources and of those valuable things doing the most valuable first
  - I.e., Value Drivers
    - *Constantly improving the performance on the way to the goal has more value than reaching the planned goal.*

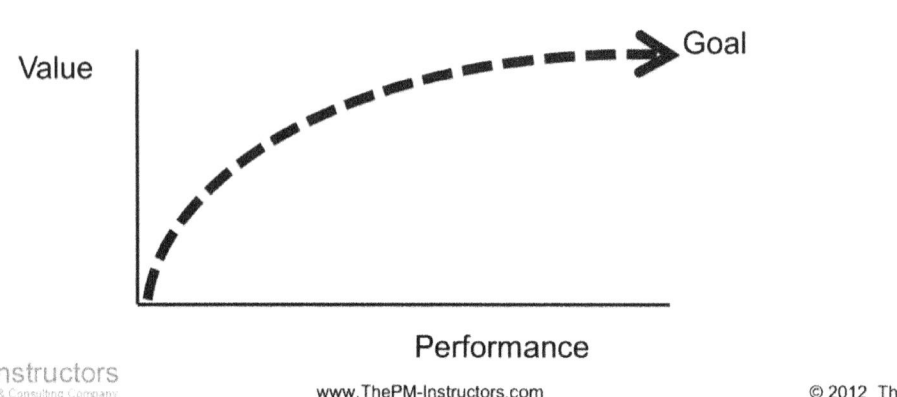

Based on the outcome of your Value-Based Analysis, you put together a Value-Driven Plan.

A Value-Driven Plan encourages you do the most valuable things with your resources and of those valuable things doing the most valuable first.

The purpose of this plan is to identify what resources you have available to achieve your goal and which tasks should be done first, based on their value.

In turn, the items on this list become your Value Drivers such as: cash flow, new products, technology advancements, sales momentum, earnings, etc.

Then, strive to constantly improve your performance while reaching the goal, instead of simply focusing on reaching the planned goal.

And upon learning how to achieve your stated goal faster, the steps you followed can be standardized into a repeatable process. This results in multiple opportunities to create valuable outcomes, thereby making perfection of your performance more valuable than reaching the goal.

# Value-Driven Planning

- **Plan-Driven Panning**
  - Establishes a target(s) that must be reached, and aids in devising a plan to get you there
    - I.e., Planning Drivers
      - *Achieving the planned goal is more valuable than how the goal was achieved.*

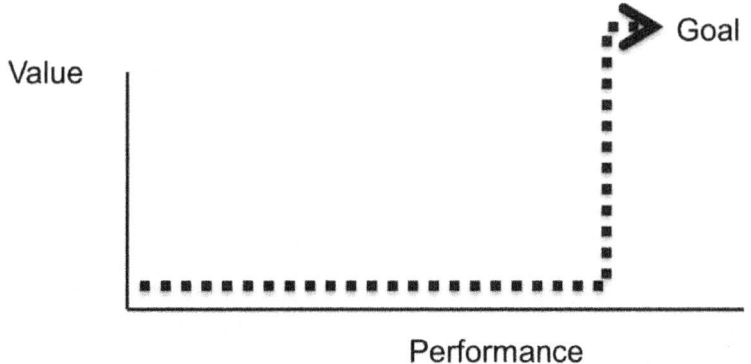

In contrast to Value-Driven Planning, Plan-Driven Planning focuses on simply achieving the goal.

It establishes a targeted that must be reached, and aids in devising a plan to get you there.

Items on target list become your Planning Drivers such as: completing a set of documents, completing a task, arrival of new resource, getting a document signed off, etc., and, achieving the planned goal is more valuable than how the goal was achieved.

In this case, how you achieve the goal doesn't matter as much as simply saying that the goal has been achieved. For example, if two people are assigned the task of delivering a product within a 1-year timeframe, a Plan-Driven individual would be content to use the entire time to reach the goal, whereas a Value-Driven person would not only work to achieve the goal, but also seek to reduce the amount of time it takes to accomplish the goal—and possibly release two products within one year.

# Value-Driven Planning (continued)

## ■ Product and Innovation Development

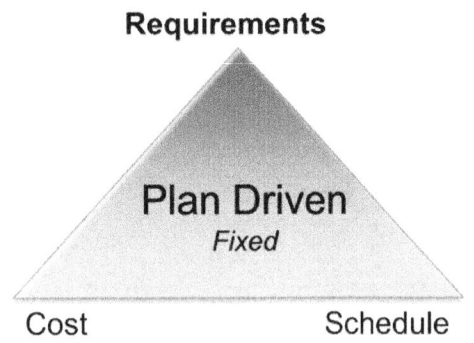

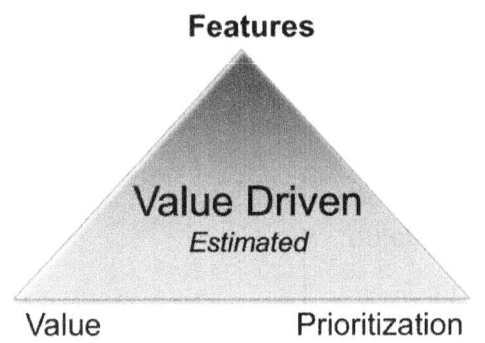

Estimates to complete requirements are usually driven by cost and schedule

Estimates to complete features are driven by value and release prioritization.

---

Notice that in the Plan-Driven approach, estimates to complete requirement are usually driven by cost and schedule.

When using the Value-Driven approach, estimates to complete feature are driven by value and release prioritization.

The difference between the two approaches is that Plan-Driven programs may find themselves constrained to sticking within a concrete cost and schedule structure. Meanwhile, a Value-Driven program focuses on achieving value, or a quicker ROI, by identifying and removing time-consuming concrete constraints.

# How to Identify Value

## Building What Matters

- The key to delivering high perceived value is attaching value to each of the customers or organizations

  - Ensure they feel that what you are offering is beyond expectation
  - Emphasizing that you're helping them solve a problem
  - Offering a solution
  - Producing results
  - Making them happy

---

In Agile, prioritization can be used to establish the sequence of delivery, or to even rule out features. When the criteria for prioritization is based on the ROI, an

Agile practitioner may decompose the value of a feature according to things like: company strategy, market comparison, value analysis, or user feedback. In turn, that will help you focus on building what matters, first.

The key to delivering high perceived value is attaching value to each of the customers or organizations.

You must ensure they feel that what you are offering is beyond their expectation.

You can do this by: constantly emphasizing that your objective is to solve their problems, by offering solutions that will produce the results they want, and have a happy outcome.

# How to Identify Value (continued)

## ■ Value Is the Mental Estimation a Consumer Makes of Something

1. The value of something is how much a product or service is worth to someone relative to other things.
2. It may be conceptualized as the relationship between the consumer's perceived benefits in relation to the perceived costs of receiving these benefits.

■ It is often expressed as the equation:

Value = Benefits / Cost

■ In Agile value can be very subjective because is based on the prioritization of a collection of valuable items
  ■ Thus, the value of an iteration may be quantified based on each features return on investment (ROI)

---

Given that, we can refine the concept of value further by saying:

The value of something is how much a product or service is worth to someone relative to other things.

It may be conceptualized as the relationship between the consumer's perceived benefits in relation to the perceived costs of receiving these benefits.

And we can express value in the equation: Value is equal to something's benefit, divided by it's cost.

In Agile, value can be very subjective because it is based on the prioritization of a collection of valuable items. Thus, the value of an iteration may be quantified based on each features return on investment (ROI).

# How to Identify Value (continued)

- **Examples**
    - For an **individual** to deliver value...
        - One has to increase their skills and knowledge as a means of showing they can contribute to an organization by delivering some type of useful benefit (e.g., getting paid for a job)
    - For an **organization** to deliver value...
        - It has to improve its value-to-cost ratio
        - It has to deliver high value, at a low price, to be perceived as high value.
        - Conversely, if it delivers high value, at a high price, the perceived value may be low.

For an individual to deliver value they have to increase their skills and knowledge as a means of showing they can contribute to an organization, by delivering some type of useful benefit (e.g., getting paid for a job).

For an organization to deliver value...

1. It has to improve its value-to-cost ratio
2. It has to deliver high value, at a low price, to be perceived as high value.
3. Conversely, if it delivers high value, at a high price, the perceived value may be low.

 Discussion Note: As a consumer, what is your personal measure of value? Time? Money? How are the projects you are currently working on being measured in terms of delivering value?

# How to Identify Value (continued)

## Other Types of Value

- Something can have Intrinsic Value:
    - The value of melting down a gold coin

- Something can have Extrinsic Value:
    - The value that arises out of an agreement

- Something can have Market Value:
    - What others are willing to pay

- Something can have Book Value:
    - The legally defined value

# Increase Value through Quality

- **Quality**

    *Quality is the measure of value added by a productive endeavor. Potential quality is the maximum possible value added per unit. Actual quality is the current value added per unit of input. The difference between potential quality and actual quality is muda."*

    – Thomas Pzydek

- **Six Sigma** provides:
    - A general approach to reduce muda
    - A collection of methods to analyze cause-and-effect relationships
    - A strategy for discovering opportunities for improvement

- **Lean** is a set of pre-packaged, proven techniques used to reduce muda

---

An integrated approach to process improvement using Lean principles and Six Sigma provides a holistic way to maximize the entire supply chain by eliminating waste, controlling variation, and improving quality. It accomplishes this objective by understanding the Value Stream or, more specifically, performing Value-Based Analysis.

# Increase Value through Quality (continued)

- **Drivers of Quality**
    - **Customers** – In a customer-driven organization, quality is established with a focus on satisfying or exceeding customer requirements, expectations, needs, and preferences

    - **Products/Services** – A culture of product/service-driven conformance to requirements and zero defect concepts
        - Has roots in producing a product/service that meets stated or documented requirements

    - **Employee Satisfaction** – Organization takes care of employees' needs so they can be free to worry about only the customer

    - **Organizational Focus** – Total organizational quality instead of using a segmented approach to implementing quality

---

In the previous section we examined Value Drivers, now we are going to examine several types of quality drivers.

First, there are Customers. In a customer-driven organization, quality is established with a focus on satisfying or exceeding customer requirements, expectations, needs, and preferences.

Then, we have Products/Services. A culture of product/service-driven conformance to requirements and zero defect concepts. These types of organizations have their roots in producing product or service that meets stated or documented requirements.

Next, there is the Employee Satisfaction driver. These organization take care of employees' needs so the employees can be free to worry about only the customer.

Last, is the Organizational Focus driver. In these organizations, the focus on total organizational quality instead of using a segmented approach to implementing quality.

# Customer Valued Prioritization

- **Applying Lean to Build-In Quality**
  Sec. 7
  - Lean "process improvement" reduces production time.
    - Quality and revenues increase, while decreasing waste caused by delays
  - Lean focuses on maximizing the efficiency of the entire process flow, from concept to consumption
    - Focusing on the results of large inventories between each step
      - *i.e., requirements are fully completed, but the code is not designed or tested*
    - Inventories hide errors in the process
  - Involving customers during the Lean "improvement process" allows them to prioritize the value in their product
    - This not only increases quality but also reduces waste that results from building the wrong product

---

In order for organizations to be globally competitive, they must focus on speed, efficiency, and customer value. Six Sigma and Lean are both powerful tools for improving quality, productivity, profitability, and market competitiveness. While Lean focuses on eliminating waste and improving flow, Six Sigma focuses on reducing variation using a problem-solving approach and statistical tools.

Lean "process improvement" reduces production time. As a result, quality and revenues increase, while decreasing waste caused by delays.

Lean also focuses on maximizing the efficiency of the entire process flow, from concept to consumption; doing so minimizes large inventories between each step. For example, a set of requirements for a project may be fully completed, but if code is not designed or tested, then the idle requirements become inventory in the software development process. Additionally, these hidden inventories hide errors in the production process.

It is also critical to involve customers during the Lean "improvement process". This will allow them to prioritize the value in their product, which will not only increase quality, but also reduce waste that results from building the wrong product.

# Anti-Value

- **Risk Erodes Value**
  1.13
  - The preservation or creation of value is usually the primary objective for an organization
    - Therefore, managing risk can add value to an organization.
  - Risk is closely related to value
    - Project risk can be equated as anti-value.
      - i.e., things that can erode, remove, or reduce value if they are to occur
      - If value is the fire, then risk is the water that can put it out.
  - Since risk has the potential to reduce value, we must minimize it in order to maximize value

---

When high levels of risk are taken without increasing revenues or reducing costs, less value is provided to the customer. Therefore, risk management can add value to an organization. Value-Driven Delivery provides many risk reducing practices that organically minimizes a project's exposure to risk.

The preservation or creation of value is usually the primary objective for an organization. Therefore, managing risk can add value to an organization.

This is because risk is closely related to value.

Project risk can be equated to anti-value, because the more things the can jeopardize the success of a project, that are not removed, will reduce the value of the project if they occur.

In other words, if value is the fire, then risk is the water that can put it out.

Therefore, since risk has the potential to reduce value, we must minimize it in order to maximize value.

# Anti-Value (continued)

## Risk Erodes Value (continued)

- Risk management can add value to an organization in the following areas:

  - **Continuously Improving Risk Management**
    Reducing overall risk exposure of the organization, thereby increasing value

  - **Revenue Growth**
    Improved risk management allows organizations to make better decisions around customer service and strategic acquisitions

  - **Cost Reduction**
    Replacing inefficient manual risk management activities (controls) with efficient automated activities

---

Consider Value-Driven Delivery like deposits being paid into your bank account, and risks as re-occurring withdrawals.

To offset these withdrawals, risk management adds value to an organization in the following areas:

Continuously Improving Risk Management allows originations to actively reduce overall risk exposure of the organization, thereby increasing value.

Risk Management improves Revenue Growth by allowing organizations to make better decisions around customer service and strategic acquisitions.

Risk Management improves Cost Reduction by replacing inefficient manual risk management activities (controls) with efficient automated activities.

# Anti-Value Planning

Although customers have visibility into the development process while the software is being created, they have limited ability to incorporate changes through feedback.

*Requirements → Design → Implementation → Verification → Maintenance*

---

Think back onto the relationship between this diagram and what we discussed about the Waterfall approach. Specifically, in Waterfall, although customers have visibility into the development process while the software is being created, they have limited ability to incorporate changes through feedback.

Well, unlike the Waterfall approach where the customer's involvement is leveraged heavily during the onset and requirements gathering of a project, the Agile Customer-Value Prioritization approach encourages, and ideally requires, the customer to be actively involved in directing the product development process based on their needs, and highest priority values. Such that, regardless of which phase a project may be in, the customer's needs are always the primary objective.

This is also expressed in the Agile Manifesto as: "Agile processes harness change for the customer's competitive advantage."

# Early Value

- **Incremental Delivery**
  - Allows the client to direct the development process in order to get the software features they want
    - By delivering high value early, the team demonstrates an understanding of the stakeholders' needs
      - Shows recognition for the most important aspects of the project, and displays an ability to deliver

Once you have learned how to identify value and increase value, it would be nice to obtain the value faster, right? Well, this is the purpose of incremental delivery.

Incremental delivery allows the client to direct the development process in order to get the software features they want.

This results in delivering high value early, and enables the team to demonstrate an understanding of the stakeholders' needs, while showing they recognize the most important aspects of the project; and more importantly, it displays that they have the ability to deliver.

# Early Value (continued)

- **Incremental Delivery** (continued)
  - Deliver Value As Soon As Possible
    - The longer you run a project, the greater the horizon of risk for:
      - Failure
      - Reduced benefits
      - Opportunity erosion, etc.
    - Conversely, quick results:
      - Build rapport
      - Create circles of support
      - Increase speed to market
      - Minimize financial exposure
      - Get stakeholders on board early
      - Increase stakeholders' confidence

---

Agile corporations that effectively manage risk are able to rapidly adjust to change, focus on customer-value prioritization, and reliably increase their speed to market.

So when you are in involved on an Agile project, you goal is to deliver value as soon as possible!

This is because the longer you run a project, the greater the horizon of risk for things like: Failure, reduced benefits, opportunity erosion, etc.

Conversely, quick results:

Builds rapport with the customer, create circles of support, increase speed to market, minimize financial exposure, get stakeholders on board early and increase stakeholders' confidence.

# Release Early, Release Often

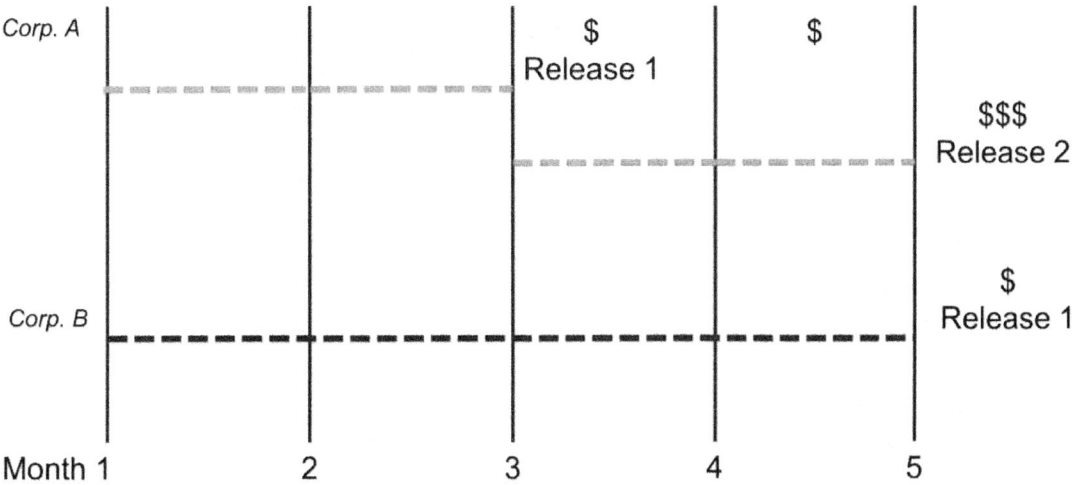

This example illustrates that if Corp A and Corp B are working to release the same project, and Corp A uses early release schedules---Corp A is able to start generating money faster, and over a longer period of time, than Corp B.

This is an obvious value increasing benefit to releasing early, and releasing often.

# Positive Value

- **Incorporating Customer Feedback Loops**
    - To get the best indication of how well or poorly your business and team is performing, reach out to your customers by creating a customer feedback loop
        - Be proactive about identifying your customers' needs and encouraging open discussions, and handle customer concerns promptly

- **Conditions of Customer Satisfaction**
    - Agile teams are able to quickly obtain a positive ROI for customers by prioritizing features based on customer feedback
        - The Kano Model separates customers' satisfaction level toward a product into the following three levels of qualities: Basic Features, Linear Features, Exciter Features

1.12

1.2

---

To get the best indication of how well or poorly your business and team is performing, reach out to your customers by creating a customer feedback loop.

Be proactive about identifying your customers' needs and encouraging open discussions, and handle customer concerns promptly.

Agile teams are able to quickly obtain a positive ROI for customers by prioritizing features based on customer feedback.

The Kano Model separates customers' satisfaction level toward a product into the following three levels of qualities: Basic Features, Linear Features, Exciter

Features, which we will be looking at later.

Another benefit of prioritizing features based on the needs of the customer is that it provides a way to remove complexity from a project. It's common during the initial phases of a project for a customer to request every "bell and whistle" feature they can conceive. To satisfy their needs, yet keep them manageable, offer to take all of their requests—but in the form of a prioritized list. Doing so will help remove complexity from the project, and simultaneously allow them to *self-filter* their requests by having to place a strategic value on them.

# Positive Value (continued)

## ■ Collecting the Voice of the Customer

- The Kano model is a two-dimensional quality model used to analyze customer requirements.
  - It uses two types of questionnaires and an evaluation table to classify the requirements into different categories (Kano, 1984).
    - The methodology is based on a structured characterization of the product features with the help of a user questionnaire.
- The goal of the questionnaire is to determine the customer satisfaction level.
  - Both functional and dysfunctional questions are included in the survey.
- When the survey is completed, a result table is produced and the answers from the customer are evaluated.

---

How do you know what's valuable to your customers?

As a consumer, how much would you pay for a car that didn't come with windows as the standard package? Would you be willing to purchase the car if it saved you $1000 more a year than your current mode of transportation? Would you pay an extra $1000 for the car if it included an audio connector for your hand-held mobile device?

Well, the Kano model is a two-dimensional quality model used to analyze customer requirements.

It uses two types of questionnaires and an evaluation table to classify the requirements into different categories

# Positive Value (continued)

- **Conditions of Customer Satisfaction Categories**
  - **Basic, Threshold, or Must-Have Features**
    Represent the features that must be present in a product for it to be successful
    - When you purchase a car, you expect it to have windows. However, if there were no windows you **would** be dissatisfied.
  - **Linear Features**
    Represent the features that increase the level of customer satisfaction in direct proportion to the quantity of the feature
    - A super-super-sized meal for just an extra $0.29 cents
  - **Exciters and Delighters**
    Represent the features a customer wouldn't expect but gets excited over if provided
    - Voice-to-text email application on mobile phone

# Positive Value (continued)

## ■ Collecting the Voice of the Customer

- The relationship between the presence of a distinct quality element and customer satisfaction can be shown on a two-dimensional Kano plot.
    - The x-axis represents the degree of functionality the particular quality attribute has in the product service.
        - The Dysfunctional level measures whether the feature Quality is or is not implemented at an acceptable Functional level (i.e., requirement fulfillment).
    - The y-axis measures the level of customer satisfaction – from Dissatisfied to Satisfied.

---

Identifying what your customers associate with value (is willing to pay for) is the purpose of the Kano Model of Satisfaction. Understanding this is important because the things you place a value on may not be the same things your customers place a value on. While this may seem obvious within the context of a traditional vendor customer relationship, how often do IT teams actively engage the customer when the product is being developed for an internal department? Aren't they still a customers? For example, an organization may want to migrate their entire business to a Service Oriented Architecture (computer based), however, each department in the organization currently feels they are operating at maximum efficiency using the legacy system (old method). How would you approach getting them to accept the migration?

# Positive Value (continued)

## ■ The Kano Model of Customer Satisfaction

- **Basic:** Regardless of how much this feature is increased, it will not increase customer satisfaction. That is because customers consider it a must-have feature.

- **Linear:** The more of this feature you add above the expected level of Quality, the more satisfied the customer will be.

- **Exciter:** Adding even a miniscule amount of this feature above the expected level of Quality, immediately increases the customer satisfaction level.

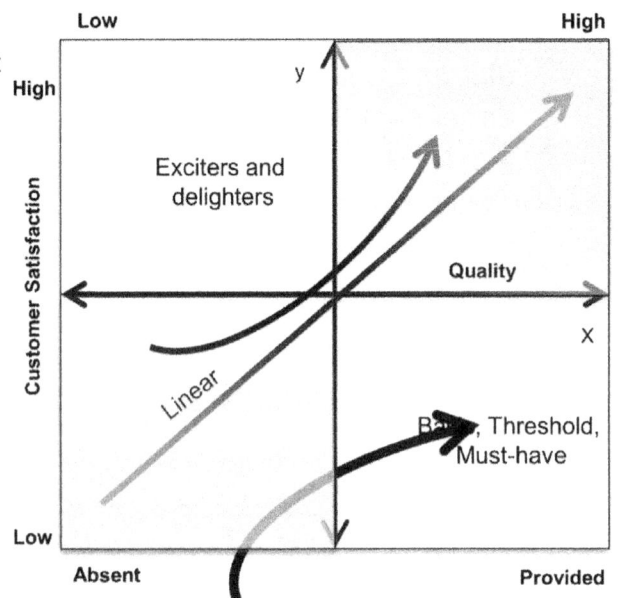

Agile organizations leverage the Kano Model to help their teams uncover, classify, and integrate customer needs and attributes into the products or services they are developing. Missing any of the three types of needs will jeopardize the success of the product offering.

# Customer Feedback Techniques

- **Collecting the Voice of the Customer (VOC)**
  - The Kano Model is a VOC technique that provides five categories into which customer requirements can be classified by questionnaire.
    - Each question has two parts…
      *How do you feel if the feature is present in the product?*
      *How do you feel if the feature is not present in the product?*

The process of capturing a customer's expectations is known as the Voice of the Customer (VOC). It's a term used in business and IT to describe the likes and dislikes of your customers.

VOC is used to produce a detailed set of customer wants and needs, organized into a hierarchical structure, then prioritized in terms of relative importance and satisfaction.

The Kano Model is a VOC technique that provides five categories into which customer requirements can be classified by questionnaire

Each question has two parts…

*How do you feel if the feature is present in the product?*

*How do you feel if the feature is not present in the product?*

# Value Stream Analysis

- **Value Chain**
    - Describes how the worker in the current step of the workflow enables the worker in the next step to create value for the customer  Sec. 10
        - At each step the worker is the customer of the previous worker.
        - The goal of each worker is to create value for the next customer.

- **Value Stream**
    - The sequence of steps that describe a workflow from start to finish
        - **Value stream mapping** is then used to analyze the flow of information required to bring a product or service to a consumer.
            - The goal is to add value at each step until the work is complete.

 Understanding the value stream of an organization can also be used to motivate employee by allowing them to see the big picture of how they add value to the organization, and possibly answering the most basic human question, "What's in it for me?"

# Value Stream Analysis (continued)

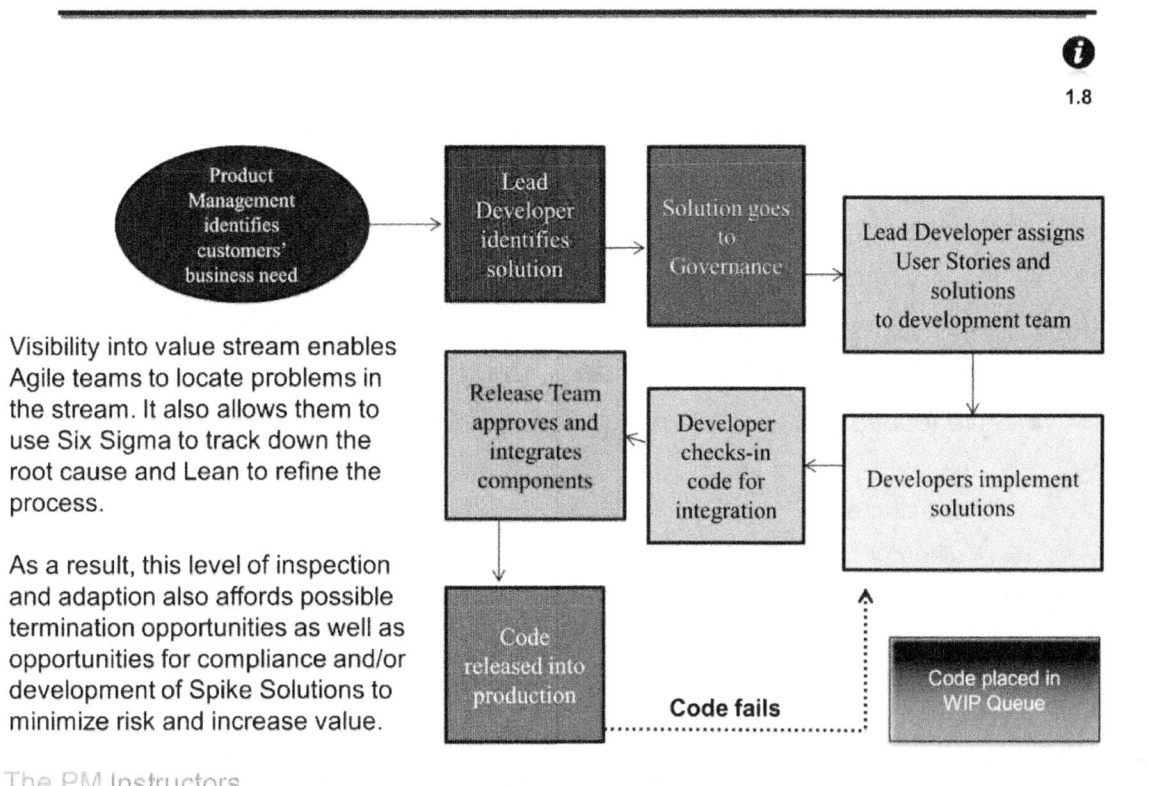

Visibility into the value stream enables Agile teams to locate problems in the stream. It also allows them to use Six Sigma to track down the root cause and Lean to refine the process.

As a result, this level of inspection and adaption also affords possible termination opportunities as well as opportunities for compliance and/or development of

Spike Solutions to minimize risk and increase value.

When Lean, Agile and Six Sigma (LASS) are incorporated into the value stream, organizations can increase their 1) speed and agility, 2) customer-value prioritization, and 3) process enforcement and compliance.

Additionally, by having visibility into the entire end-to-end process, organizations can simplify their auditing and reporting with the use of metrics as a way of documenting Compliance.

# Value Stream Analysis (continued)

- **Make the System "Fast-Flexible-Flow"**
  - Prioritized and sustainable, value streams are created in Lean enterprises through a coordinated effort among:
    - Business
    - Management
    - Delivery team
  - Lean focuses on improving communication as a whole, through the end-to-end creation of value.
    - Agile focuses on the communication at lower levels among the:
      - Team
      - Product owner
      - Customer
      - etc.

# Value Stream Analysis (continued)

- **Make the System "Fast-Flexible-Flow"** (continued)  1.9
  - Lean emphasizes that software teams are only as capable as the processes that have been established for them to follow.
    - Leverages the Emergent Design methodology to focus on delivering small pieces of working code with business value
    - Performs activities just before they are needed (Just in Time) to:
      - Reduce risk
      - Eliminate waste
      - Shorten time-to-market

---

The internal design of a development process is created for the purpose of future maintenance so that enhancements can be performed throughout development. Documentation may be internal or external and consists of value stream maps for business or writing of APIs for the software. The engineering process selected by the developing team will determine how much internal documentation (if any) is required. Plan-driven models like the Waterfall method typically generate more documentation than Agile models.

Lean emphasizes that software teams are only as capable as the processes that have been established for them to follow, and leverages the Emergent Design methodology to focus on delivering small pieces of working code with business value.

It focuses on performing activities just before they are needed (Just in Time) to:

Reduce risk

Eliminate waste

Shorten time-to-market

# Value Stream Analysis (continued)

- **Value Stream Mapping**
  - A value stream map looks quite complicated but its concept is quite simple.
    - It is basically a map showing how the product's lifecycle begins and ends. The customer is usually the start and end point.

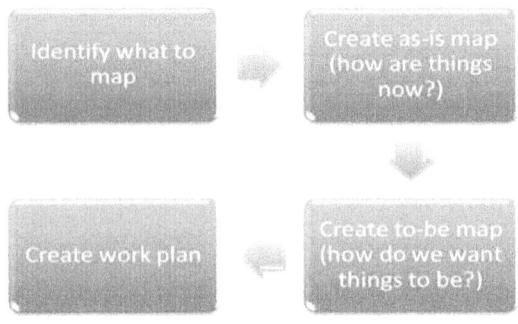

A value stream map looks quite complicated but its concept is quite simple. It is basically a map showing how the product's lifecycle begins and ends. The customer is usually the start and end point.

# Optimizing the Value Stream

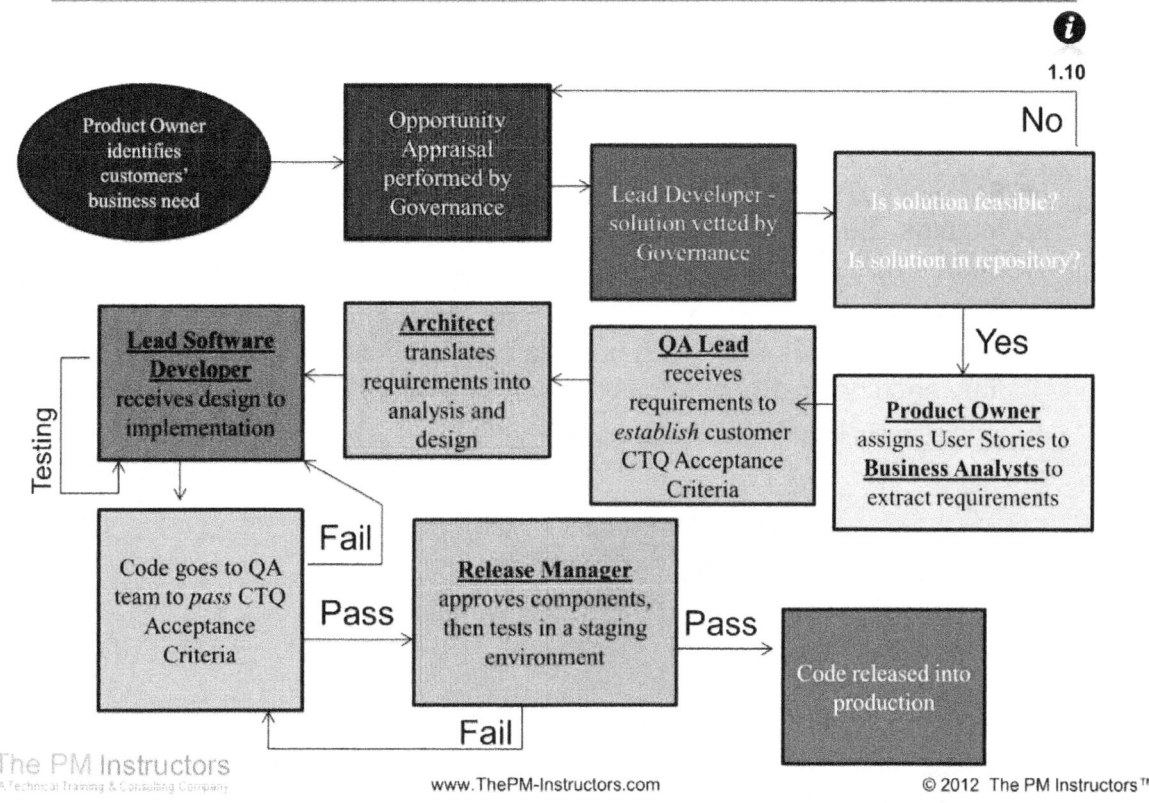

Value stream mapping allows the business team to capture things like supplier, input, process, and output as customer diagrams. It can also reveal failure modes as well as provide a starting point to perform effects analysis, to perform a technical feasibility study (Spike Solutions), and to solicit feedback from customers.

Having access to the big picture of your project's inputs and outputs can also provide a great starting point where you can look to analyze the root cause of problems taking place on your project.

# Optimizing the Value Stream (continued)

- **Takt Time/Cycle Time**
  - A term for the beat or rhythm of the activities that make up a value stream
    - For example, if the takt time of a value stream is set at 30 minutes, then all of the activities in the process are designed and resourced to be completed within 30 minutes.
    - When every role of a value stream executes to the same beat or takt time, the output of each upstream role is finished at the same time each downstream role is ready for the input.
      - This helps to achieve a balanced flow.

Takt Time, or Cycle Time, is a term used to describe the rhythm of the activities that make up a value stream. For example, if the takt time of a value stream is set at 30 minutes, then all of the activities in the process are designed and resourced to be completed within 30 minutes

When every role of a value stream executes to the same beat or takt time, the output of each upstream role is finished at the same time each downstream role is ready for the input, and this helps to achieve a balanced flow

In order for this to be effective, the time required to complete work at each station must be less than the takt time required for the product to be completed within the allotted time.

There are obviously going to be reasons for stoppages, so the reality is that no human or machine will ever be able to maintain 100% efficiency. However, padding should be built in to the schedule for these instances and thus the production line will need to be designed to run at a faster rate. As such, takt time may be adjusted according to requirements within the company.

# Optimizing the Value Stream (continued)

- **Emergent Design**
    - Design patterns are used to create other design artifacts, resulting in an emergent phenomenon.
        - The properties of the artifact created are more than the sum of its parts.
            - In software, the result of this creative input is a flexible and resilient architecture
    - Can only be achieved by paying close attention to code quality
        - Uses only the essential elements required to achieve the desired outcome

# Optimizing the Value Stream (continued)

- **Emergent Design** (continued)
  - Automated Acceptance and Unit tests must also be incorporated.
    - Improve the thought process by creating test harnesses
      1. Agile Team 1 develops and tests a process resulting in *Product A*.
      2. Agile Team 2 develops and tests a process resulting in *Product B*.
      3. Agile Team 1 and Agile Team 2 re-factor commonalities between Products A & B to create an even better Product C.

# Optimizing the Value Stream (continued)

## ■ Acceptance Testing

Sec. 5

- A method of Test-Driven Development (TDD) that involves writing an executable test before the solution is coded.
    - The Product Manager and/or customer typically develop tests in conjunction with each other.
    - Conducted to determine whether or not a feature satisfies its acceptance criteria
    - Requires discussion about how the acceptance tests are done upfront
        - Focuses the development discussion among customers, developers, and testers
        - Reinforces "Definition of Done" and CTQ

> **Critical to Quality (CTQ):** Links customer needs gathered with process drivers and with specific, measurable characteristics

---

Acceptance tests describe requirements identified by your stakeholders with which they expect the product to conform. They're executable specifications that may verify things like the business rules, features, and non-functional requirements, ensuring that the product is completed to customer satisfaction.

# Operating as a Lean/Agile Organization

- **Know the Health of Your Project**
  - There must be a bidirectional line of communication between the customer and the company.
    - Customers must be able to ask questions, make suggestions, give product reviews, and offer other feedback.
    - As customers respond, businesses must in turn respond to their feedback in a timely manner.
    - This allows for quicker changes while gauging the health of the project.

Like Agile practices, project management techniques can also be tailored to achieve extreme results or extreme project management. In this approach, deliverables are adapted to the characteristics of the organization or product and are submitted in different stages of the iterative lifecycle. For example, since Agile management derives from Agile software development and follows the same standards, the turnaround time of Agile deliverables can be modified into weeks, rather than iterative months.

Lean organizations maintain a bidirectional line of communication between the customer and the company. Customers must be able to ask questions, make suggestions, give product reviews, and offer other feedback. As customers respond, businesses must in turn respond to their feedback in a timely manner. This allows for quicker changes while gauging the health of the project.

# Operating as a Lean/Agile Organization (continued)

- **Know the Health of Your Project** (continued)
  - Getting feedback early can prevent wasted development efforts by providing information about the health of the project
    - If the project is moving too slowly…
      - Resources can be added
      - The project can be de-scoped
      - Deadlines can be extended and the project can even be canceled
    - Reduce costly efforts by stopping the wrong projects early or if it doesn't produce enough benefit-to-cost
      - Agile advocates "fail fast" to prevent wasted effort
      - Lean advocates "learn fast" in hopes of preventing failure

# Operating as a Lean/Agile Organization (continued)

- **Enterprise Risk Management**
  - Quality requirements for inputs and outputs along the value stream represent a substantial benefit to practicing ALSS.
    - By clearly establishing assumptions on the inputs and outputs, we expose the risks and have an opportunity to assess, mitigate, and control them.
      - Accomplished with tools and techniques like:
        - *Spike Solutions and Risk-Based Spikes*
        - *Prototypes*
        - *Acceptance Tests*
        - *Definitions of Done*
    - Discuss transition indicators with customers to preemptively learn about project-specific risks in an effort to prevent total failures.

---

Obtaining quality requirements for inputs and outputs along the value stream represent a substantial benefit to practicing Agile, Lean, Six-Sigm (ALSS).

By clearly establishing assumptions on the inputs and outputs, we expose the risks and have an opportunity to assess, mitigate, and control them.

This type of risk management is accomplished with tools and techniques like: Spike Solutions and Risk-Based Spikes, Prototypes, Acceptance Tests and Definitions of Done.

Another opportunity of risk management is to discuss transition indicators with customers to preemptively learn about project-specific risks in an effort to prevent total failures.

Agile teams strive to provide high-value and high-quality outcomes for their customers. To achieve this aim they are constantly triaging the product backlog to ensure they implement the highest-value requirements first—with the least amount of risk—to maximize stakeholder ROI. However, since requirements change frequently throughout the life of the project, Agile teams need a flexible approach to change management. As a result, Agile is more about adapting to change and risk management, than it is about delivering a product.

# Operating as a Lean/Agile Organization (continued)

- **Enterprise Risk Management** (continued)
  - It promotes discussions about…
    - Regulatory and compliance requirements
    - Response to emergency and business continuity requirements
  - With this approach, operations are able to incorporate both quality and risk, while maintaining maximum agility.

# Operating as a Lean/Agile Organization (continued)

- **Just in Time (JIT)**
  - Is a production strategy that strives to improve business return on investment by reducing in-process inventory carrying costs
    - Focuses on continuous improvement
    - Areas of waste Agile teams must constantly monitor are:
      - Excessive waste times (i.e., meetings)
      - Inflated inventories (i.e., Work in Progress Queues or "WIP Queues")
      - Unnecessary hand-offs (i.e., developer-to-manager code reviews)
  - JIT relies on signals, or Kanban, between the different points in the value chain regarding when to make the next part

---

Just in Time is a production strategy that strives to improve business return on investment by reducing in-process inventory carrying costs. It focuses on continuous improvement, and sure the areas of waste constantly monitored. Examples of waste on project may come in the form of:

Excessive waste times (i.e., meetings)

Inflated inventories (i.e., Work in Progress Queues or "WIP Queues")

Unnecessary hand-offs (i.e., developer-to-manager code reviews)

Just in Time relies on signals, or Kanban, between the different points in the value chain regarding when to make the next part

As previously stated, one of the key components of JIT is to add value with the relentless pursuit of reducing waste, or being firmly committed to continuous improvement.

# Operating as a Lean/Agile Organization (continued)

- **Kanban**
  - Is a scheduling system that tells you…
    - What to produce
    - When to produce it
    - How much to produce
      - …by initiating a demand signal that immediately propagates through the supply chain.
  - A Kanban board is a visual indicator that can be used as an information radiator.
    - Visually provides Agile teams with information backlogs and work-in-process
      - Allows for incremental delivery of products

Kanban (pronounced kahn-bahn) is a Just-In-Time (JIT) technique used for the purpose of minimizing inventory and increasing throughput. This is achieved through the use of highly visible "Signals" which function as indicators to inform other workers in the value stream that more input is needed during a phase of processing.

It is akin to a scheduling system that tells you: What to produce, When to produce it, How much to produce. Each step in the cycle is initiates a demand signal that immediately propagates through the supply chain.

For example, if a book repository uses multiples stations of bins to fulfill their orders, when a bin is empty or in a partial state of fullness a Signal in the form of a colored marker may be placed in the bin to inform the person responsible for keeping the bins full that it needs to be refilled. Likewise, if the book inventory runs low, then the storage department needs to send a similar signal up the chain to re-order books from the supplier. A Kanban board is a visual indicator that can be used as an information radiator to visually provide Agile teams with information backlogs and work-in-process. The Kanban board allows for incremental delivery of products.

# Operating as a Lean/Agile Organization (continued)

## Kanban (continued)

| Backlog | Todo | Dev | Test | RTS |
|---------|------|-----|------|-----|
| M | J | A | G | I |
|   | K | B | H |   |
|   | L | C |   |   |
|   |   | E D |   |   |
|   |   | F |   |   |

Kanban boards are used heavily in Agile/Lean/Six Sigma (ALSS) development methodologies, with the focus on the signaling through the use of Kanban Boards. Kanban is duplicated by using things like a whiteboard, index cards on a bulletin board, sticky notes, or more elaborate means to keep members of the team aware of the current status of their project deliverables.

In the example above, a user story or task is being represented as a sticker on the board. The whiteboard is divided into columns and given labels such as still in the "Backlog", "To Do.", in "(Dev)elopment,", "Test" and "(R)elease (T)o (S)tagging." As the project moves forward, tasks are moved along from one column to the next, and everyone on the team can see what the status is and what task is due next.

This level of visibility into the development process aids to empower the development team to be a "pull" system. In other words, a developer can pull a card from the "To Do" column, take responsibility for it, and own it until it's DONE. Additionally, the product manager can see what the status is at any moment.

# Operating as a Lean/Agile Organization (continued)

- **Incremental Delivery**
  - Lean organizations use JIT demand-driven systems to allow for Incremental Delivery.
    - Produce faster turnarounds
    - Lower inventory levels
  - Delivers based on the information the customer is clear about
  - Focus on the core functionality that drives the business process
    - Pareto Principle: 80% of the value will come from 20% of the work

Incremental Delivery can be thought of as a project lifecycle strategy used to reduce the risk of project failure by dividing projects into smaller, more manageable pieces. The resulting sub-projects may deliver parts of the full product, or product versions. These will be enhanced to increase functionality or to improve product quality in subsequent sub-projects.

Lean organizations use JIT demand-driven systems to allow for Incremental Delivery which, produces faster turnarounds, and lower inventory levels.

An important aspect to remember is that Incremental Delivery, delivers based on the information the customer is clear about, and focuses on the core functionality that drives the business process.

This narrow band of focus is in alignment with the with the Pareto Principle which advocates that: 80% of the value will come from 20% of the work.

# Operating as a Lean/Agile Organization (continued)

- **Incremental Delivery** (continued)
    - Reduces requirement speculation from the customer
        - Reduces the risk of uncertainty and develops unused features
    - Agile prescribes short iterations with lots of customer feedback.
        - Enables the business to focus on quickly improving their ROI
        - Products can be released by providing "Minimal Marketable Features."

Sec. 7

---

Agile teams develop software in small, usually time-boxed, portions at a time (incremental) through a series of repeated cycles (iterative). Using this approach allows the team to build upon the knowledge and experience acquired during the previous development phases.

Other benefits of incremental delivery is that it:

Reduces requirement speculation from the customer

Reduces the risk of uncertainty and development of unused features

Similarly, Agile prescribes short iterations with lots of customer feedback which enables the business to focus on quickly improving their ROI, and rroducts can be released by providing "Minimal Marketable Features."

A key step in the process is the continual prioritization of a subset of Backlog Items (aka features, software requirements) that iteratively enhance and evolve until the full system is implemented. High levels of customer satisfaction and higher ROI can be achieved using this approach because as the customer is learning more about their own needs, they are able to share refinements into Minimal Marketable Features with the Agile team. Such refinements can then be implemented and available for use (or testing) by the next end of the iteration.

# Operating as a Lean/Agile Organization (continued)

- **Minimal Marketable Feature**
  - The smallest set of functionality that must be realized in order for the customer to perceive value
    - Characterized by these three attributes:
      - Minimum
      - Marketable
      - Feature

Sec. 7

To achieve a faster ROI on large projects or on a project that may have an extended development life, businesses can prioritize and release incremental pieces of the software based on the customer-valued functionality, or Minimum Marketable Features.

# Value-Based Prioritization

- **Minimally Marketable Feature** (continued)
  - **Minimum:** Requires a mutual agreement of "Definition of Done"
  - **Feature:** Something that is perceived as value by the user
  - **Marketable:** Provides significant value to the customer
  - Value may include revenue generation, cost savings, competitive differentiation, brand projection, or enhanced customer loyalty.
    - Allows features to be delivered according the customer needs

Value obtained from releasing Minimum Marketable Features may include revenue generation, cost savings, competitive differentiation, brand projection, or enhanced customer loyalty

In short, it allows features to be delivered according the customer needs.

# Value-Based Prioritization (continued)

- **Customer-Value Prioritization**
  - Allows the client to direct the development process in order to get the software features they want
    - Elicits information from the customer to decide what should be delivered and when
  - Addresses not only basics such as the good or service's price, but also related issues such as:
    - Prompt delivery of products
    - Quality of service and support provided to the client
    - The relationship that is established between the customer and the supplier

---

Customer-Value Prioritization allows the customer to direct the development process in order to get the software features they want. It elicits information from the customer to decide what should be delivered and when and addresses not only basics, such as the good or service's price, but also related issues such as:

Prompt delivery of products.

Quality of service and support provided to the client.

The relationship that is established between the customer and the supplier.

Agile teams make it their responsibility to elicit the information required to not only build what the customer wants, but also help the customer with what will create the most value. This can also be referred to as identifying a customer's CTQ's, or Critical To Quality factors.

In order for this level of rapid flexibility to occur, the development processes must be open to change.

As the customer, business, and stakeholders become more informed about their target market it often becomes necessary to adjust requirements. The necessity for such readjustment may occur at any point in the development process. Given this need for flexibility, Agile teams are better suited to adapt to these changes given their acceptance of the empirical design process model.

# Value-Based Prioritization (continued)

- **Net Present Value (NPV)**
  Sec. 7
  - Represents the amount an organization has to invest today in order to realize a certain amount in the future
    - Measures how much money a project can be expected to return in today's present value
    - Allows organizations to look at cash flow streams as a single present value amount.

$$NPV = -Principal + \sum_{i=1}^{n} \frac{payment_i}{(1+rate)^i}$$

Net Present Value represents the amount an organization has to invest today in order to realize a certain amount in the future.

The formula is used to measure how much money a project can be expected to return in today's present value, while allowing organizations to look at cash flow streams as a single present value amount.

In Agile development, if the business is deciding whether it should sponsor a project, the prospective project should be positive. On the hand, the project should be rejected if the NPV is negative, because cash flows will also be negative.

For example, if a food retailer wants to develop a custom application to improve their business, first, they should estimate what the future cash flows of that application will generate; then, discount the cash flow into a lump-sum present value amount. We will use $900,000 for our example. If the cost to develop the software is less than $900,000, then developing the software would be a viable idea because the NPV is positive. Conversely, if it is discovered that it would cost more than $900,000 to develop the application, the CEO should not pursue the project, because the investment would present a negative NPV at that time, and reduce the overall value of the project.

# Value-Based Prioritization (continued)

## ■ Return On Investment

Sec. 7

- Expresses how quickly money invested on a project will increase in value
    - The calculation for return on investment can be modified to suit the situation—it all depends on what you include as returns and costs.
        - In Agile, ROI can be used to measure the time effectiveness of retrospective meetings from the team members' perspective.

$$ROI = \frac{(\text{Gain from Investment} - \text{Cost of Investment})}{\text{Cost of Investment}}$$

---

Return On Investment expresses how quickly money invested on a project will increase in value. The calculation for return on investment can be modified to suit the situation, because it all depends on what you include as returns and costs.

In Agile, ROI can be used to measure the time effectiveness of retrospective meetings from the team members' perspective

# Calculating Financial Operational Efficiency

- **Payback Period**
  - The amount of time required to earn back the initial investment
    - How long something takes to "pay for itself"
  - Has limitations and qualifications for its use, because it does not account for:
    - Time value of money
    - Risk
    - Financing
    - Opportunity cost
    - etc.

# Calculating Finical Operational Efficiency (continued)

- **Payback Period** (continued)
  - Advantages:
    - Easy to use
    - Measures the amount and duration of financial risk taken on by the organization
      - *The longer the payback period, the higher the risk*
  - Disadvantages:
    - It values money in the future the same as money today.
    - It doesn't measure the profitability of a project.

# Calculating Finical Operational Efficiency (continued)

- **Discounted Payback Period**
    - Gives the number of years it takes to break even from undertaking the initial expenditure
        - Future cash flows are considered as discounted to time "zero."
        - Similar to a payback period, however, the payback period only measures how long it takes for the initial cash outflow to be paid back, ignoring the time value of money.
        - Solves the payback period problem of valuing money in the future the same as money today

# Reinforcement Training

## Questions & Exercises

### Time to Test your New Knowledge!
Take the next PMI-ACP practice quiz.

# Exercise 1

**Match the Description with the Role**

Guides direction of the project to make sure the team delivers now and in the future

**Team Member**

Has a set of specific interests, skills and strengths, and can function as a generalist-specialist

Implements stories with high business value using good techniques and practices

**Product Manager**

Helps the customer identify usability needs

Responsible for organizing the product backlog by highest priority

**Customer**

Defines the charter by explaining what the product is and why it is valuable

Assists the team with Agile skills, removing impediments and implementing conflict resolution

**Agile Coach/Facilitator**

Works to ensure the team focuses on delivering stories that generate the highest business value possible

Manages the team

Develop acceptance tests in conjunction with each other

# Module 1 Quiz

## Exam Practice Questions

1. The project has been going well until you recently discover a member of your development team has wasted 6 days working to complete his favorite feature of the project, even though that feature only has to be 50% implemented for the business to release it after the first iteration. This discovery comes as a shock to the entire team. How could this situation have BEST been avoided on an Agile project?
    A. By managing and monitoring the team closer
    B. By helping the customer understand that the completed feature will save time in the long run
    C. By making sure everyone on the team understands the charter of the project
    D. By making the developer check in their code at the end of the night

2. One of your colleagues is experiencing trouble managing his project, which is already showing signs of poor performance. He feels that the project is too complex and has asked for your advice. As an Agile project manager, what is the BEST direction you can provide him?
    A. Offer to help him manage the project, even though you are currently at max capacity
    B. Direct him to his functional manager, since it is his manager's job to provide him with training
    C. Direct him to the project management office (PMO)
    D. Explain that he should take steps to prioritize the backlog based on the customer's values to reduce the complexity of the project

3. Sally is currently assigned to a project involving the construction of a new luxury condominium. A project team member has just informed Sally that out of the 210 bags of cement that were ordered to complete the first section of the building, 78 remain unused and must be stored somewhere until they are needed next month. As an Agile project manager, which of the following should Sally do to improve the value stream of this project?
    A. Tell the team member to send the extra packages back to the supplier and re-order them again once they are needed
    B. Rent an offsite storage facility for the extra supplies so they don't interfere with the work
    C. Analyze what caused the error in the product overage
    D. Ask the supplier for a refund on the order

4. Who has the MOST power on an Agile team?
    A. The developers
    B. The project manager
    C. The customer
    D. The entire team

5. All of the following are advantages of using Six Sigma, EXCEPT:
    A. It reduces waste
    B. It is automatically updated once installed
    C. It provides ways to analyze cause-and-effect relationships
    D. It provides a strategy for discovering opportunities for continuous improvement

6. Customers have the most amount of influence within a project during which phase?
    A. Initial phase
    B. Intermediate phase
    C. Final phase
    D. All phases

7. The CFO of Ultra Sweet Confectionary Solutions needs to assess the value of the corporate portfolio for a presentation he is going to provide to the Board members next week. He asks the senior project manager to provide him with a chart that will allow him to visually explain what chocolates are being produced, when they're being produced, and how much is being produced on an hourly basis in the Salt Lake City, UT facility. Where would be the BEST place for the project manager to start looking for this information?
    A. Organizational breakdown structure (OBS)
    B. Resource breakdown structure (RBS)
    C. Kanban board
    D. RACI chart

8. Which of the following BEST describes how an Agile organization would utilize Value-Based Analysis for its customer?
    A. Using a cross-function feature board to reveal the availability of various types of resources, including human and equipment
    B. Drafting policies and procedures relating to staffing, rental, or purchase of supplies
    C. Creating factors that impact or influence resource availability and skills
    D. Asking a set of Critical to Quality (CTQ) questions to determine what the customer needs and what resources are available to meet those needs

9. An Agile product manager understands that:
    A. Change is inevitable
    B. A well-constructed schedule requires no changes
    C. The baseline is fixed
    D. Many projects are alike

10. Jason is currently working on a project that will soon release a new GPS mobile imagine solution. A member of the development team asked Jason if adding support for web-based access to the imaging solution would be of value to the project in light of the upcoming release. Based on this information, what is Jason's role?
    A. Customer
    B. Product manager
    C. Facilitator
    D. Developer

11. A quality control process that is used to evaluate whether a product, service, or system complies with regulations, specifications, or conditions imposed at the start of a development phase can BEST be described as:
    A. Validation
    B. Verification
    C. Compliance
    D. Inspection

12. A quality assurance process of establishing a high degree of evidence that a product, service, or system accomplishes its intended requirements can BEST be described as:
    A. Validation
    B. Verification
    C. Compliance
    D. Inspection

13. Which of the following is NOT and Agile Principle?
    A. Our highest priority is to satisfy the customer through early and continuous delivery of valuable software.
    B. Welcome changing requirements, even late in development
    C. Deliver working software frequently, from a couple of weeks to a couple of months, with a preference toward a more accurate and longer development cycles.
    D. Business people and developers must work together daily throughout the project.

14. Which of the following BEST describes an Agile practice-based methodology for modeling and documenting of software-systems
    A. Agile UML
    B. Agile Requirements Gathering
    C. Agile Modeling
    D. Agile Features

15. Value-Based Analysis can BEST be described as:
    A. A decision process that relates the needs of the company with the specific resources available on the project.
    B. A decision process that relates the needs of the customer with the specific resources available in the marketplace.
    C. A decision process that relates the needs of the team with the specific resources available in the company.
    D. A decision process that relates the needs of the project with the specific resources available in the company.

16. Two companies are assigned the task of delivering a product within a 1-year timeframe. Company A is content to use the entire time to reach the goal. In contrast, Company B not only works to achieve the goal but also plans to complete the activities that return the greatest ROI first, while reducing the amount of time it takes to accomplish each task. Company B is a good example of:
    A. Agile Driven Planning
    B. Target Driven Planning
    C. Value-Driven Planning
    D. Performance-Driven Planning

17. Which of the following BEST describes the Agile technique used to establish a sequence of delivery for generating the highest ROI?
    A. Affinity Estimates
    B. Prioritization
    C. Sizing
    D. Planning Poker

18. Select the equation that MOST accurately expresses Value:
    A. Value = Benefit x (Cost x 2)
    B. Value = Benefit – Expense / Cost
    C. Value = Benefit x Cost
    D. Value = Benefits / Cost

19. Six Sigma provides all of the following, EXCEPT:
    A. A general approach to reduce muda
    B. A collection of methods to analyze cause-and-effect relationships
    C. A strategy for improving intrinsic value
    D. A strategy for discovering opportunities for improvement

20. Agile organizations must focus on speed, efficiency, and customer value to be globally competitive. Six Sigma and Lean are both powerful tools for improving quality, productivity, profitability, and market competitiveness. While Six Sigma focuses on reducing variations, Lean focuses on:
    A. eliminating waste and improving flow
    B. finances and improving positive cash flow
    C. increasing ROI and improving positive cash flow
    D. eliminating paperwork and improving employee moral

# Module 1 Quiz Answers

1. Answer: C

   Explanation: Since Agile methods are often used on projects where uncertainty around requirements and high rates of change exist, there is typically less certainty around scope. To avoid this tendency, it is important that everyone understands the project charter. Answer A is incorrect because Agile teams are expected to be self-empowered and self-organizing with no need for direct management. Answer B is incorrect because it is not the role of the Agile project manager to tell the customer what his values should be. Answer D is incorrect because simply checking in the code every night would not have prevented this problem either.

2. Answer: D

   Explanation: In this case D would be the appropriate answer because it encourage Customer-Prioritization and the Lean principle of removing complexity. While answer A would be the kind thing to do it would potentially place your project at risk due to stretching your own capacity is already at its maximum. Answers B and C could be viable answers but they do not directly address the problem as well as answer D.

3. Answer: C

   Explanation: Although all of the answers would provide a solution to the problem of how to deal with the product overage, only C answers the question as to how to improve the value stream. Remember, in addition to solving project problems, Agile project managers need to identify what caused the problem. To accomplish this aim, Lean and Six Sigma techniques should be used to track down the root cause and refine the delivery process.

4. Answer: D

   Explanation: Agile is about collaboration, not hierarchical structures of authority and management. In a projectized organization, the project manager has the greatest amount of authority. But this tendency often leads to controllism and doesn't encourage the development team to be self-organizing. On the other hand, some companies give all the power to the developers. But once again, collaboration is the essence behind the Agile principle that states, "Business people and developers must work together daily throughout the project."

5. Answer: B

   Explanation: Six Sigma is a methodology use to improve quality; it's not a piece of software that gets installed. It is maintained through a commitment to perform continuous improvement efforts within an organization.

6. Answer: D

   Explanation: Customer-Value Prioritization allows the customers to direct the product development process based on their needs and what they believe to be of the most value or of the highest specialty. As such, regardless of which phase of a project you're in, the customer needs are always at the forefront of the project. This is also expressed in the Agile Manifesto as: "Agile processes harness change for the customer's competitive advantage." Furthermore, don't confuse "influence" with "authority." Authority would imply that the customer can tell the team what do to, whereas influence requires collaboration.

7. Answer: C

   Explanation: A Kanban board is a visual indicator that can provide information about what to produce, when to produce it, and how much to produce.

8. Answer: D

    Explanation: Value-Based Analysis is a decision process that relates the needs of the customer with the specific resources available in the marketplace. It asks a set of Critical to Quality (CTQ) questions to determine what the customer needs and what resources are available to meet those needs.

9. Answer: A

    Explanation: The Agile Manifesto states that there is more value in responding to change than there is in following a plan. It is impossible to plan out a project to perfection. There are too many moving parts and factors, regardless of the similarity a project may have to others managed in the past. An Agile product manager understands that change is inevitable, which is why visibility, inspection, and adaptation are so important on projects. That's not to say that this tendency should be an excuse for poor planning. All other statements made within the remaining options are false.

10. Answer: A

    Explanation: The customer works to ensure the team focuses on delivering stories that generate the highest business value possible. The product manager guides the direction of the project to make sure the team delivers now and in the future. The facilitator assists the team with Agile skills, removing impediments and implementing conflict resolution. The developer implements stories with high business value using good techniques and practices.

11. Answer: B

    Explanation: The key words in this question are "at the start of a development phase". Validation is quality assurance process of establishing a high degree of evidence that a product, service, or system accomplishes its intended requirements. Compliance means conforming to a rule, such as a specification, policy, standard or law. Inspection involves the measurements, tests, and gauges applied to certain characteristics in regard to an object or activity.

12. Answer: A

    Explanation: The key words in this question are "accomplishes its intended requirements". Verification is a quality control process that is used to evaluate whether a product, service, or system complies with regulations, specifications, or conditions imposed at the start of a development phase. Compliance means conforming to a rule, such as a specification, policy, standard or law. Inspection involves the measurements, tests, and gauges applied to certain characteristics in regard to an object or activity.

13. Answer: C

    Explanation: The key words that make this the incorrect answer are "more accurate and longer development cycles". The actually principle states a "shorter timescale" which drives the Agile values of using shorter iterations.

14. Answer: C

    Explanation: Agile Modeling is an Agile practice-based methodology for modeling and documenting of software-systems. UML is often used in software modeling but is not specific to Agile thus making Agile Modeling the best answer. Agile Requirements Gathering and Agile Features are not used for modeling.

15. Answer: B

    Explanation: Relating the needs of the customer with specific resources available in the marketplace is the best example of Value-Based Analysis. The important concept to remember about Value-based analysis for the exam is that you are striving to meet the needs of the customer.

16. Answer: C

    Explanation: Value-Driven Planning is where you plan to do the most valuable things with your resources, and of those valuable things you try to do the most valuable thing first. Target driven planning is where you plan to simply reach the target. Value-Driven Planning emphasizes that improving ones performance is what creates the value. Therefore, the better we perform the more value we generate and the more likely we are to place a higher priority on activities that progressively increase our performance.

17. Answer: B
Explanation: The key word here is ROI. Prioritization encourages customers and Agile team to focus on completing features that are of the most importance, typically those that will generate the quickest ROI for the customer. While the other techniques can also be used to plan a sequence of delivery they focus more on planning—determined by the complexity required to complete the feature.

18. Answer: D
Explanation: Value may be conceptualized as the relationship between the benefits a customer perceives they will receive from a product, in relation to the perceived *cost of obtaining the benefits*.

19. Answer: C
Explanation: Six Sigma provides a means to improve the quality of production by removing things like waste (muda), identifying causes of waste and discovering opportunities for improvement. It has nothing to do with improving intrinsic value.

20. Answer: A
Explanation: Lean focuses on increasing value for customers by eliminating waste and improving the flow of production. Any action required to complete a process that a customer is not willing to pay for is considered waste and would be a target for elimination under Lean.

# Module 1
## Summary

- ✓ Assessed Ways to Maximize Value and Minimize Waste
- ✓ Discussed How to Increase Value through Quality
- ✓ Explained Customer Valued Prioritization
- ✓ Compared Value to Anti-Value
- ✓ Interpreted Release Early, Release Often
- ✓ Described Value Stream Analysis
- ✓ Optimized the Value Stream
- ✓ Demonstrated Value-Based Prioritization
- ✓ Illustrated Financial Operational Efficiency

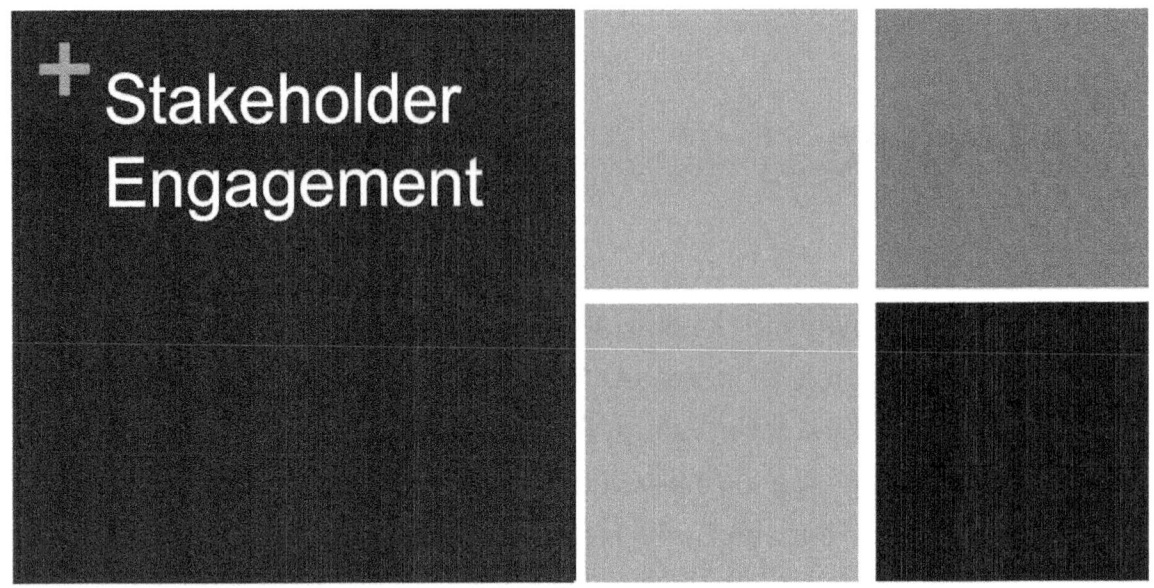

# Stakeholder Engagement

## Module 2
- PMI-ACP Exam Preparation Course

# Module 2
## Objectives

- ✓ Evaluate What it Means to Manage Stakeholders
- ✓ Explain Collaboration and Participation
- ✓ Identify Who Are the Stakeholders
- ✓ Define Continuous Involvement
- ✓ Develop an Agile Business Case
- ✓ Compare Agile Progress Reports that Provide Value to a Project

# Managing Stakeholders

## Identifying the Stakeholders

- A stakeholder is anyone who can be affected by or affects the Agile team but may not participate in the work directly
  - Stakeholders may come in the form of...
    - Customers
    - Owners
    - Fellow employees
    - Advisors
    - Community members

---

Stakeholder management is a strategy for dealing with potential scenarios that could be encountered with key stakeholders. This generally includes strategies to increase the support of stakeholders and to minimize negative impacts. The Agile product manager should determine the needs of the stakeholders and define a collaborative and open approach to communication.

Stakeholder management should include the following:

1. Identify stakeholders and information about them.
2. Identify the potential impact or support of each stakeholder.
3. Assess stakeholder reactions and responses given various scenarios.
4. Identify information, such as name, position, location, contact information, and project role.
5. Assess information, such as expectations, major requirements, individual project interests, and potential influence in the project.
6. Classify stakeholders, such as whether they are internal or external, and are a supporter, neutral party, or resistor of the project.

# Empowering Stakeholders

- **Stakeholder Management vs. Engagement**
    - Active stakeholder participation is imperative to ensure that the team addresses the dynamic needs of the stakeholders to maximize business value.
        - Stakeholder engagement decreases the probability of the project veering off course.
    - Teams are encouraged to communicate problems that are not in their power up the management chain.
        - Though the team is empowered to solve most problems on their own
    - Although similar to the *PMBOK* that teaches "Stakeholder Management," Agile advocates Stakeholder Engagement.
        - Stakeholders are engaged on a more frequent basis, such as at the end of each iteration.

---

An open dialogue between the Agile team and stakeholders is required for any project to be successful. Since traditional methods rarely involve stakeholders being involved through the development cycle, it's important that Agile product managers actively engage stakeholders to participate and share information with them.

The distribution method used is tied into the communication type appropriate for the given scenario.

Examples of communication methods include:

Face-to-face meetings, information radiators, reports, phone conferencing, web-conferencing, email, etc.

**For The Exam:** always remember that face-to-face communication is the preferred method of communication.

**Agile Principle:** "The most efficient and effective method of conveying information to and within a development team is face-to-face conversation."

# Empowering Stakeholders (continued)

## ■ Make Issues Highly Visible and Readily Available

- Issues can be brought up by the Agile Product Manager using shared tools.
  - Place issues on easily readable Task Board.
  - Keep stakeholders abreast of changes that take place in the product backlog through:
    - Planning meetings
    - Stand-ups
    - Retrospectives
  - Face-to-face meeting are encouraged in addition to utilizing reports.

---

Communication involves combining the various types and formats of the information needed. The aim is to provide a summary of the information needed by the project stakeholders to make informed decision (for example, communicating the progress and capabilities of the team in relation to the project or current iteration). Here, the focus is on communicating information that contributes to the success of the project and communicating information that, if not communicated, would lead to the failure of the project.

By ensuring stakeholders have a steady flow of information and engaging them during knowledge-sharing activities such as planning meetings, product demos, reviews, and retrospectives, you not only increase their confidence and build trust in the team, but you also increase project value and reduce risks.

Meetings such as retrospectives can be used to engage stakeholders by asking them questions such as how they felt the current processes worked or didn't work toward reaching their project objectives.

## Empowering Stakeholders (continued)

### ■ Stakeholders Generally Align with Particular Roles
- Roles can be on the business and technical side of the house.
  - The key steps in engaging stakeholders for an Agile project include:
    - Correctly identifying stakeholders
    - Mapping stakeholders to understand their current level of support
    - Understanding what is needed from each of the stakeholders
    - Developing and implementing an action plan to influence and get the required support from the stakeholders

In the real-world, the stakeholders of a project are not always easy to identify. From a technical definition, a stakeholder can be anyone affected by the outcome of the project the Agile team is working on or someone who affects the Agile team. For example, there may be stakeholders who contribute expertise to the project in the form of a business analyst that will be using the product created by the development team. Conversely, a lead architect on the project team may be a stakeholder because he's going to end up using the product to manage his own team upon completion.

**For the Exam:** The important thing to remember about stakeholders is that they assist best by ensuring the project remains on track with its chartered purpose, in order to maintain its value.

# Commitment Required from Stakeholders

- **Stakeholder Engagement Differs from Stakeholder Management.**
  - Express that business involvement is critical within Agile projects.
    - Traditional projects usually imply minimal business involvement after the minimal requirements are gathered.
      - An Agile project is unlikely to succeed if these expectations are not set early on with the stakeholder.
  - Establish a working relationship with stakeholders to where they feel like "active collaborators" instead of "managing overseers."
    - Encourage the participation of the stakeholders by inviting them to review and demo meetings.

Establishing stakeholder relationships involves collecting, sharing, and distributing information. Distribution methods include the mediums used to get stakeholders the information they need. Out of these methods, the preferred and best type is face-to-face meetings, which is a form of collaborative communication. A face-to-face meeting is also the preferred method used when dealing with stakeholders or complex situations.

# Use the Value Stream to Ensure User Knowledge

- **Remember Multiple Stakeholders will Derive Value from your Product**
    - Agile teams work closely with their stakeholders to include not only the people paying for the project, but also the end users, managers of end users, enterprise architects, support staff, etc.
    - By working in a prioritized order, Agile teams maximize the return on investment (ROI). They accomplish this by ensuring they are working on the high-value functionality as defined by their stakeholders.
    - For example:
        - Customers and end users have a stake in achieving low incremental cost and fast incremental time to market.
        - End-users want the right solution to their problem.

**Real World:** Keep in mind that there may be a lot of stakeholders counting on your Agile team to deliver, what they committed to delivering. These people may not only be sponsors of the project, but also other projects that have dependencies on the outcome of your project. Therefore it is important to establish a prioritized delivery list, least you find yourself being pulled into multiple directions.

# Promoting Collaboration and Participation

- **Improving the Stakeholder Engagement Value Stream**
    - The big picture of stakeholder engagement can be thought of as a value stream.
        - Each role can then be mapped into the value stream.
        - The roles are more present in every development phase because of Agile's emphasis on feedback and Lean's emphasis on consistency.
    - The primary consideration should be on supporting the *change* that occurs in the long term.
        - This requires close communication and feedback loops.
        - If you can change you can improve the value stream.

For successful collaboration and participation to occur, Agile product managers must actively identify, listen, and analyze the needs and expectations of the stakeholders. In turn this allows the Agile team to prioritize requirements using insight into the stakeholders' goals and objectives. Understanding stakeholder priorities is important to release and iteration planning.

# Who Are The Stakeholders

- **The Key Stakeholders Can Be Found in 5 Categories:**
  - **Business:** Executive Sponsors, Board of Directors, Sales, Marketing
  - **Customer:** Product Owners, Product Managers
  - **Domain Experts:** Architects, Business Analysts
  - **Developers:** Designers, Coders, Testers
  - **End Users**

When you are trying to identify your stakeholders, the key stakeholders can normally be found in these 5 basic categories.

# Who Has What at Stake?

- **The Business**
  - Good businesses usually have a stake in growing their customer base and in giving good returns to investors.
    - The enterprise will have a diversity of end users or customers to support in the market.
    - If the business can serve more customers, it grows its stake in its customer base and increases revenue.

Through constant communication and collaboration between the Agile product manager, the business, and the customer, a shared understanding of the project scope and deliverables can be accomplished. Additionally, the use of a Vision Statement, a roadmap that reinforces the customer values using the 5W's, can be used as a guideline to set acceptance criteria and to identify acceptable trade-offs. Adhering to the Agile principle "Our highest priority is to satisfy the customer through early and continuous delivery of valuable software" sets the stage for the Agile team to organically conduct risk management efforts and to be empowered to remove constraints in order to continuously deliver valuable products to the customer.

# Who Has What at Stake? (continued)

- **The Business** (continued)
  - One of the most important functions of the business is deciding on the scope of the project.
    - Scoping has to balance the expectations of all customers and users against financial objectives.
      - Should the scope be the union of the entire market's expectations?
      - Or should the business focus on the 20% of the market where 80% of the revenues lie?

**Discussion Note:** What other types of decisions do you think the business stakeholders will be expected to make?

How about things like vendor agreements? Project cost? Timing of the project in relation to their long term strategic path?

# Who Has What at Stake? (continued)

- **The Business** (continued)
  - The product scope can't take development into a technology-dependent area beyond the maturity in the product's lifetime.
    - Such insight comes from domain experts and developers.
  - The business is responsible for holding down costs by making buy-versus-build decisions.
    - Decisions should be made by informed customers and end users who desire selected standards
    - Domain experts who can advise the business on the feasibility of integrating third-party software
    - Developers and testers who do the work and are responsible for testing it

In short, the business must leverage the knowledge of the expertise of others to make their decisions.

# Who Has What at Stake? (continued)

- **Customers**
  - Are the individuals who have responsibility for the program and project budgets
    - They put forward the business case for undertaking these programs and projects.
  - Separate the customer role from the end user role.
    - Customers are more about process while end users are more about products and services.
  - If Agile methods are going to be adopted successfully on the projects, then customers need to understand:
    - How Agile can help them meet cost targets
    - How Agile delivers functionality to the business within given timelines
    - How Agile can rapidly deliver critical functionality to their business

The customers are responsible for ensuring the project delivers what it was chartered to do, according to the needs of the business; and equally important, within the budget.

Remember that the customer is not necessarily the end user. Rather, they are concerned with the process required to deliver the product to the customer.

# Who Has What at Stake? (continued)

- **Customers** (continued)
    - In terms of stakeholder engagement, these individuals have to be supportive of adopting Agile methods.
        - They are the first stakeholders to be addressed when stakeholder engagement is undertaken.
    - The customer is essentially a middleman.
        - *Customers are not the consumers of the service.*

Remember to keep the customer engaged throughout the project because their support is critical for adopting Agile methods.

Also, they are not the consumers of the service, but rather that middle man in the delivery of the service.

# Who Has What at Stake? (continued)

- **Customers** (continued)
  - When engaging customers, consider their stake as opportunistic.
    - A product is being developed for which there is not yet an end user.
  - Customers are averse to risk.
    - They are interested in delivery times and development costs rather than functionality.
  - The customer has a large stake in your development process.
    - Customer engagement will take place more in the area of process improvement than in development.
      - Provide a place in your enterprise for such activities using retrospectives.

Customers will typically take on projects in order to take advantage of market opportunities. As such, customers are averse to risk. Why? Because while new opportunities provide a means to increase or generate new revenue, it also introduces the potential of new problems.

# Who Has What at Stake? (continued)

- **Domain Experts**
  - These individuals come from the business or the technical side of the house.
    - The Product Manager typically comes from the business side.
      - Although the business and technical project management roles can be combined
  - Innovation in the solution domain goes hand-in-hand with long-term experience.
    - Trust someone as an expert only if they are good at telling a balanced story.
    - Encourage active dialogue between the innovators and the solution domain experts.

Domain experts are the individuals the business turns to in order to understand how things actually get done within the business. In other words, the business may look at a chart to see how the organizations onboarding process takes place, however, the Human Resources manager is the boots on the ground individual that fills in the unseen details in the chart.

# Who Has What at Stake? (continued)

- **Domain Experts** (continued)
  - Keep the team balanced so that both problem domain experts and solution domain experts have an equal say.
    - Stovepipe development between innovators and domain experts often results in a war because one over-constrains the other.

The business must also be aware of finding a balance between problem domain experts and solution domain experts. Problem domain experts will focus on solving the day to day problems of the business, whereas solution domain experts may be tempted to focus on identifying a solution first, then solving the problems last.

# Who Has What at Stake? (continued)

- **Developers**
  - Execute on the visions of the business and domain expertise
    - Should own the development estimates
    - Are the main source of technical feasibility and domain expertise
      - Opinions aren't informed enough to make long-term business or architecture decisions, they need input from developers
    - Help by building prototypes that compare architectural alternatives
  - The tester's stake is to make sure the architecture is testable.
    - Usability testing can validate regardless of whether the team has captured the end user mental models.

Developers are the team members responsible for actually getting the work done. They execute on the vision of the business. As such, their stake in the project is making sure the proposed solutions to the problems are doable, and testable. Because up until they get involved, everything is just based on assumptions and opinions; and we all know what happens with assumptions.

# Who Has What at Stake? (continued)

- **Developers** (continued)
    - Ongoing testing is required during development.
        - Testers as well as the developers need to know requirements.
    - The developer and tester engage with the business to come to an agreement on the requirements.
        - The tester codes up tests for the new feature.
        - The developer implements the feature.

Remember that on Agile teams, testing is built into development, so there needs to be an on-going dialog between the developers and the business, to ensure they are fulfilling the requirements set by the business.

# Who Has What at Stake? (continued)

- **End Users**
  - Customers and end users are very different stakeholders
    - They seek service from the software you are developing
      - That is the value you supply for them
    - The end users' value to the development organization is that they are usually the source of revenues that feed your team members
      - It's a good deal for them if your software provides services that increase their quality of life
    - Their stake in the system is that it does what they expect it to
      - A tacit expectation that goes beyond conscious assumptions

Let's start by stating that the end user is not the customer. End users are the stakeholders that are expecting to receive value from the service [or software] being created. In terms of Agile, the customer is the one responsible for shepherding the services to the end user, using the most efficient ways possible. Thus, the end user is the stakeholder that is the source of revenue that feeds your team, by allowing the business to pay the bills and keep the stockholders happy. Their stake in the system is that your service, does what they expect it to do.

# Who Has What at Stake? (continued)

- **End Users (continued)**
  - Most software requirement techniques start by asking customers what they want the system to do rather than focusing on what the end user expects it to do.
    - By having a chance to use the product, end users can tell you whether it does what they expect it to.
  - Too many projects collect lists of potential features that are driven by the business view of what the customer is willing to pay for.
    - Instead of depending on exhaustive compilations of use case scenarios, consider the <u>end user's cognitive mode</u>l.

Unfortunately the business may forget that they are working to please the end user, and instead focus on pleasing the customer. When that happens the product that gets built contains a list of features that are of no use to the end user because they were created by the customer.

# Continuous Involvement

- **Managing Stakeholder Expectations**
  - Agile increases the level of direct involvement from the business on projects and in project teams.
    - This direct involvement ensures the stakeholders have more visibility into the project.
      - Provides them with a greater assurance that the outcome will meet their business objectives
    - To accomplish this aim, a dedicated customer should be provided with the opportunity to prioritize the feature list.
      - Set goals for each iteration.
      - Write and prioritize stories.
      - Create acceptance tests.

Since Agile projects primarily operate using adaptive planning methods, Agile teams must constantly work with the customer to manage their expectations against estimations. This is achieved by making sure the customer is involved during product backlog prioritization and by writing acceptance tests. As a result, when estimations are provided to the customer, it will come as no surprise that a balance must be struck between the minimal and most likely outcomes, based on the CURRENT INFORMATION THAT IS AVAILABLE. When this approach to planning and customer engagement is taken, stakeholders are given a greater assurance of the team's competency and their ability to achieve the project objectives.

Conversely, if the business, customer, stakeholders, and/or team do not deliver on their commitments, then even an Agile project with the best team of developers will fail.

**Agile Principle**: "At regular intervals, the team reflects on how to become more effective. It then tunes and adjusts its behavior accordingly."

# Continuous Involvement (continued)

- **Managing Stakeholder Expectations** (continued)
    - Participants from the business need to be part of the project team to provide timely input and feedback to the developers.
        - A lack of commitment to providing business resources is often the source of failure for Agile projects.
        - Engaging stakeholders so that the business delivers on these commitments is critical.

Inviting stakeholders to the daily stand-up meeting is a good way to keep them engaged on the project. Allowing them to see the status of the tasks discussed in the meetings, and how they are progressing toward completion of tasks for that day, is an ideal way to build and maintain their confidence in the team. The caveat, however, is that stakeholders need to be aware that the stand-up meeting is for the benefit of the team and that they are not allowed to side track the meeting with extraneous issues that don't directly relate to the tasks at hand.

Additionally, show them the status reports that were taken during the meeting and how progress is being made toward their desired outcome. This will help maintain their confidence in the team.

That said, the business must make a commitment to be engaged by attending the meetings, yet not being there as a distraction.

# Continuous Involvement (continued)

- **Both Lean and Agile Can Help Us**
  Sec. 6
  - "Individuals and interactions over processes and tools" and "Customer collaboration over contract negotiation" comprise half of the values of the Agile Manifesto.
    - Lean teaches us the importance of the value stream and that every activity/artifact should contribute to end-user value
    - Agile's "customer collaboration" reinforces the importance of the value stream during the software development process
      - User needs are explicit and visible

In many cases, traditional product managers must negotiate with others to get the resources needed for the project, to satisfy the resource requirements, and to accomplish their project goal. And this negotiation may take place with functional managers, product managers, or external vendors. As such, most of the agreements between the partners are negotiated and signed upfront, with each party going to their respective corner until the project is completed, or more realistically, until a problem comes up that wasn't addressed in the contract.

However, with Agile projects the emphasis is on maintaining constant contact with the customer throughout the entire project. This is so much so that it is expected that the customer (or authorized person to make important decisions for the customer) is embedded into the team. As a result, there is less need for road blocking constant contract negotiation. That is because collaboration requires talking to the customer on a regular basis and listening. In turn, your customers are more inclined to listen and work with you to resolve problems.

# Continuous Involvement (continued)

## Seven Principles of Stakeholder Engagement
- Acknowledge legitimate stakeholders.
- Listen and openly communicate.
- Adopt processes and behaviors.
- Recognize interdependence, risks, and rewards.
- Work cooperatively.
- Avoid unacceptable risk.
- Acknowledge and address conflicts.

In order to encourage active stakeholder engagement, you must foster strong relationships. If building relationships on a project is not something that comes naturally to you, following the seven principles of engagement can assist you by treating it as a functional task.

# Agile Business Case Development

- **Making Your Business Case**
  - The business case justifies to stakeholders the reasons for proposing the project
  - Outlines the benefits a project will provide in terms of:
    - Cost of project vs. benefits to the organization
    - Return on investment
    - How the project will further improve strategic business objectives
    - Strengthening the existing business portfolio
    - Supporting information should also be provided to cover:
      - Risk mitigation
      - Resource requirements
      - Project environment assumptions
      - Team resourcing

Risk mitigation, resource requirements, project environment assumptions, and team resourcing information should also be provided to back up a business case.

Gaining the support of an influential project sponsor would also be good start toward getting your project approved and funded.

In order to guarantee buy-in from your organization in order to get your project approved, it is helpful to garner support from the most influential sponsors.

# Elements of an Agile Project Charter

- **Capturing the Values of Stakeholders**
  - The output of the Initiation phase of the project allows the stakeholders to state their needs.
    - At minimum, a good project charter should contain:
      1. Vision Statement
      2. Mission Statement
      3. Success Criteria
    - Traditional inputs that are fed into the Initiation phase:
      - Product Requirements Document (PRD)
      - Marketing Requirements Document (MRD)
    - The Agile equivalent of these documents is the Product Overview Document.
      - It is similar to the project charter.

---

Project charters formally authorize the initial requirements of the project to satisfy stakeholder needs and expectations. Because the project charter is the most important project document created, it is essential that all stakeholders participate in its creation. Stakeholder alignment, balance intentions and an agreed-upon definition are supposed to be defined in the charter. And even though it is a short one-page document, getting everyone in agreement can be a challenging undertaking. Having a project charter in place, however, will be time well spent because it will prevent potentially endless weeks of revision to realign the project.

At a minimum, a good project charter should contain:

1. Vision Statement
2. Mission Statement
3. Success Criteria

# Agile Business Case Development (continued)

- **Product Overview Document** (continued)
  - As more information is needed, it can be obtained from the product roadmap or product backlog.
  - Agile projects rely on the iterations' output to function as the traditional PRD artifact.
    - Formal documentation can be provided based on the agreement between the team and the customer.
  - Agile projects can start sooner than traditional projects.
    - Features that are going to be worked on are based on prioritized business value.
    - Stakeholders can continue to elaborate as needed.

---

The product overview document provides a means for everyone involved on, or interested in, the product, to get a high level understanding of what the product will do. This information is worked-on and prioritized by value, and updated as needed.

# Meeting the Business Objectives

- **Participatory Decision-Making (PDM)**
  - Good organizations support effective communication through group autonomy, collocation, and group functions.
    - PDM is a model in which organizations encourage employees to participate in organizational decision-making.
      - The process can be formal or informal, and the degree of participation can range from zero to 100% through varying stages of the project.
    - PDM is used on Agile teams in the form of:
      - Customer demos
      - Review meetings
      - Iteration planning
      - Retrospections
    - In order for PDM to be most effective, workers need to feel a sense of belonging to an organization or team.

PDM gives workplace influence to individuals who are typically viewed as hierarchically unequal. In other words, the basic concept involves sharing power. Co-determination of working conditions, problem-solving, and decision-making are examples of such power-sharing arrangements, but they can vary from organization to organization. PDM has the "perceived motivational effects of increased employee involvement" throughout the organization.

PDM is known by many names, including employee involvement, shared leadership, employee empowerment, dispersed leadership, participative decision-making, open-book management, Participative Management (PM) and industrial democracy.

# Progress Reports

- **Information Radiators**  Sec. 1
    - Are highly visible pieces of information that provide insight into what the team is doing  3.9
        - Provide for easy sharing of information among the team and build trust with stakeholders
            - Also maintain the confidence of the stakeholder that the team is on the right track
    - **Vision Statement:** the document that provides the context for other progress reports
        - Created and updated by the onsite customer.
        - Explains what you're doing, why you're doing it, and how to know when you've successfully achieved your goal
    - **Demos:** allow your stakeholders to see what you've been building

The Lean concept of minimizing waste and the Agile philosophy of "barely sufficient" are still applicable when it comes to creating project documentation and reporting. That isn't to say that thorough reporting shouldn't be provided to the customer and team to keep them informed about the progress of the project. Rather, the intent is to remain consistent in the Agile philosophy of staying focused on value, which, in the case of documentation, can be exemplified in the Agile principle that states: Simplicity—the art of maximizing the amount of work not done—is essential.

# Progress Reports (continued)

- **Information Radiators** (continued)
    - **Release and Iteration Plans:** provide a means for the team to coordinate their activities
        - Communicate the stories that will be accomplished during the iteration from the release plan
    - **Burn-up Chart:** shows how much work was actually accomplished during a given iteration in contrast to how much work remains to be completed
        - Shows how much total work the project contains
        - Shows how much the scope has increased each iteration

This new approach to tracking and reporting information can be disorienting to traditional PMOs and product managers who have grown accustomed to the project plan and Gantt charts. But once again, this cultural transitional challenge is addressed in the **Agile Principle**: "At regular intervals, the team reflects on how to become more effective, then tunes and adjusts its behavior accordingly."

# Progress Reports (continued)

- **Optional Reports**  Sec. 4
    - **Product Roadmap:** provides more detail than the vision statement, but not as overwhelming as the release or iteration plan; can be used to provide a summary of the release plan and the features provided by each one
    - **Status Email:** can be used to provide information about the stories completed during an iteration, schedule changes, and changes from other reports

# Managerial Reports

- **Productivity:** created around what the business values
  - The team and the organization must agree upon an objective value to measure, such as:
    - *Cost savings*
    - *Revenue generated by software*
- **Throughput:** the amount of time required to turn an agreed-upon idea into a completed and ready-to-use product
- **Defects:** measuring how many defects are found in a story after it has been declared as "done-done"
- **Time Usage:** tracking how and where hours were used to complete a task during an iteration
  - Tracking this information should be the exception instead of the rule since the team is trusted to be self-organizing

Reports that may provide insight to removing waste and increasing productivity may be classified as managerial reports.

# Reports to Stay Away From

- **Counterproductive Reporting**
    - **Source Lines of Code:** Good programming is about reuse and modularization.
        - Measuring how much code is written provides little benefit.
    - **Number of Stories:** Stories can be split or removed from an iteration so they provide little value in measuring.
        - An average team will complete about 4-10 stories per iteration.
    - **Velocity:** can be misleading because it may lead to shortcuts that result in technical debt or inaccurate estimates
        - Since various teams will have various ways of creating estimates, velocity should never be compared across different teams.

Once again, just as we do not want to over document, we do not want to over report; or create reports because information is available. As such, counterproductive reporting may sneak in as these reports.

**For the Exam:** Velocity should never be compared across different teams because teams will have different ways of creating estimtes.

# Reinforcement Training

## Questions & Exercises

### ■ Time to Test your New Knowledge!
Take the next PMI-ACP practice quiz.

# Exercise 2

Identify the Top 3 High-Quality Project Deliverables You Would Recommend to Stakeholders to Get the Highest ROI and Explain Your Answers

|    | Requirement | Priority | ROI% | Risk |
|----|-------------|----------|------|------|
| 1  | Add Content and Content metadata |  | 9.0  | Med  |
| 2  | Administrator defines User Role |  | 14.0 | High |
| 3  | Administrator edits Roles assigned to CPS user (add/remove) |  | 16.0 | High |
| 4  | Administrator edits the actions that a Role allows |  | 15.0 | High |
| 5  | Assign a pricing Policy to an Asset |  | 10.0 | Low  |
| 6  | Assign a Subscription Policy to a Channel or Channels |  | 16.5 | Med  |
| 7  | Create a discount Coupon |  | 11.0 | High |
| 8  | Create a one-time-use Coupon |  | 12.0 | High |
| 9  | Create a Subscription Policy |  | 6.0  | Low  |
| 10 | Create pricing Policy |  | 1.8  | Med  |
| 11 | Link related Assets |  | 4.0  | Low  |
| 12 | Load Content media files and images |  | 5.0  | Low  |
| 13 | Use one-time-use Coupon |  | 13.0 | High |
| 14 | User logs into CPS Administrative System |  | 2.0  | Low  |
| 15 | User logs out of the CPS Administrative System |  | 3.0  | Low  |

# Module 2 Quiz

## Exam Practice Questions

1. A project manager has requested an increase to her project budget based on a confident belief that developers will be needed to assist the Help Desk with technical support calls once the project has been released. Based on the complexity of the new application and the current experience of the existing Help Desk staff, she believes the project's success will be at risk due to poor customer satisfaction. The project stakeholders have denied her request because they believe her concern falls outside the scope of the project. All of the following are benefits of engaging stakeholders during a project, EXCEPT:
    A. Stakeholder engagement decreases the probability of the project veering off course
    B. Stakeholders may have influence over the project budget
    C. Stakeholder engagement encourages collaboration with the development team
    D. Stakeholders are responsible for providing technical details to the development team

2. Last year, Janet successfully managed a $4.5 million project for her company from beginning to end using a compressed schedule. This project was based on an inordinate amount of risk, and it held a high level of visibility amongst the executive team. Part of her strategy was to ensure that the stakeholders were engaged throughout the project while constantly utilizing Enterprise Risk Management techniques. Which of the following would be considered the LEAST effective technique to engage stakeholders with respect to risk management?
    A. Provide information to stakeholders about spike solutions that have been completed during planning meetings
    B. Provide stakeholders with information about prototypes that have been completed during Retrospective meetings
    C. Make information easily accessible to stakeholders on the Task Board regarding acceptance tests that have been completed
    D. Send stakeholders an e-mail when a problem arises

3. Your manager has just informed you that a new project is under consideration. In order to assist in making the decision on whether the technical goals of the project are achievable, you have been tasked with conducting a study on the project's existing potential. What is this type of research called?
    A. Monte Carlo analysis
    B. Cost performance index
    C. Feasibility study
    D. Cost plus fee

4. In order to maintain communication among the business team lead, the development team, the testing team lead, and the release team lead, the Strike First software development company requires each team to participate in group discussion at the end of each iteration. The purpose of this discussion is to see where each team's processes may have worked best and where they may have worked least. In Agile, this type of discuss would BEST be characterized as:
    A. Kill points
    B. Phase gates
    C. Retrospectives
    D. Phase exits

5. Daily work typically occurs before which of the following in the Agile SDLC?
    A. Release planning
    B. Task completion
    C. Visioning and chartering
    D. Iteration planning

6. All of the following are likely to exist before the completion of the first iteration on an Agile project, EXCEPT:
    A. Roadmap
    B. Pareto Prioritization Matrix
    C. Vision
    D. Project charter

7. When a workplace encourages individuals who are typically viewed as hierarchically unequal to get involved in co-determining working conditions and sharing power, it can BEST be described as:
   A. Team work
   B. Agile churn
   C. Sprint meetings
   D. Participatory decision-making

8. All of the following can be characterized as information radiators that provide value to a project, EXCEPT:
   A. Burndown chart
   B. Vision statement
   C. Release plan
   D. Source lines of code report

9. A dedicated customer on an Agile project should be used to provide all of the following, EXCEPT:
   A. Creation of acceptance tests
   B. Setting goals for each iteration
   C. Writing and prioritizing of stories
   D. Management of the development team

10. A list of prioritized features has been converted into actual stuff to do. Where are you in the Agile SDLC?
    A. In the Iteration Planning meeting
    B. In the Release Planning meeting
    C. In a Demo meeting
    D. In the Feature Decomposition

11. Agile stakeholder management should include all of the following, EXCEPT:
    A. Identifying stakeholders and information about them.
    B. Identifying the potential impact or support of each stakeholder.
    C. Assessing stakeholder reactions and responses given various scenarios.
    D. Guaranteeing stakeholders the accuracy of your estimates.

12. By ensuring stakeholders have a steady flow of information and engaging them during knowledge-sharing activities such as planning meetings, product demos, reviews, and retrospectives, you not only increase their confidence but also:
    A. reduce trust in the team
    B. reduce project value
    C. reduce risk
    D. reduce communication

13. Stakeholders contribute MOST to a project by:
    A. Facilitating the meetings necessary to gather teams together to build thorough requirements
    B. Providing technical guidance for the development team to build the right products
    C. Ensuring the project remains on track with its chartered purpose in order to maintain its value
    D. Continually funding the project even in the event of overruns

14. Which of the following BEST describes a responsibility of the business?
    A. The business is responsible for taking the product beyond the current technology maturity.
    B. The business is responsible for selecting the best third-party software to integrate with.
    C. The business is responsible for holding down costs by making buy-versus-build decisions.
    D. The business is responsible testing the software.

15. Agile teams can build stronger stakeholder relationships by doing all of the following, EXCEPT:
    A. Collecting information
    B. Marketing information
    C. Sharing information
    D. Distributing information

16. Understanding stakeholder priorities is important to release and iteration planning because it allows the Agile team to prioritize requirements using insight into the stakeholders' goals and objectives. All of the following are example of how an Agile project manager can assist with this, EXCEPT?
    A. By engaging the stakeholder to understand their needs
    B. By listening to the stakeholder to understand their needs
    C. By analyzing the needs of the stakeholders
    D. By managing the needs of the stakeholders

17. Agile increases the level of direct involvement from the business on projects and in project teams. This direct involvement ensures the stakeholders have more visibility into the project. To accomplish this a dedicated customer should be embedded into the project with the opportunity to provide all of the following, EXCEPT:
    A. Work with the team to set goals for each iteration
    B. Write and prioritize stories with the team
    C. Create acceptance tests
    D. Manage the work done by the team

18. When creating a business case all of the following should be included, EXCEPT:
    A. Technical implementations
    B. Risk mitigation
    C. Resources needed
    D. Project environment assumptions

19. Two traditional inputs that feed into the initiation phase are the Products Requirements Document and the Marketing Requirements Document. In Agile, these are equivalent to the:
    A. Agile Project Requirements
    B. Output of iterations
    C. Use Cases
    D. Stories

20. Participatory Decision-Making (PDM) is a model in which organizations encourage employees to participate in organizational decision-making. All of the following are examples of PDM used on Agile teams, EXCEPT:
    A. Review meeting
    B. Customer demos
    C. Iteration planning
    D. Stage gates

# Module 2 Quiz Answers

1. Answer: D

    Explanation: A stakeholder can be anyone who can be affected by or who affects the Agile team but may not participate in the work directly. So although there may be stakeholders who can contribute technical expertise to the project, they are not responsible for providing technical implementation details to the development team. Stakeholders assist best by ensuring the project stays on track and maintains value. The technical implementation required to deliver that value is the responsibility of the development team.

2. Answer: D

    Explanation: Sending an e-mail is the least effective means of communicating on a project, especially when communicating risk. The ideal form of communication is through face-to-face contact such as meetings. If face-to-face contact is not available, then information should be provided through the use of highly visible information radiators.

3. Answer: C

    Explanation: The study that the question refers to is something that is done *before* a project begins. Monte Carlo analysis is an analysis that takes into account project risk. This is irrelevant, since the project has not yet begun. The same applies to the cost performance index, which is a measure of a project's cost efficiency. Cost plus fee, the last option, is related to the procurement activities. A feasibility study is a preliminary study conducted to determine a project's viability, which is a match and the correct answer.

4. Answer: C

    Explanation: Agile methodologies are adaptive rather than prescriptive or defined. By incorporating frequent feedback from stakeholders and team members through Retrospectives, the methodologies encourage modification and/or incorporation of new practices while discarding practices that are not beneficial.

5. Answer: B

    Explanation: Task completion is when the fine-grained details required to implement the features are completed on the project. It takes place after the daily Work and daily Stand-Up meetings. All other answers occur before the daily Work meeting.

6. Answer: B

    Explanation: There is no such item as a Pareto Prioritization Matrix, although a Pareto Analysis and Prioritizations may be done at the beginning of an Agile project.

7. Answer: D

    Explanation: Participatory decision-making gives workplace influence to individuals who are typically viewed as hierarchically unequal. In other words, the basic concept involves sharing power. Co-determination of working conditions, problem-solving, and decision-making are examples of such power-sharing arrangements, but they can vary from organization to organization.

8. Answer: D

    Explanation: Measuring how much code is written provides little benefit to a project because good programming is about reuse and modularization.

9. Answer: D

    Explanation: Agile development teams are self-organizing and self-managing. All of the other options are benefits of having a customer on the team.

10. Answer: A

    Explanation: A list of prioritized features is converted into actual stuff to do during the Iteration Planning meeting. This meeting can be divided into two parts. During the first part, the team determines what features should be worked on during the iteration. The second part involves determining which tasks are required to realize completion of these features.

11. Answer: D
    Explanation: Since Agile relies on value-driven and adaptive planning the value provided to stakeholders from using Agile is not about how accurate an estimate will be, but rather, what actions will the team take to ensure the best ROI on a project. Part of understanding what is valuable to stakeholders also requires identifying who your stakeholders are and assessing how they will respond to various outcomes.

12. Answer: C
    Explanation: The organic checkpoints built into the Agile process reduce risk by ensuring stakeholders are engaged throughout the entire process. All of the activities mentioned increase visibility into the project and allow time for inspection and adaptation, which ultimately aids in reducing project risk.

13. Answer: C
    Explanation: Stakeholders contribute most to project by making sure it stays on track with the chartered purpose. Too often, projects can become sidetracked with scope creep and over documentation resulting in a loss of focus on its intended value. The other options are incorrect because collecting thorough requirements is not tenant of Agile; and not all stakeholders are required to provide financial or technical input to a project.

14. Answer: C
    Explanation: Holding down costs by making buy-versus-build decisions are responsibilities of the business. The other answers are incorrect because the business should not be making decisions about technology that are beyond the maturity of the current technology or making implementation specific IT decisions.

15. Answer: B
    Explanation: Collecting, sharing and distributing information all aid in building trust with the stakeholders. To build strong stakeholder relationships you must have the courage to provide them with honest and accurate information, even if the information is not always pleasant. So in comparison to the other options, Marketing is the best answer.

16. Answer: D
    Explanation: While "managing" the needs of the stakeholders may sound correct it is not the *best* answer. Agile project management is less about managing and more about engaging. As a result, this was the best answer through a process of elimination.

17. Answer: D
    Explanation: Managing is the key word to this option. Remember the goal of an Agile team is to be self-managing, self-empowered and self-organizing.

18. Answer: A
    Explanation: The business case is created during the initial phase of the project and as a result there is not enough information to provide technical implementation details.

19. Answer: B
    Explanation: Agile projects rely on the output of iterations to function as the traditional Product Overview Document. If more information is needed it can be obtained from the product roadmap or product backlog. Formal documentation can be created if agreed upon by the team and customer.

20. Answer: D
    Explanation: Stage gate is incorrect because it is a process for implementing structured project management where the project must pass through a "stage" in order to proceed to the next. In contrast, all of the other options provide a means for Participatory Decision-Making between the team, customer and stakeholders.

# Module 2
## Summary

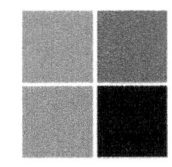

- ✓ Evaluated What it Means to Manage Stakeholders
- ✓ Explained Collaboration and Participation
- ✓ Identified Who Are the Stakeholders
- ✓ Defined Continuous Involvement
- ✓ Developed an Agile Business Case
- ✓ Compared Agile Progress Reports that Provide Value to a Project

# Boosting Team Performance Practices

## Module 3
- PMI-ACP Exam Preparation Course

# Module 3
## Objectives

- ✓ Examine the Characteristics of a High-Performance Team
- ✓ Compare the Traditional Team Roles and Responsibilities
- ✓ Use Coaching Techniques to Increase Team Success Rates
- ✓ Recommend Ways to Deal with Conflict
- ✓ Describe Close Communication on Agile Projects
- ✓ Judge What Team Commitment Means
- ✓ Integrate Work Practices to Keep the Team Together

# Characteristics of a High-Performance Team

- **High-Performance Teams Are the Special Forces of an Agile Organization**
  - The team is built around the principles of self-organizing, collaboration, empowerment, and continuous improvement.
    - As a self-organized and self-empowered team, team members are able to make decisions about the goals they have committed to.
      - However, giving a team this type of freedom can also compete with traditional ideas of management and business roles.
    - Controlling the complexity and chaos of a project requires a variety of skills that individuals do not inherently possess.
      - This requires team collaboration where the whole is greater than the sum of its parts.
    - As a cohesive team, the team members support each other and make use of each others' strengths.

---

Agile teams are usually set up to be cross-functional and self-organizing. Existing corporate hierarchy or corporate roles should not be used in deciding the team's composition on an Agile project. The objective is to gather team members who are generalized specialists and who are willing to take responsibility for tasks they commit to deliver. They then decide individually how to meet an iteration's requirements.

# Characteristics of a High-Performance Team (continued)

## ■ Clearly Defined Vision

Sec. 5

- In pulling from the Six Sigma principle that "what gets measured is what gets improved," higher-performance teams always establish measurable tasks that are clearly prioritized and enacted into team-agreed-upon tasks.
  - Team members establish a Definition of Done that quantifies the amount of time that will be spent on a task and the expected level of quality.

The stakeholders, sponsors, and team establish a Definition of Done that quantifies the amount of time that will be spent on a task, the expected level of quality, and the velocity.

Teams that are able to follow through on their commitment build stronger levels of trust between team members and the stakeholders. A technique used to accomplish this trust can be found in velocity tracking. By measuring and monitoring the velocity during each iteration, teams are able to more accurately provide estimates and keep their commitments.

**Agile Principle**: "Build projects around motivated individuals. Give them the environment and support they need, and then trust them to get the job done."

# ✛ Characteristics of a High-Performance Team (continued)

- **Established Levels of Competence**
  - Although the team is formed to be cross-functional, individual team members have a clear level of competence and expertise in certain areas so that power struggles are avoided.
    - Team members are still expected to meet, or exceed, the threshold of competency required to perform any task the team may be expected to undertake.
    - The boundaries between organizational management groups and the ability to work autonomously as a team are clear.
      - It is the responsibility of the Agile Product Manager to protect the team from changes to the product backlog once an iteration has started.

---

So as mentioned, within your high performance (HP) teams, not only is each team member expected to meet the minimum level of competence to be able to fill in for another team member, they also have an expertise in a specific area. That said, while team members can swap roles, they maintain a clearly defined separation of responsibilities. This prevents power-struggles from occurring because team member respects what each of them brings to the team.

# Characteristics of a High-Performance Team (continued)

- **Empowered to Solve Problems**
  - In addition to having the skills to identify problems and find solutions, team members are empowered to execute their solutions.
    - The team establishes a set of guidelines that allows them to perform their work, with the primary objective of finding a solution.
      - What use is it to be a highly skilled individual, working as part of an autonomous team—but still have to wait for a drawn-out formal approval process to solve the problem?

---

In addition to having the skills to identify problems and find solutions, team members are empowered to execute their solutions.

The team establishes a set of guidelines that allows them to perform their work, with the primary objective of finding a solution.

What use is it to be a highly skilled individual, working as part of an autonomous team—but still have to wait for a drawn-out formal approval process to solve the problem?

Therefore, the third characteristic of an HP team is that they are empowered to solve problems. The purpose of this is that it allows the constant flow of productivity to take place. When your HP teams are given the power to do what they were set out to do (identify and solve problems) they also need the power to execute solutions. This results in an unimpeded flow of work from self-organizing and self-managed, problem solvers.

# Traditional Team Roles and Responsibilities

- **The Team Decides When They're Done**
  - A group of people with a high degree of interdependence geared toward the achievement of a goal or the completion of a task
    - Members of a team agree on a goal and concur that the only way to achieve that goal is to work together.
    - Some groups have a common goal but they don't work together to achieve it.
      - Some groups work together but they don't have a common goal.

Another organic means of strengthening bonds and commitment in an Agile team is through the use of the Definition of Done (DoD). Prior to starting a project a high-performance team establishes a Definition of Done that quantifies things like the amount of time that will be spent on a task, the expected level of quality, and the velocity. Doing this is a collaborative effort that ensures that everyone on the team is committed to contributing their full share of effort to the project, and that the team is all being measured against the same levels of quality, performance and accountability standards that are in-line with the value committed to be delivered to the customer.

# Traditional Team Roles and Responsibilities (continued)

- **Types of Teams**
  - Knowing the type of team you are on can help you choose how to plan your work and what you expect as outcomes.
  - There are many types of teams:
    - Traditional Model
    - Team Spirit Model
    - Task Force Model
    - Distributed Model
    - Cutting-Edge Model

Keep in mind that with the exception of the distributed model, you are not required to know the other team models for the exam. They have only been included to provide a context for understanding the other models, specifically, distributed and collocated teams, which are covered on the exam.

# Traditional Team Roles and Responsibilities (continued)

- **Traditional Model**
  - This model consists of a group of people who have a traditional boss but who also share some of his/her responsibility and authority.
    - How much is shared is usually dependent on the topic under discussion.
    - One person is in charge, but on various issues that person may allow other team members to take the leadership role.
    - Easily associated with being collocated
      - Located in the same work sphere and with quick and easy access to a designated team space

# Traditional Team Roles and Responsibilities (continued)

- **The Team Spirit Model**
  - This model consists of a group of people who are happy working for one boss and for whom everything seems to be going well.
    - Team members have team spirit but in reality they aren't a team because one person calls all the shots.
    - No sharing of authority or responsibility exists.

- **Task Force Model**
  - This model consists of a group that comes together for a specific period of time to work on a special project or task.
    - Traditionally called a task force or committee and may include quality circles as used in TQM efforts

The two other models we will compare against are the team spirit and task force model. In the team spirit model there is still only one boss, but there is no sharing of power. In this model, everyone follows the boss for the sake of team spirit. Then there is the task force model where a group comes together for a specific period of time to accomplish a task, then disbands; similar to a party planning committee. The task force model is also similar to an Agile team, with the exception that the goal of Agile teams is to stay together, so that the experience, and team bonding, can be transferred from one project to the next.

# + Traditional Team Roles and Responsibilities (continued)

Sec. 1

- **Distributed Team**
  - Members see one another infrequently or not at all.
    - These are called "cyber" or "virtual" teams.
    - What makes these teams different is that they have to work together to accomplish goals, but they may meet only at the beginning of their project and thereafter interact through e-mail and telephone.
      - They can also fit any of the four models listed above.
    - Easily classified as being a distributed team by…
      - Being located beyond the normal conversation proximity to other team members
        - *Can be located in different buildings, floors, geographical areas, etc.*

Distributed Agile can work, but it is risky. The communication, however, rarely lends itself well to collaboration. True collaboration flourishes when people can make the kind of face-to-face contact that enables them to read body language, make eye contact, and engage in group laughter. The reality, however, is that we live in a virtual world where team members may span the globe. As such, a self-empowered Agile team is responsible to adapt, make the necessary adjustments, and fill in the distance gaps.

**For The Exam:** Keep in mind that distance gaps between none collocated teams can be filled in with video-conferencing tools, instant-messaging software, meeting adjustments to accommodate different time zones, and arranging for members to fly in on a regular basis to meet with each other.

# Traditional Team Roles and Responsibilities (continued)

- **Cutting-Edge Model**
  - This model consists of a group of people who manage themselves.
    - No one person within the group has the authority to make all the decisions about the events that impact the group as a whole.
    - This is referred to as a self-organizing work team because everyone has authority and responsibility for all the decisions that have to be made.
    - Easily classified as a High-Performance Agile Team by..
      - Being self-organizing and empowered to make their own decisions based on the needs of the project.

Self-organization rarely happens on its own. Shared goals, boundaries, and knowledge of some simple rules are starting points for creating self-organizing teams. It's not a process that happens overnight, and the behavior required to become self-directed and motivated isn't something that can always be taught from a textbook. Becoming a fully competent, self-organizing, self-empowered, and self-managed team takes determination. Different styles of support will be required to take a whole team from novices that need directions to "roll-up your sleeves and just get it done, RIGHT," experts.

Conversely, since an experienced Agile coach knows not to ever tell a team what needs to be done from day one, s/he must walk the line in teaching the team the core fundamental of being Agile and in leading them toward the path of true adoption. Even so, in order for a team to learn this new way of not being managed, some level of management, and controllism, will likely be required. What the Agile coach has to remember is that controllism isn't the long-term objective. As such, s/he must remain conscious of not falling into a controlling pattern to get things done. Rather, the Agile product manager must clearly state to the team that his or her control is temporary and is needed only because the team is new to the process. This, in turn, will require a level of trust between the team and the business that the Agile product manager will take them where they need to be to truly become a High-Performing Agile Team.

# Traditional Team Roles and Responsibilities (continued)

## ■ Advantages and Disadvantages of Teams

| Advantages | Disadvantages |
|---|---|
| • Can get more varied ideas<br>• Can get more creative solutions<br>• Can get more done<br>• Can be more fun<br>• Can take more risks | • Can be dominated by one strong person<br>• Can take more time<br>• Can waste time talking, trying to be democratic<br>• Hard on members' egos<br>• Requires more skilled leadership |

Agile Teams are built on collaboration and close communication. However, this can't happen if one person is constantly taking charge of the team and others are afraid to speak up. Techniques such as Planning Poker and Participatory Decision-Making are used to make sure all Agile Team members are engaged on the project.

# Factors that Increase Success

## Team Space

Sec. 1

- Success in the workplace depends on your ability to build a team and to interact with others on that team.
    - Together, people can accomplish what one person alone cannot.

| Highly effective teams have: |
|---|
| • Unified commitment to being Agile and to understanding what it means to be Agile |
| • A clear, elevating goal to deliver high-quality products |
| • Internal standards of excellence that drive their behavior |
| • A results-driven structure |
| • Competent members |
| • A collaborative climate |
| • External support and recognition |
| • Principled leadership |

 **Note: This Topic was Touched Upon in Module 2:**

*Traditional Team Roles and Responsibilities – Distributed Teams*

Dynamic, real-time communication is a key component of Agile projects. The use of low-tech communication tools and collation of the team is a 'recommended' way to accomplish this aim. The reason being is that having the team gather in front of something like a corkboard where the group members can physically touch the user stories on index cards creates a greater bonding experience and better team collaboration. Given that, how does an organization that is new to Agile go about creating a team space that is conducive to Agile development?

As mentioned, the most effective layout for the physical team location is collocated desks and shared access to plans, status, next steps, and other project planning and management tools. The close proximity encourages face-to-face interactions and allows team members to subconsciously listen to sidebar conversations that may be taking place in the team space. It also enables them to contribute to the conversation if needed. (**For the exam:** This is known as Osmotic Communication.)

# Factors that Increase Success (continued)

- **Falling Short of Success**
    - When teams fail to perform, the typical reaction is to point the blame exclusively on the team members.
        - However, the answer doesn't always lie in replacing the team or firing the 'scapegoat.'
        - Rather, seek to answer the question, '*What went wrong with the group as a whole and why?*'
        - Start by looking at several contributing factors:
            - Environmental Influences
            - Goals
            - Roles
            - Processes
            - Relationships

When projects fail, and fail they will, the easy thing to do is point the finger and find a scapegoat to take the blame. But as a Lean/Agile advocate, your goal is to find out what caused the problem, and improve the process so that it does not happen again.

# Why Teams Fall Short of Success

- **Environmental Influences**  Sec. 1
    - The team is not given adequate resources to do the job.
    - There is no recognition of team effort.
        - There is a lack of recognition by the organization or its leaders that a team exists.
    - Physical separation prevents members from meeting frequently.
    - **In contrast:** Agile teams leverage osmotic communication among team members to solve problems and collaborate.

By keeping the team members close together and replacing offices and cubicles with shared desks, traditional separation gives way to an open concept environment—and, open communication.

For teams that must be geographically dispersed, conference calls, instant messaging, shared electronic documents, and information portals are used to minimize the separation. Moreover, these tools should be set up and made easily accessible in a war room. A war room affords the team a private area to conduct meetings, to share project-planning tools dynamically, and to share information in real time. Ideally, this is a physical meeting space near the team area.

# Why Teams Fall Short of Success (continued)

- **Goals**
    - Members do not participate in setting goals.
        - Goals are unclear.
        - Goals are not communicated.
        - Everyone is doing their thing without attention to team goals.
    - **In contrast:** Agile teams collaborate as a group to make decisions and they take responsibility for the outcomes of their actions.

 **Note: This Topic was Touched Upon in Module 2:**
*Participatory Decision-Making (PDM)*

Agile teams use Participatory Decision-Making (PDM). PDM gives workplace influence to individuals who are typically viewed as hierarchically unequal. In other words, the basic concept involves sharing power. Co-determination of working conditions, problem-solving, and decision-making are examples of such a power-sharing arrangement but can vary from organization to organization.

# Why Teams Fall Short of Success (continued)

- **Roles**
  - No clear leadership structure is identified.
    - Responsibilities are poorly defined.
    - There is buck-passing of responsibility.
    - Members engage in power plays for authority and control.
    - Members refuse to recognize their interdependence and act as if they were independent.
  - **_In contrast:_** Agile teams are cross-functional, whereby each member is a generalist such that teamwork in maximized and bottlenecks are reduced.

**Note: This Topic was Touched Upon in Module 3:**
*High-Performance Teams Are the Special Forces of an Agile Organization.*

Agile teams are usually set up to be cross-functional and self-organizing. Existing corporate hierarchy or corporate roles should not be used in deciding the composition of the team on an Agile project. The objective is to gather team members who are generalized specialists and who are willing to take responsibility for tasks they commit to deliver. They then decide individually how to meet an iteration's requirements.

# Why Teams Fall Short of Success (continued)

- **Relationships**
  - Members are unwilling to be identified with the team.
    - Relationships are competitive.
    - There is disguised conflict between members.
    - There are severe personality conflicts.
  - ***In contrast:*** Agile teams facilitate a safe environment where open communication encourages conflict as a means of proactively resolving problems and addressing concerns.

By fostering open communication in an open environment, team member feel safe to bring up issues and address conflicts. In turn, a trust is built between the members and stronger relationships are formed. Again, we see a cyclical effect in the Agile teams can become even better at self-managing because they are willing to address conflicts head on.

# Why Teams Fall Short of Success (continued)

- **Processes**
    - Decision-making is dominated by one person.
    - Communication is one-way channeled through the leader.
    - Members work individually and ignore each other.
    - Actions are taken without planning.
    - Minor points are debated endlessly.
        - Meetings are unproductive with the issues remaining unresolved.
        - Meetings cover trivial versus significant issues.
        - Members are late for meetings or do not attend.
- *<u>In contrast</u>:* Agile teams participate in well-structured, time-boxed daily stand-ups where all members are given the opportunity to report on their current situation and impediments.

---

One preconceived notion that people who are unfamiliar with Agile is that it does not have a formal process. And that could not be further from the truth. Agile is in fact a very structured. The difference is that the structure is done through we defined cycles of planning, and pre-planning. The outcome of this planning defines the constraints within the which the team can work their magic. I like to think of it by using the saying, "Discipline, is Freedom". Such that when a team has the discipline to follow the steps of Agile, such as adaptive planning and following through on their commitments, they have the freedom to get their work done as they see fit.

# Increasing Team Success Rates

- **Team Contracts**
  - The creation of a team contract outlines the ground rules for the team.
    - It is created and then monitored by the team.
    - As a group, team members discuss the possible advantages and disadvantages of such a contract.
    - Some people get offended by the idea of a team contract.
      - It's not ideal in every situation.

A great way to build relationships on a team is to work at understanding the members' different perspectives. Nonetheless, in order for the team to accomplish their goals as a group they must agree on a set of group rules, established in a team contract. For example, if a team member prefers to avoid conflict, you can't really accept that preference if you expect him to provide expert opinions that may not match the general consensus. This is why establishing a clear set of behaviors, communication expectations, and guidelines for conflict resolution are an important aspect of high-performance team coaching.

A team contract, or charter, can be a great way to formalize these expectations. The contract outlines a set of behavioral rules that everyone is expected to follow and support.

# Increasing Team Success Rates (continued)

- **Team Contracts** (continued)
  - **Code of Conduct**

    *As a team we will:*
    - Operating in a proactive manner, anticipating potential problems and working to prevent them before they happen.
    - Keep other team members informed.
    - Focus on what is best for the team as a whole.

  - **Ground Rules: Participation**

    *We will:*
    - Be honest and open.
    - Encourage a diversity of opinions on all topics.
    - Give everyone the opportunity for equal participation.
    - Be open to new approaches and listen to new ideas.
    - Have one conversation at a time.

Team members must feel safe to offer opinions when needed and to talk directly when feeling wronged. Here are several examples of ground rules that should be implemented.

# Increasing Team Success Rates (continued)

## Sample Contract (continued)

### Ground Rules: Communication

*We will:*

- Seek first to understand and then to be understood.
- Be clear and to the point.
- Keep discussions on track.
- Use visual means such as drawings, charts, and tables to facilitate discussion.

### Ground Rules: Problem-Solving

*We will:*

- Encourage everyone to participate.
- Encourage all ideas (no criticism) since new concepts come from outside our normal perceptions.
- Build on each other's ideas.

---

As an added measure, processes for team members to follow can be defined to ensure the charter expectations are met. For example, when one team member feels offended by another, a conflict resolution process would define the steps to take. In that scenario, the process could state that before going to the team as a whole, or the product manager, the offended person speaks with the offender first. Building trust among colleagues and creating a more unified team are the end results of these types of tools and techniques.

# Increasing Team Success Rates (continued)

- **Sample Contract** (continued)
  - **Meeting Guidelines:**
    - The meeting begins and ends on time.
    - We have an agenda for every meeting.
    - Cell phones and pagers are muted.
  - Each member then signs and dates the contract.

Once the team has agreed upon their expected behavior, reaffirm that commitment by signing and dating the contract. You may also consider placing it in a highly visible are in the team space, and as a reminder to help others outside of the team understand how your team functions.

# Connecting with Your Team

- **Emotional Intelligence (EI)**  Sec. 6
  - Refers to the ability to identify, assess, perceive, control, and evaluate emotions
    - This can be in relation to how one interacts with oneself and with groups.
    - Some scientific literature states that EI can be learned and strengthened, while others claim it is an inborn characteristic.
  - Various definitions and EI models have been proposed. Salovey and Mayer proposed a model that identified four different factors of emotional intelligence:
    - The perception of emotion
    - The ability to reason using emotions
    - The ability to understand emotion
    - The ability to manage emotions

---

Experience plays a large role in EI. It can be considered one of the most important aspects of leading a high-performance Agile team and of determining the leadership style of an Agile product manager. Getting "the job done" frequently takes more work than just completing the technical pieces. It requires a savvy means of adaptive leadership whereby you intuitively know how to engage others in order to build relationships. This ability of an Agile product manager is what ultimately determines how successful the team will be.

**For the Exam:** At times, this may require having a bigger purpose for the goal and becoming a Servant Leader.

A Servant Leader is one who invites the wisdom of the team instead of just dropping commands. In this type of leadership role, you strive to make your team operate at 110% and have very little tolerance of imperfection. At the same time, you also understand the impact of being accepting and having empathy as they relate to the team and the company.

# Expanding your Emotional Intelligence

- **Parker Team Player Survey (PTPS)**
  - The PTPS is an 18-item, easy-to-use self-assessment instrument that helps individuals identify their primary team player style.
  - The PTPS yields scores for four team player styles:
    - The Contributor
    - The Communicator
    - The Challenger
    - The Collaborator

**Note:** The PTPS is not required learning for the exam. It has been included to provide a context for discussing: Team Contribution, Communication and Collaboration.

# Players on the Team

- **The Contributor**
  - This is the detailed person who keeps track of everything and who makes the greatest use of checklists and guidelines.
    - You can count on this team member to know what the assignment is and when it will be due.
    - This individual gets frustrated with those who lose sight of the details or who want to try something new.
    - This person follows recipes, knows where his or her tools are, and doesn't like surprises.
    - This team member's motto might be "Why reinvent the wheel?"

# Players on the Team (continued)

- **The Communicator**
  - This type of team member is a people person.
    - This individual doesn't want to rock the boat; s/he just wants to enjoy the boat ride.
    - This person is usually more concerned about harmony than results.
    - "If it's not broke, don't break it" would be this team member's motto.

- **The Challenger**
  - This person wears the hat of the Devil's Advocate.
    - This individuals delights in challenging authority and has the uncanny knack of finding the weakest link in any argument.
    - This team member believes in constantly asking "Why?" and their motto might be "Who says so?"

# Players on the Team (continued)

- **The Collaborator**
  - This team member is the visionary who is always looking to the future and for a better way of doing things.
    - This person is a "big picture" thinker who doesn't always consider the feelings of others in his or her quest for "the better way."
    - For this individual, titles aren't important as long as goals are reached.
    - This team member will pitch in and do what has to be done.
    - "Build a better mouse trap" is this person's motto.
    - This individual can persuade and get others motivated, but don't bore him or her with the details of it all.

# Team Dynamics

- **Balancing between Contributor and Collaborator**
  - Focused on both the short- and long-term aspects of the job
    - Do whatever it takes to complete the immediate task and reach the team's overall goals.
    - Sharing your expertise, training, pitching in, and working outside your designated roles that come naturally to you.
  - *Be careful of:*
    - Focusing so intently on the strategic and tactical issues that it comes at the expense of not giving sufficient attention to the internal dynamics of the team
    - Being so focused on the work that you fail to raise important questions about the team's efforts

In looking at the previous team member types, you want to find a balance between being a contributor and a collaborator. That means focusing on both the short and long term goals, and doing whatever it takes to accomplish your tasks to reach the team goals. Contribute by training, and sharing your expertise, and being willing to work outside of roles that come naturally to you. It also means not neglecting the needs of your team because all you can see is your own strategy, and failing to raise important issues that would benefit the team.

# Interpersonal Growth Within Team Growth

- **Self-Assessment**
  - Affirm your strengths.
    - Acknowledge that you're OK. Look for ways to add to your strengths. Be the best Contributor, Collaborator, Communicator, or Challenger.
  - Look for teams and organizations where your strengths are appreciated.
    - Avoid those situations where they are not valued. For example, Challengers should avoid conservative, risk-adverse environments.

2.11

---

Becoming Agile depends on you and your organization's ability to seize external opportunities, proficiency in planning for the long haul, eagerness to remove complexity, and capability to bounce back from unforeseen changes. More importantly, as a team you must not only have a strategic plan but you must capitalize on market trends as well as anticipate and respond to change more rapidly.

An Agile self-assessment can stimulate learning and change as well as build enthusiasm for Agile development. On a team level, self-assessments expose key areas of improvement and identify performance improvement opportunities. On an organizational level, they identify gaps in business process and establish development needs. With these pieces of information identified, it becomes easier to create a cost-benefit analysis and get key stakeholders and sponsors to commit to an Agile transformation.

James Shore provides a great online Agile Assessment based on his book, *The Art of Agile* available at: http://jamesshore.com/Agile-Book/assess_your_agility.html

# Interpersonal Growth Within Team Growth (continued)

- Extend your repertoire by incorporating more of the strengths of other styles.
  - For example, if your least active style is Communicator, develop a plan to increase your skills as a group facilitator.
- Develop your ability to analyze your team.
  - How Agile are you willing to be?
    - Observe the need for a particular strength.
      - *(i.e., challenge complacency)*
    - Provide an appropriate intervention and/or encourage others to do the same.

# Team Growth

- **Building Team Trust through Commitments**
  - Trust is an Agile team mainstay virtue.
    - It is the bond that allows any kind of significant relationship to exist between people.
      - Once a commitment is broken, regaining trust is not easily, if ever, fully recovered.
  - Trust is produced in a climate that includes four elements:
    - Honesty: Integrity, no lies, no exaggerations
    - Openness: A willingness to share and receptivity to information, perceptions, ideas
    - Consistency: Predictable behavior and responses
    - Treating people with dignity and fairness

**Note: This Topic was Touched Upon in Module 3:**

*Characteristics of a High-Performance Team – Clearly Defined Vision*

The stakeholders, sponsors, and team members establish a Definition of Done that quantifies the amount of time that will be spent on a task, the expected level of quality, and the velocity.

Teams that are able to follow through on their commitment build stronger levels of trust between team members and the stakeholders. A technique used to accomplish this trust can be found in velocity tracking. By measuring and monitoring the velocity during each iteration, teams are able to more accurately provide estimates and keep their commitments.

**Agile Principle:** "Build projects around motivated individuals. Give them the environment and support they need, and then trust them to get the job done."

# Team Growth (continued)

- **Building Team Trust through Commitments** (continued)
  - The problem is that trust is so fragile.
    - If any one of the previously listed elements is breached even once, a relationship is apt to be severely compromised, even lost.
    - With trust gone between individuals, teams have little hope of functioning well and of realizing their true potential.
    - Do-Say
      - Do what you say you're going to do!

# Team Growth (continued)

## ■ Protecting your Team

- Four themes emerge to help explain why a climate of trust fosters teamwork.

  ___ Trust allows team members to stay problem-focused.
  ___ Trust improves the quality of collaborative outcomes.
  ___ Trust leads to compensating.
  ___ Trust promotes more efficient communication and coordination.

It is the responsibility of the Agile product manager to protect the team from changes to the product backlog once an iteration has started. A misconception about being Agile is that teams are supposed to be able to change their focus at a moment's notice. The reality is that change is only allowed to happen up until the iteration has started. The reason being is that prior to the start of the iteration, the team has already devoted time and effort to planning and prioritizing the work that will be done in order to meet the customers' needs and has made a commitment to do so. And that commitment is expected to be reciprocated by the customer—otherwise work would never get completed. Nonetheless, it's often tempting for stakeholders outside the core development team to make "one small request," which eventually sets the stage for rendering it acceptable to keep making last-minute modifications, thereby resulting in wasted efforts and time over the duration of the project.

# Coaching and Mentoring with Teams

## The Stages of Team Development

- Every group of people, whether they are a team or just a group working together, grows and evolves.
- The four stages of this development are:
  - Forming
  - Storming
  - Norming
  - Performing

---

Having access to an experienced Agile coach makes the transition to becoming Agile much easier. Agile coaches provide teams with guidance throughout the developmental work and proactively build collaboration within their team and the organization. An important thing to remember is that like all aspects of Agile, even coaches must continuously seek to improve themselves and learn new ways to solve problems. Coaching and mentoring are ongoing processes.

An easy way to remember this is by thinking of Tuckman's four stages of group development: Forming, Storming, Norming, and Performing.

# Team Development

- **The Stages of Team Development** (continued)
  - Forming
    
    *Characteristics of this stage:*
    - Group members may adopt a wait-and-see attitude, or they may be formal.
    - No clear idea of goals or expectations exists.
    - Team members are not sure why they are there.
    
    *What you can do to help:*
    - The team writes its own charter or mission statement and clarifies goals. Remember, goals must have personal buy-in.
    - Help the team establish boundaries and determine what is expected.
    - Teams get to know each other doing non-conflict-laden tasks.
      - This builds commitment to one larger goal.
    - Help them know what to expect; communicate and reassure.

**Also Discussed in section Module 2:**

*Who Has What at Stake? – The Business*

Through constant communication and collaboration between the Agile product manager and the customer, a shared understanding of the project scope and deliverables can be accomplished. Additionally, the use of a Vision Statement, a roadmap that reinforces the customer values using the 5Ws, can be used as a guideline to set acceptance criteria and to identify acceptable trade-offs. Adhering to the Agile Principle "Our highest priority is to satisfy the customer through early and continuous delivery of valuable software" sets the stage for the Agile team to organically conduct risk management efforts and be empowered to remove constraints in order to continuously delivery valuable software to the customer.

# Team Development (continued)

- **The Stages of Team Development** (continued)
  - Storming

    Sec. 6

    *Characteristics of this stage:*
    - Team members are eager to get going.
    - Conflict can arise as people bring different ideas of how to accomplish goals and notice differences rather than similarities.
    - Some members may drop out mentally or physically.

  *What you can do to help:*
  - Continue with no surprises and communicate.
  - Tensions will increase; this is normal, so recognize and publicly acknowledge accomplishments.
  - Participate in meetings.
  - Value diversity.
  - Gather information, offer assistance, and be supportive.

**Also Discussed in section Module 3:**

*Connecting with Your Team – Emotional Intelligence*

Experience has a large role to play in EI. It can be considered one of the most important aspects of leading a high-performance Agile team and of determining the leadership style of an Agile product manager. Getting "the job done" frequently takes more work than just completing the technical pieces. It requires a savvy means of adaptive leadership whereby you intuitively know how to engage others in order to build relationships. This ability of an Agile product manager is what ultimately determines how successful the team will be.

At times, this may require having a bigger purpose for the goal and becoming a Servant Leader.

A Servant Leader is one who invites the wisdom of the team instead of just dropping commands. In this type of leadership role, you strive to make your team operate at 110% and have very little tolerance of imperfection. At the same time, you also understand the impact of being accepting and having empathy as they relate to the team and the company.

# Team Development (continued)

## The Stages of Team Development (continued)

- Norming

    *Characteristics of this stage:*
    - People begin to recognize ways they are alike.
    - They realize it's sink or swim; we're in this together.
    - People get more social.
    - Team members may forget their focus in favor of having a good time.

    ***What you can do to help:***
    - Recognize how they are alike.
    - Help with training if applicable.
    - Encourage them to feel comfortable with each other and with the systems.
    - Help the group stay focused on the goal.

---

In the norming stage the team becomes more social and are more comfortable with being themselves. They let their defenses down and instead of focusing on their differences, they realize they are able to get more done, and have a good time, when they focus on their similarities.

# Team Development (continued)

## ■ The Stages of Team Development

### ■ Performing

*Characteristics of this stage:*

- Team members are trained and competent, able to do their own problem-solving.
- Now the leader will ask for critical self-assessment and look at ways to both challenge team members and develop them.
- Team members are mature and understand their roles and responsibilities.
- They are self-motivated and self-trained.
- They want more input in processes.

**What you can do to help:**

- Recognize efforts.
- Encourage growth.
- Give new challenges.

During the performing period the team will have matured into the roles and responsibilities. They are competent and able to self-motivate and self-train in order to solve problems, and contribute to improving the process.

To encourage continual growth in this stage, recognize their efforts, and give them challenges to help the team grow.

# High Performance Teams

- **Forming a High-Performance Team**
  - Not all of us will take the same approach to forming a successful work team.
    - There is a tendency to want to surround ourselves with people who are just like us.
      - If you get to choose a team rather than organize a pre-formed one, then you'll want people with a variety of strengths.
    - For a team that is already in place, organizing may be more subtle.
      - Consider calling all the workgroups together to discuss what you want to accomplish (goals) and how everybody can help.
      - Imposing goals on people doesn't work as well as having them tell you what goals they will strive for.

The relationship between motivation and job satisfaction is not overly complex. The problem is that many organizations only look for short-term solutions and do very little to motivate their employees for the long haul (for example, with money). Traditional managers like to use this approach because they think people are more financially motivated than intrinsically motivated. And for the average team that might be true. But motivating a team to become an Agile High Performer is far more complex. It may require a company policy so that the team is truly self-organizing and empowered; or, it may even require redefining jobs for maximum satisfaction and performance. All the same, the team has to respect the culture of the company and first show that it can be trusted. So, it is wise to start by motivating your team by firstly getting rid of the things that are annoying them about the company and the workplace. Make sure they're treated fairly and with respect, and that they are acknowledged for getting their job done. As an Agile product manager, once you've done this, look for ways in which you can help the team grow within the project, and give them opportunities to do so.

# Conflict Resolution

## High-Performance Communication

Sec. 6

- Two of the most powerful communication skills to resolve conflict is to **listen** and **ask** questions.
  - These are the tools everyone uses to overcome miscommunication problems.

**For the Exam:** Part of the requirements that you need to be aware of for the exam are soft skills. In this section we are going to examine tools and that everyone can use to overcome miscommunication and conflict. Specifically, we are going to look at the skills of listening and asking questions.

# Conflict Resolution (continued)

## ■ High-Performance Listening
- One thing most people do is make a lot of assumptions about the people they come into contact with.
  - Team members often assume they have interpreted others' comments correctly
  - They assume others understand perfectly what they are trying to say.
  - They also assume that others will react as they would to different situations.

When it comes to communication, remember this: you have two ears and one mouth, so use the proportionately.

If you want to be understood, make it a habit of listing to others first, making sure you understand what they are saying. Reinforce your listening, by asking questions to confirm that you understood them correctly. This way you will not make assumptions about what you thought you heard.

# Roles and Responsibilities

- **Know Who Is On Your Team**
    - Customer – ensures the team works on stories that deliver the highest business value possible
    - Customer Proxy – helps the Agile customer ensure the team works on stories that deliver the highest business value possible
    - Team Lead – does whatever it takes to ensure the team delivers now and in the future
    - Product Manager – does whatever it takes to ensure that valuable projects are delivered now and in the future
    - Business Analyst – helps the Agile customer discover the goals and needs of the product's customer

Part of being a generalized specialist is not only knowing your roles and responsibilities, but also understanding the roles and responsibilities of those on your team. The benefit to knowing this not only allows you to be more empathetic towards each other, but it also reinforces the concept of the value chain, but understanding how your outputs impact another person's inputs.

# Makeup of an Agile Project Team

- **Teams of 5-10 Members with Cross-Functional Skills**

  - Project Manager/Product Manager/Product Owner
  - Testers
  - Analyst
  - Technical Writer
  - Architects
  - Developers
  - Facilitator/Agile Coach

  - Each being a generalized specialist

Up until now we have been using the term team in a generic since, and you mave have assumed that we were only referring to the development team. Well, in Agile, the term team is not exclusive to just the developers. Team can encompass everyone that contributes to the development of the product.

# Building an Agile Project Team

- **Agile Team Member Qualities**
  - Not afraid to take risks, make decisions on their own, and be accountable for their actions
    - In order for this to happen, the team needs a set of common ground rules and processes.
  - Strive for a mix of backgrounds and personalities to get organizational buy-in as a whole
    - Pro-Agile mentality
    - Positive attitude toward change
    - Can see the big picture and still execute the details when needed

# Building an Agile Project Team (continued)

## ■ Project Manager vs. Agile Coach

*"A Project Manager's success equals the success of the project. An Agile coach's success equals the team's continual improvement and their pursuit of high performance"*

— Lyssa Adkins, Coaching Agile Teams

- PMs are typically accustomed to using command-and-control techniques to accomplish the project goals.
    - Agile coaches strive to help the team members reach their goal by encouraging self-organization and empowering them to be self-directed.
- PMs maintain control of their project through the project plan.
    - Agile coaches encourage the team to control the outcome of the project by applying Agile values and principles.
- PMs juggle between the triple constraints to correct for unknowns.
    - Agile coaches adjust scope to account for unknowns while holding time and budget constants.

---

Facilitated meetings are a way to identify the ineffective and inefficient practices that may be holding an organization or team back. A time-boxed agenda should be prepared by the facilitator and shared with all participants in order to make the goals of the meeting clear and keep it on track. The meeting should be conducted by a neutral participant, for example an Agile coach, but in the real world it's more likely that it would be conducted by a designated team member or as an open forum. However, for the exam, don't confuse the term Agile product manager with the term Agile coach. It is important that the facilitator not be the product manager because such an individual is not really neutral, especially if the team needs to bring up issues and deal specifically with him or her.

# Team Inspiration

- **Adaptive Leadership**  Sec. 6
  - The goal of an Agile manager IS NOT to motivate their team!
    - The Product Manager is responsible for providing an environment where team members can find their own intrinsic motivators to keep them focused on reaching their objectives.
  - The Agile manager's focus should be on setting up the conditions to maximize the probability that team members will develop an interest in their work.
    - The PM does this by removing impediments to the team.
  - The first step in accomplishing this aim is to facilitate a set of clearly defined team:
    - Values
    - Principles
    - Practices

Since everyone is motivated differently, and Agile practitioner must adapt as a leader to motivate team members. But more importantly, manager must understand it is not their responsibility to motivate the team. Rather, it is their job to ensure the team environment encourages the team to through intrinsically motivate. This is achieved by removing obstacles that the may keep the team from being able to focus on their goal. When this type of motivating environment is in place, you increase the probability of the team's success.

# Establishing Agile Team Values

- **Agile Team Values**
  - In addition to seeking business value, Agility is about establishing values that promote ethical and sustainable work practices.
    - Laid out in the Agile Manifesto and guiding principles
  - Values are already in place from several Agile methodologies.
    - *Scrum Values*: commitment, openness, courage, and respect
    - *XP Values*: communication, feedback, simplicity, courage, and respect

III.4

# Establishing Agile Team Values (continued)

- **Agile Team Principles**
  - Provide the context around which the team wraps the values and provide an actionable tenet.

    *"We believe in <value>; therefore we will <do something>."*

- **Agile Team Practices**
  - Day-to-day activities performed by the team that reinforce the principles and values:
    - *Following Coding Standards (Discipline)*
    - *Active Listening (Respect)*
    - *Prioritization (Courage)*
    - *Planning Meeting (Open Communication)*
    - *Daily Stand-up (Commitment)*
    - *Retrospectives (Continuous Improvement)*

# Establishing Agile Team Values (continued)

- **Agile Team Practices**
  - De-motivators
    - Unclear goals, no collective responsibility, infighting

- **So How Does One Motivate a Team?**
  - Theory X and Theory Y provide insight into styles of management that create motivation in the workplace.
    - Theory X: assumes the average employee is lazy, only does the minimum amount of work required, and assumes responsibility to simply maintain employment.
      - Because people are extrinsically motivated, managers need to employ rewards and punishments to pull the most out of their employees.
    - Theory Y: assumes that if given the opportunity, people want to do well because of a self-motivation to succeed.
      - Reaffirms McGregor, Deming, and Drucker's assertion that self-esteem, creativity, curiosity, and a sense of community are the driving forces behind motivation.

III.7

**Note: This Topic was Touched Upon in Module 3:**

*High-Performance Teams – Forming a High-Performance Team*

The relationship between motivation and job satisfaction is not overly complex. The problem is that many organizations only look for short-term solutions and do very little to motivate their employees for the long haul (for example, with money). Traditional managers like to use this approach because they think people are more financially motivated than intrinsically motivated. And for the average team that might be true. But motivating a team to become an Agile High Performer is far more complex. It may require company policy so that the team is truly self-organizing and empowered; or, it may even require redefining jobs for maximum satisfaction and performance. All the same, the team has to respect the culture of the company and first show that it can be trusted. So, it is wise to start by motivating your team by firstly getting rid of the things that are annoying them about the company and the workplace. Make sure they're treated fairly and with respect, and that they are acknowledged for getting their job done. As an Agile product manager, once you've done this, look for ways in which you can help the team grow within the project, and give them opportunities to do so.

# Establishing Agile Team Values (continued)

- **Creating a Value-Driven Agile Team Environment**  Sec. 6
    - Facilitate ground rules and working agreements around which the team will operate.
        - Empowers the team to take responsibility
        - Develops itself through self-organizing, collaborative decision-making and mutual accountability

- **Servant Leadership**
    - The Agile Product Manager is responsible for coordinating the activities that encourage the team to be self-organizing and empowered.
        - Removes roadblocks that prevent the team members from reaching their goals

---

Just as the business will be moving toward value driven delivery, so should the team. Remember, in value-driven deliver, you are not merely striving to read the goal, but constantly looking for way to improve the process used to get there. This is accomplished betting ground rules and working agreements to build productive and safe environment. The result will foster an empowered, self-organizing, and collaborative team, that takes responsibility for their actions. All the same, the success of the environment is contingent upon the product manager protecting the team and removing roadblocks.

# The Art of Facilitation

## Facilitating Cross-Functional Teams

- All members are in agreement that they all bear the burden of product delivery.
- Ensure members will be fully dedicated and engaged on the project.
- Strive to produce collocated teams to reduce cost and increase productivity.
    - If not possible, utilize tools.

Since Agile is less about management and more about facilitation, it is important to understand how to facilitate cross function teams. The first thing to reinforce is that all members must share the responsibility of delivering the product, and in agreement that they will be fully engaged on the project. The best way to foster this type of agreement is through collocating team. Remember collocation allows for fact to face communication as well as open communication.

But, what happens if collocation is not an possible?

# The Art of Facilitation (continued)

- **Facilitating Distributed Teams**
  - Requires Virtual Stand-up Meetings
    - Add back some documentation because you can't rely on talking as much
    - Add detail to the product backlog
  - **Encourage lateral communication**
  - Communication Tools
    - Wikis to share commentary and photos
    - Web/Video conferencing
    - Online whiteboards
    - Instant messaging

**For the Exam:** When co-location is not an option, use communication tools such as wikis to share information, web and voice conferencing to conduct virtual stand up meetings, online whiteboard for sharing diagrams and rapid communication feedback. However, because there is less face to face communication you will need to add back some documentation and in more detail around your backlog items.

# The Art of Facilitation (continued)

- **Facilitating Distributed Teams** (continued)
  - Seeding visits
    - Ideally, the whole team meets in person at start.
    - Stay together for an iteration or more when possible.
  - Contact visits
    - Whole team, quarterly, face-to-face
  - Traveling Ambassadors
    - Individuals who travel more frequently among locations to ensure a good working relationship

**For the Exam:** The idea behind this strategy is to bring your remote teams together for a duration of time to build a bond, and level of trust. The can be done at the start of an iteration or for an entire iteration if possible. These types of quarterly, face to face visits allows team members to attach a physical person to what may otherwise simply be a thought of as Jon in the video cam.

# Creating a Safe Team Environment

- **Team Dynamic and Hierarchy**
  - Part of the Agile team dynamic is built around Servant Leadership.
    - It invites the wisdom of the team instead of just dropping commands.
    - Tolerance of imperfection
      - Continuous improvement is best achieved by not being afraid to take risks in order to learn something new.
    - Promotes acceptance, empathy, compassion, and uncompromising perfection.

**Also Discussed in section Module 3:**

*Connecting with Your Team – Emotional Intelligence*

Experience has a large role to play in EI. It can be considered one of the most important aspects of leading a high-performance Agile team and of determining the leadership style of an Agile product manager. Getting "the job done" frequently takes more work than just completing the technical pieces. It requires a savvy means of adaptive leadership whereby you intuitively know how to engage others in order to build relationships. This ability of an Agile product manager is what ultimately determines how successful the team will be.

At times, this may require having a bigger purpose for the goal and becoming a Servant Leader.

A Servant Leader is one who invites the wisdom of the team instead of just dropping commands. In this type of leadership role, you strive to make your team operate at 110% and have very little tolerance of imperfection. At the same time, you also understand the impact of being accepting and having empathy as they relate to the team and the company.

# Creating a Safe Team Environment (continued)

## ■ Team Dynamic and Hierarchy (continued)

Sec. 6

- Try to avoid having the Agile Project Manager conduct performance reviews.
    - Discourage the coach from playing the role of the Agile Project Manager/Product Owner
    - There are no management hierarchies.
        - *It respects the roles that evolve between that of a teacher (Shu), coach(Ha), and advisor(Ri)*
    - The team members negotiate work as partners and mentors.
- What happens on the team stays on the team.

---

It is also important to respect the roles that develop between the team and coaches. The team should feel comfortable approaching their mentor or coach, without the feeling of being judged or fear of being reprimanded. As such, it is important that the coach does not play the role of a product manager; this blurs the line between the person that conducts your performance review, and the person you need to confide in for assistance.

# Team Collaboration

- **Cooperation vs. Collaboration**
  - **Cooperation** promotes things like autonomy and sustainable development.
    - It discourages counterproductive long e-mails that are designed to place blame …
      - instead of solving issues.
  - Gets people to interact and leverage each other's complementary skills.
    - Increases the effectiveness of the team output.
    - When a project is incremental, cooperation is all that you really need.

Up to this point we have discussed collaboration in a loose sense of the word. So now let's begin to put some more mead on the bone, and we will do that by first, comparing it to cooperation. In terms of being Agile, cooperation is not only the idea of the output that occurs when two or more people work together, but it also focusses on the skills that each cooperating member brings to the table to enable cooperation to occur. A highly skilled individual that knows how to cooperate with in the confines of a team, may still do so, autonomously, at a sustained pace.

# Team Collaboration (continued)

- **Cooperation vs. Collaboration**
  - **Collaboration** enables people to build off each other's strengths and knowledge.
    - Enables them to create something that is beyond their individual abilities.
    - Involves negotiating, challenging assumptions, and building on each other's perspectives.
  - To build strong team collaboration skills, it's important to develop strong individual collaboration skills:
    - Improving team cooperation skills
    - Expecting members to show up prepared
    - Allowing room for team members' egos
    - Defining a collaboration zone

The augmenter to cooperation is collaboration. Such that if cooperation is the ability of a team member to be a high functioning, autonomous, contributor—collaboration builds up that by enabling people to build upon their individual strength and knowledge. The result is that by developing a strong team of collaboration, the output of the whole is greater than that of the individual. But, collaboration requires work. It involves negotiation, challenging assumptions and building on the strengths of each other.

# Close Communication

- **Agile Encourages Close Customer Communication**
  - Traditionally, the customer is represented by the requirement and design documents.
    - Agile Product Managers work to connect people through face-to-face communication.
      - As a result, formal documentation is not a huge requirement because communication is a fundamental part of the Agile framework.
    - Reinforced in the Agile Manifesto:
      - "Individuals and interactions over processes and tools"
      - "Customer collaboration over contract negotiation"
  - Requires trust to ask for information as needed

---

On traditional project, the needs of the customer are simply captured as a list of requirements, and once they have agreed to and signed off on those needs, there is little, if any room to change those needs. Agile, on the other hand, addresses the needs of the customer through close communication and collaboration. This is accomplished, once again, through face to face communication—the fundamental part of Agile.

 **Also Discussed in Section Module 2:**

*Who Has What at Stake – The Business*

Through constant communication and collaboration between the Agile product manager and the customer, a shared understanding of the project scope and deliverables can be accomplished. Additionally, the use of a Vision Statement, a roadmap that reinforces the customer values using the 5Ws, can be used as a guideline to set acceptance criteria and to identify acceptable trade-offs. Adhering to the Agile Principle "Our highest priority is to satisfy the customer through early and continuous delivery of valuable software" sets the stage for the Agile team to organically conduct risk management efforts and be empowered remove constraints in order to continuously delivery valuable software to the customer.

# Close Communication (continued)

- **Communication Stratagems**
  - **Release Planning Meeting:** communicates the up-to-date status on the strategic vision
  - **Iteration Planning Meeting:** communicates the tactical objectives of achieving the goal
  - **Daily Stand-Up Meeting:** communicates the internal progress and impediments to other team members
  - **Review/Demo Meeting:** communicates the progress of the product to the team and stakeholders
  - **Retrospective Meeting:** communicates areas of improvement to be made on the project

A critical part of achieving close communication is communication management. Agile product managers maintains open lines of communication between team members, stakeholders and sponsors, by using structured, and well defined planning sessions to foster communication; and planning session are conducted to achieve a specific goal and outcome.

# Close Communication (continued)

- **Release Planning Meeting**
  - Communicates with the team how the functional and non-functional requirements in backlog will be used to achieve the stakeholders *vision* and to estimate which features will be delivered by the release deadline
    - Initial release planning meetings rarely last longer than a day.
    - The customer presents the prioritized features to be delivered.
      - Developers should have rough estimates of how much work is required to implement each of these features.

The Release Planning Meeting communicates with the team how the functional and non-functional requirements in the backlog will be used to achieve the stakeholders' vision and to estimate which features will be delivered by the release deadline.

The Initial release planning meetings rarely last longer than a day.

During that meeting, the customer presents the prioritized features to be delivered and Developers should have rough estimates of how much work is required to implement each of these features.

# Close Communication (continued)

- **Release Planning Meeting** (continued)
  - Information from this meeting is used to decide whether or not the project will produce enough ROI and if it should proceed.
    - Using the developers' estimates and the customers' feature priorities, the team lays out a release plan.
      - Maps features very roughly to the first few iterations.
    - Developers may find low-priority features that pose design or architectural risks.
      - Ask customers to consider assigning these features to earlier iterations.

Information from the Release Planning Meeting is used to decide whether or not the project will produce enough ROI and if it should proceed.

Using the developers' estimates and the customers' feature priorities, the team lays out a release plan.

They then roughly maps features into the first few iterations, and allows developers to find low-priority features that pose design or architectural risks. If found, ask customers to consider assigning these features to earlier iterations.

# Close Communication (continued)

## ▪ Iteration Planning Meeting

- The team sets an overall goal for the iteration to help guide the selection of features.
    - The highest-priority features are selected from the release plan at the beginning of the meeting.
    - If the iteration does have an overarching goal, then some lower-priority features may be selected if they better align with the goal.
    - Knowing the team's previous velocity helps the team members determine how much they can sign up for in the next iteration.
        - If the iteration is overbooked, then the customer needs to select which features need to be delayed to a future iteration.

During the Iteration Planning Meeting, the team sets an overall goal for the iteration to help guide the selection of features.

The highest-priority features are selected from the release plan at the beginning of the meeting.

If the iteration does have an overarching goal, then some lower-priority features may be selected if they better align with the goal.

Knowing the team's previous velocity helps the team members determine how much they can sign up for in the next iteration.

If the iteration is overbooked, then the customer needs to select which features need to be delayed to a future iteration.

## Close Communication (continued)

- **Daily Stand-Up Meeting**
  - A daily team meeting to provide a status update to the team members
    - Establish a shared commitment to complete an individual portion of work on the project.
    - The 'semi-real-time' status allows participants to know about potential challenges.
    - Coordinate efforts to resolve difficult and/or time-consuming issues.

---

A Daily Stand-Up Meeting is a daily team meeting to provide a status update by the team members.

Meeting in this manner establish a shared commitment to complete an individual portion of work on the project.

The 'semi-real-time' status also allows participants to know about potential challenges and coordinate efforts to resolve difficult and/or time-consuming issues.

# Close Communication (continued)

- **Daily Stand-Up Meeting** (continued)
  - The meetings are intended to be time-boxed.
    - 5–15 minutes in length
    - Are held standing up to remind people to keep the meeting focused
  - During the meeting, each person uses their slice of time to report on:
    - What they worked on yesterday
    - What they are going to work on today
    - What impediments or obstacles are preventing them from completing their assigned work

During a standup meeting, facilitation is important so that the team is addressing members as a whole. Such meetings should be time-boxed to no more than 15 minutes. To do this, team members simple take turns addressing the group by answering the following three questions: What they did yesterday, what they are going to do today, and what impediments they are facing. Once again, it important that they address each other during the meeting and not the product manager. By doing so, the meeting focuses on building team collaboration instead of becoming a status meeting.

# Close Communication (continued)

## Review Meeting

- Opportunity for the team to demo the results of the iteration to the customers/stakeholders
  - Generally held on the last day of the iteration or the first day of the next iteration
    - The customers, project sponsor, team management, and stakeholders like Marketing, Production Support, Legal, etc. are invited.
  - Team demonstrates working features that were produced in the iteration.
    - Solicits feedback from the attendees.
    - Informs the attendees of any changes to the project or release plan.

---

The Review Meeting provides an opportunity for the team to demo the results of the iteration to the customers/stakeholders.

It is Generally held on the last day of the iteration or the first day of the next iteration.

The customers, project sponsor, team management, and stakeholders like Marketing, Production Support, Legal, etc. are invited.

During the meeting, the team demonstrates working features that were produced in the iteration and solicits feedback from the attendees, and informs the attendees of any changes to the project or release plan.

# Close Communication (continued)

- **Retrospective Meeting**
    - Held at the end of every iteration following the iteration meeting
        - The team and Agile coach meet to discuss what went well and what to improve in the next iteration.
        - Should be time-boxed to three hours
    - A time to discuss issues that affected the team's overall effectiveness, productivity, and quality as well as the team's satisfaction with the project
        - If the team did not complete all of the user stories in the iteration, then the Agile coach will discuss what and why it happened.
            - Determine whether the team can adapt its processes so that those kinds of problems are less likely to occur again.

---

Organizations often can't see their problems because they have worked around them and made them a regular part of the business culture for so long. To overcome this issue, retrospective meetings are held at the end of each iteration. A retrospective meeting can start by asking the participants questions about how they felt the last iteration went, what worked, what didn't, and more importantly, to use the 12 Agile principles as the guidelines for solutions. The facilitator may engage the team proactively by asking for their ideas about how they felt problems should have been resolved or for hypothetical scenarios with personas. In so doing, the facilitator can gently pull out underlying concerns team members may have but are not willing to outright address.

Although the scheduled retrospectives are the ideal place to conduct facilitated meetings, they can/should be held whenever impediments turn into major barriers that place the success of the project at risk.

# Team Commitment

- **Communication Creates Commitment**
  - In Agile, the people who are doing the work know best how to do it and how much time it will take to do it.
    - Traditional management styles negotiate a deadline, commit for the team, decide what will be delivered, and then tell the team to go do it.
  - The Agile approach works because the feedback loop is now directly between the team and the product owner.
    - This allows the team to be left alone.
  - Anything that does not contribute to the end mission is gradually taken out.

# Team Commitment (continued)

- **What Does It Mean to Be *Left Alone*?**
  - No one can tell the team how they should transform the requirements into functionality.
    - No one but the team can be blamed if they fail and no one but the team can bask in the glory if they succeed.
      - It is solely the team's responsibility to figure out what to do and to do it.
  - Basic checks to prevent avoidable failure:
    - The Agile coach **must protect** team members from others requesting changes to the backlog once the iteration has started.
    - Team members have to deliver what they commit to or let the product owner know if they won't be able to do so.
    - They can ask management for help in meeting their target.
      - This self-empowerment encourages brainstorming and self-organizing to meet commitments.

# Leadership Techniques

## Moving from Innocence to Mastery

✓ *Shu*
✓ *Ha*
✓ *Ri*

- Are three kanji that describe the three cycles of a student's progress in a martial arts transformation
    - The application of Shu Ha Ri can also serve as a model for any sort of learning.

# Leadership Techniques (continued)

## Moving from Innocence to Mastery (continued)

- **Shu**
  - It's a stage of innocence, where you know nothing about the practices.

- **Ha**
  - Next is the stage of sophistication, where you know enough to mimic what you have learned, yet you are still moving through a means of conditioned responses.

- **Ri**
  - There is finally an alertness or spontaneous stage, where your actions are reactions that occur naturally to changing situations.

# Work Practices to Keep the Team Together

- **Moving from Innocence to Mastery**
  - Agile coaches assist with method tailoring by:
    - Teaching
      - Laying down the law, forcefully or gently, to teach the new Agilist the rules
        - *Use your experience to show them that Agile is better; for now they just have to trust your judgment and experience to get them to where they want to be.*
    - Coaching
      - Teaching Agilists how to transition from simply following the rules to internalizing what they've learned and becoming mindful of what being Agile means.
        - *It is showing them how to solve the same problem, in multiple ways, without breaking Agile principles.*
    - Advising
      - Once the team has learned to embody the values, principles, and practices of Agile, they can function without the need of a coach to provide them with rules.
        - *They operate as a self-organizing, self-empowered and self-monitoring team.*

# Team Maintenance

- **Building and Maintaining High-Performance Teams Is One of the Principal Goals of Agile Organizations.**
  - This often means getting the right people on board and in the right seats …
    - *…and getting the wrong people off.*
  - Requires setting a good example
    - Coaches must clearly articulate the principles of Agile in writing and in their own actions.
    - Explain what is required for individuals and the team to excel.
    - Reinforce the value of delivering on time by starting and stopping meetings on time.
    - Use the daily stand-up meeting to reaffirm team commitments and to touch base to ensure team expectations are being met.
    - Inspire your employees with your own enthusiasm, positivity, and competence.

## Team Maintenance (continued)

- **Gratuitously Offer Genuine Positive Feedback**
  - Provide criticism fairly but firmly.
  - Remember, in order to become a fully functional self-organizing and empowered team … improvement is not only the employee's responsibility; it's the team's responsibility.
  - Solicit feedback from the team and ask for it as well.
    - Tell them to keep you honest about falling into the habit of controllism
  - Ask them to verbalize their expectations and career goals.
    - Maintain clear and accessible lines of communication.
    - Such interaction will create organic and dynamic information exchange.

# Team Maintenance (continued)

- **Insist on Excellence but Understand that Your Employees Are Human.**
    - Avoid over-familiarity but get to know individual team members as humans who are trying to be their best.
        - Convey compassion and empathy as team members fulfill their duties.
    - Create an environment where people know they will be supported even when they falter—as long as they remain committed to improvement.
        - Mistakes are inevitable but competence is non-negotiable.
        - Remember, no one is perfect.

# Reinforcement Training

## Questions & Exercises

### ■ Time to Test Your New Knowledge!
Take the next PMI-ACP practice quiz.

# Exercise 3

**Match the Description with the Role**

Assists the team with Agile skills, removing impediments and implementing conflict resolution

**Customer**

Manages the team

Does whatever it takes to ensure the team delivers now and in the future

**Distributed Team**

Ensures the team works on stories that deliver the highest business value possible

Develop acceptance tests in conjunction with each other

Defines the charter by explaining what the product is and why it is valuable

Guides direction of the project to make sure the team delivers now and in the future

**Coach**

Works to ensure the team focuses on delivering stories that generate the highest business value possible

Has a set of specific interests, skills and strengths, and can function as a generalist-specialist

**Team Member**

Responsible for organizing the product backlog by highest priority

They have to work together to accomplish goals, but they may meet only at the beginning of their project and thereafter interact through e-mail and telephone

**Product Manager**

Helps the customer identify usability needs

Is responsible for protecting the team

Implements stories with high business value using good techniques and practices

# Module 3 Quiz

## Exam Practice Questions

1. Which of the following BEST describes an important characteristic of a High-Performance Agile Team?

    A. Self-organizing
    B. Fast
    C. Technical
    D. IT specialist

2. Erica has been working on the same project for one of her largest clients for the past 2 years. Of that time, she has spent the last year facilitating meetings and coaching team members. In the process, she has ensured Agile best practices and has removed impediments from the team. Which role is Erica most likely involved in on the project?

    A. Agile coach
    B. Business analyst
    C. Customer
    D. Project manager

3. Which of the following BEST describes what would be expected from a high-performance team prior to starting work on the feature list?

    A. Establishing Definition of Done
    B. Conducting a Kano model survey to get feedback about what users will find of most value in the product being delivered
    C. Recommending ways to increase the performance of the product being delivered
    D. Establishing a milestone list

4. Sonya is a project manager for the Optical Performance Consulting Company. During her final visit with the CEO and business development team, they agree to hire her company to assist them with the release of their new product. To get the project moving and to help her identify the right people for the team, Sonya asks the customer to provide her with a list of all the technologies the team is planning to use on the project. Which of the following BEST describes how Sonya would use this information to build a high-performance team?
    A. To ensure individual team members have a clear level of competence and expertise in certain areas so that power struggles are avoided
    B. To purchase books to learn about the project
    C. To decide if there is a need for product using the technologies the team members identify
    D. To engage the customer by showing how interested she is in succeeding

5. Which of the following team model consists of a group of people who have a traditional boss but who also share some of his/her responsibility and authority?
    A. Team Spirit Model
    B. Traditional Model
    C. Task Force Model
    D. Distributed Model

6. Which of the following teams work together to accomplish goals, but may meet only at the beginning of their project and thereafter interact through e-mail and telephone.
    A. Team Spirit Model
    B. Traditional Model
    C. Task Force Model
    D. Distributed Model

7. All of the following are advantages of the Traditional team model, EXCEPT:
   A. Can get more varied ideas
   B. Can get more creative solutions
   C. Can be dominated by one strong person
   D. Can be more fun

8. All of the following environmental influences could be factors as to why an Agile team would become dysfunctional, EXCEPT:
   A. The team is not given adequate resources to do the job.
   B. There is no recognition of team effort.
   C. There is a lack of recognition by the organization or its leaders that a team exists.
   D. The teams are forced to sit in close proximity to one another and engage in osmotic communication.

9. A project manager working on a mid-level pharmaceutical project is currently in the process of making project assignments. After identifying and selecting the right candidates to be on the team, he suggests the team members come up with a set of ground rules and a code of conduct they can use to govern themselves by. The output of this activity would be an example of:
   A. Team contract
   B. Negotiation
   C. Pre-assignment
   D. Strategy

10. Which of the following refers to one's ability to identify, assess, perceive, control, and evaluate emotions.
    A. Foresight
    B. Compassion
    C. Emotional Intelligence
    D. Friends Psychic Network

11. Agile teams are usually set up to be cross-functional and self-organizing. Existing corporate hierarchy or corporate roles should not be used in deciding a team's composition on an Agile project. The objective of this is to:
    A. create teams of generalized specialists that can work on multiple projects at once
    B. create teams of specialists that are willing to work until the project is done
    C. create teams of generalized specialists that are willing to take responsibility for tasks they commit to deliver
    D. create teams of specialists that are willing to take responsibility only for the task they are assigned

12. The stakeholders, sponsors, and team establish a Definition of Done that:
    A. quantifies the amount of time that will be spent creating viable solutions using risk based spikes
    B. quantifies the amount of time that will be spent on testing and preparing the product for deployment
    C. defines what time the team is free to stop working on the project and go home
    D. quantifies the amount of time that will be spent on a task and the expected level of quality

13. In order for a team to learn how to operate as being self-managed, some level of management, and controllism, will likely be required to get the team started. Which of the following BEST describes what an Agile project manager must remember when this approach is taken?
    A. The team will adjust to becoming controlled
    B. Controllism isn't the long-term objective
    C. The team lead will ultimately take control
    D. Controllism is the long-term objective
    E.

14. Which of the following activities BEST ensure that Agile team members have a time to discuss issues that affected the team's overall effectiveness?
    A. Demo meeting
    B. Creating team space
    C. Poker planning
    D. Retrospectives

15. Using low-tech communication tools in a collocated team space is a 'recommended' way to increase the success of teams. By being able to gather in front of something like a corkboard where the team can physically touch the user stories on index cards allows for all of the following, EXCEPT:
    A. ownership of commitments
    B. increased team collaboration
    C. a greater bonding experience among the team
    D. more accurate estimating for stakeholders

16. Which of the following BEST describes why a geographically dispersed Agile team would use conference calls, instant messaging, shared electronic documents, and information portals?
    A. to minimize the separation.
    B. increase the speed of decisions making
    C. create a recordable paper trails
    D. increase the scalability of the team

17. Which of the following BEST describes a great way to build relationships on a team?
    A. Taking the time to understanding each members' different perspectives
    B. Creating a hierarchy within the team so that everyone knows who to ask for advice
    C. Allowing team members not to participate in decision making processes
    D. Consistently sticking to one approach to solving problem to keep everyone on track

18. An example of a ground rule that should be implemented in a team contract is?
    A. Avoid confrontation at all costs if it will disrupt the project.
    B. Only allow new members to contribute ideas after have gone through one iteration.
    C. Ensuring that team members feel safe to offer opinions and be able to talk directly when feeling wronged.
    D. Allow the discussion go on until a solution has been solved and everyone it satisfied.

19. Someone who invites the wisdom of the team instead of just dropping commands can BEST be described as:
    A. A Project Leader
    B. A Servant Leader
    C. A Team Manager
    D. A Listening Leader

20. In order for an organization to become Lean and Agile it must be able to do all of the following, EXCEPT:
    A. Be able to seize external opportunities
    B. Be proficient in planning for the long haul
    C. Be eager to remove complexity
    D. Be able to create comprehensive requirements

# Module 3 Quiz Answers

1. Answer: A

   Explanation: Although a high-performance team can be all of these things, the best answer in relation to Agile is self-organizing.

2. Answer: A

   Explanation: Due to the fact that Erica functions as a facilitator, Agile coach is the best answer. In order to remain neutral the project manager shouldn't function as a facilitator on the team. The stakeholders, sponsors, and team establish a Definition of Done that quantifies the amount of time that will be spent on a task, the expected level of quality, and the velocity.

3. Answer: A

   Explanation: The high-performance team establishes a Definition of Done that quantifies the amount of time that will be spent on a task, the expected level of quality, and the velocity. The other tasks mentioned could also be performed but would fall under the responsibility of the customer or the project manager.

4. Answer: A

5. Answer: B

6. Answer: D

7. Answer: C

   Explanation: Agile Teams are built on collaboration and close communication. However, this can't happen if one person is constantly taking charge of the team and others are afraid to speak up. Techniques such as Planning Poker and Participatory Decision-Making are used to make sure all team members are engaged in the project.

8. Answer: D

   Explanation: By keeping the team members close together and replacing offices and cubicles with shared desks, traditional separation gives way to an open concept environment—and, as a result, open communication. In turn, this situation increases the opportunity for team members to resolve problems and work together.

9. Answer: A

   Explanation: In order for the team members to accomplish their goals as a group, they must agree on a set of group rules, which are established in a team contract. A contract establishes a clear set of behaviors, communication expectations, and guidelines for conflict resolution and team coaching.

10. Answer: C

    Explanation: Emotional Intelligence (EI) requires a savvy means of adaptive leadership, whereby you intuitively know how to engage others in order to build relationships. This ability of an Agile project manager is what ultimately determines how successful the team will be.

11. Answer: C

    Explanation: Agile teams are made up of generalized specialists that take responsibility for delivering on their commitments. This is the best answers because being a high performing team requires more than just being willing to work until the job gets done, it's also about being able to deliver within your timeboxed commitments. Additionally, Agile discourages assigning team members to multiple projects because it reduces their efficiency—context switching creates waste. However, team members are expected to contribute to other areas during the iteration, such as testing, if needed.

12. Answer: D

    Explanation: The Definition of Done (DoD) quantifies the amount of time that will be spent on a task and the expected level of quality. This definition ensures that when the team says they are done, the feature will be delivered in the agreed upon state, thus preventing slippages do to hidden work.

13. Answer: B
    Explanation: In order for the team to become self-managing and self-empowered, the project manager must remember that controllism is not the long-term objective. On Agile teams, power does not reside in the hands of one person so assuming it will be transferred to the Team Lead is incorrect.

14. Answer: D
    Explanation: Retrospective meetings provide a time to discuss issues that affected the team's overall effectiveness, productivity, and quality—as well as the team's satisfaction with the project.

15. Answer: D
    Explanation: The best answer from these options can be obtained through a process of elimination. The purpose of creating a collocated team space with low-tech communication tools is to encourage team members to take ownership for their tasks, increase collaboration and build stronger team bonds. That said, this would be of little value toward increasing the team's ability to create more *accurate* estimates for stakeholders.

16. Answer: A
    Explanation: By keeping the team members close together and replacing offices and cubicles with shared desks, traditional separation gives way to an open concept environment—and, open communication. For teams that must be geographically dispersed, conference calls, instant messaging, shared electronic documents, and information portals are used to minimize the separation.

17. Answer: A
    Explanation: Taking time to understand each members' different perspectives is the best answer based on the process of elimination. Agile discourages hierarchies in order to promote self-managing teams and to ensure that all members actively participate in making decisions. Sticking with one approach is incorrect because Agile teams encourage new approaches to solve problems.

18. Answer: C
    Explanation: Ensuring that team members feel safe to offer opinions and be able to talk directly when feeling wronged, is the best answer through a process of elimination. Avoid confrontation at all costs is incorrect because teams that encourage open communication, means that members should not be afraid to confront issues needing to be addressed. Making new members wait to contribute is not the best answers because it does not encourage being open to new approaches and ideas. Allowing group discussions to continue is incorrect because meetings should be timeboxed, and issues that cannot be solved immediately need to be taken offline or dealt with in a separate meeting.

19. Answer: B
    Explanation: A Servant Leader is one who invites the wisdom of the team instead of just dropping commands. In this type of leadership role, you strive to make your team operates at 110% and have very little tolerance of imperfection. At the same time, you also understand the impact of being accepting and having empathy as they relate to the team and the company.

20. Answer: D
    Explanation: Seizing external opportunities, planning for the long haul and removing complexity are all in alignment with the objectives of Lean and Agile. Being able to create comprehensive requirements is not. The Agile Manifesto state: Working software over comprehensive documentation.

# Module 3
## Summary

- ✓ Examined the Characteristics of a High-Performance Team
- ✓ Compared the Traditional Team Roles and Responsibilities
- ✓ Used Coaching Techniques to Increase Team Success Rates
- ✓ Recommended Ways to Deal with Conflict
- ✓ Described Close Communication on Agile Projects
- ✓ Judged What Team Commitment Means
- ✓ Integrated Work Practices to Keep the Team Together

# Adaptive Planning

## Module 4
- PMI-ACP Exam Preparation Course

# Module 4
## Objectives

- ✓ Explain Why Discipline is Required to Make Agile Work
- ✓ Analyze How to Plan at Multiple Levels
- ✓ Perform Project Decomposition
- ✓ Examine Estimating Tools and Techniques

- ✓ Compare Release Planning, Iteration Planning and Daily Planning Concepts

# Adaptive Planning in Action

- **Agile Software Development**
  - Requirements are described at a very high level and the rest of the planning is driven by priority.
    - Less time is spent figuring out the details of low-priority requirements.
      - Large high-priority requirements are split into smaller ones so their details can be explored.
      - Relative sizing of the estimates is done to get an idea of how "big" the work is.

IV.2

Agile planning usually consists of 5 levels. More often than not, the team will only be engaged in Release Planning, Iteration Planning, and Daily Planning. During the release planning, the team and customer identify features and functionality are going to be delivered for the next several iterations. This is driven by the priorities of the customer (*see also: Customer-Driven Prioritization*) and the capabilities of the team (*see also: Velocity*).

# Adaptive Planning in Action (continued)

- **Agile Software Development** (continued)
  - Upon quantifying the tasks required to complete the work, estimates are created for the highest-priority requirements.
    - The team members now have an idea of how much work they can deliver in an iteration.
      - The idea is tested in the first iteration and gives the team a better understanding of its velocity.
      - Now knowing their velocity, the team is in a better position to give commitments for later iterations.

# Adaptive Planning in Action (continued)

## ■ Just-Enough-Planning

Epics/Themes/Big Stories

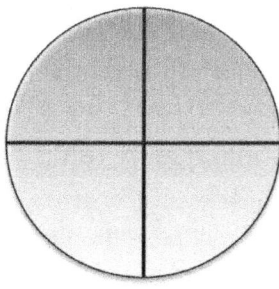
Split Big Stories
Small Stories

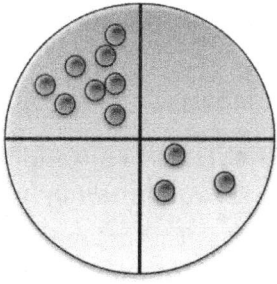
Split Smaller Stories
into Tasks

How do you eat an elephant? One bite at a time. Well, in Agile the same holds true for planning. As illustrated above the best way to plan your projects is to systematically dissect your stories into manageable parts. But more importantly Agile planning can be used to decompose problems domains in numerous areas of your project, beyond the software development phase. Can you think of a few? For example, many organizations require a long process to bring a project in front of a review committee to get approval, what are some ways Agile and Lean could be used to optimize that process?

# Adaptive Planning in Action (continued)

- **Adaptable Plans Allow for Better Visibility to Stakeholders**
  - Size estimates are done in accordance to requirement changes as the product backlog evolves.
    - The product burn-down chart shows how much work is remaining based on the revised scope in the product backlog.
    - The work remaining is controlled by removing low-priority requirements from the scope.
      - This approach ensures that scope is managed continuously based on highest-priority requirements.

The multi-level planning that takes place on Agile projects allows the team a chance to learn from the previous iterations and adjust their approach to account for changes in priorities. It gives both the team and the customer an opportunity to inspect their development processes, adapt required changes, and reprioritize any items in the backlog as needed. Additionally, upon having a better idea of their velocity and sharing it with the customer, team members are able to create more accurate delivery estimates and adjust the project plan.

# Adaptive Planning in Action (continued)

- **At the Beginning of Each Iteration the Team Makes a Commitment on the Functionality It Can Deliver.**
  - In order to make a commitment, the team may need some time to investigate certain aspects and risks in the preceding iteration.
    - It may make sense to plan ahead and reserve some time for investigation on risky backlog items in the next iteration.
      - Insight into high-risk backlog items helps the product owner make a conscious decision on the item's priority.
  - New functionality requests by customers can be expected at any point during the project.
    - Complex functionality rarely has enough details to give quick commitments at the beginning of a new iteration.
      - Helps to groom the scope during a previous iteration, which makes sense.

For the current iteration, detailed planning can be performed by the team to identify the tasks that need to be delivered. It is reasonable to expect this level of detailed planning from the team, at least 2–4 weeks out, and to provide an achievable commitment to the stakeholders. Anything beyond that timeframe will be difficult for them to commit to because of changes that may be made by the business, changes in the team, and experience acquired from the past iterations.

# Adaptive Planning in Action (continued)

- **Trust, Commitment, and Collaboration**
  - Working with an adaptive plan requires trust among the team, the product owner, and other key stakeholders.
    - Individual stakeholders have different motivating factors and it requires time to build the trust.
  - If trust is lost, planning becomes difficult and unsustainable.
    - Could result in ...
      - Poor quality
      - Reduced velocity
      - Inability to meet commitments
      - High attrition
      - Loss of face in front of the customers

---

Estimate ranges can be refined based on the functionality required to support the value needs of the business. The list of features that are expected to be produced during the project is modified by adding or removing functionality as the project proceeds. A main driver behind this need to adapt may be a result of both the business and team gaining a better understanding of the problem the project is trying to solve or even improvements to the automation process that the product is delivering.

Having visibility into the development process and the flexibility to adjust in accordance to the needs of the business increases the trust required for the team, product owner, and customer to balance the stakeholders' expectations with the reality of the actual work that can be performed in a given amount of time.

# Adaptive Planning in Action (continued)

- **Trust, Commitment, and Collaboration** (continued)
  - The product owner and management should give the team the freedom to decide how much it can deliver in an iteration.
    - The product owner needs to set the right expectations between the customers and the team.
      - Setting unreasonable expectations can result in the team members being pressured into committing more functionality than they can actually accomplish.
      - Results in success by cutting quality or introducing loads of technical debt

A critical factor teams must consider when creating their estimates is the team's velocity. The number of features team members believe they can complete within a given iteration is known as velocity. Velocity is estimated by assigning the team an agreed-upon means of measuring the relative size (complexity) of a story (requirement) then assigning "story points" to each story and estimating the number of story points team members can complete in an iteration, as a measure of their velocity. From there, the team can adjust their release plan based on the features that will be delivered within each iteration. Although this process isn't an exact science, it prevents the team from over-committing to an iteration by ensuring team members adjust their plan according to the team's capacity and resourcing needs, in addition to technical feasibility.

# Adaptive Planning in Action (continued)

- **Trust Requires Commitment and Collaboration.**
  (continued)
    - The Agile Product Manager needs to support the team by guarding the scope and Agile practices.
        - The team must understand the needs of the product owner and help to achieve such goals.
    - Can help by improving engineering practices
        - Act on feedback from Retrospectives.
        - Highlights issues that are beyond control.

# Why Discipline is Required

- **The Mechanism of "Inspect and Adapt" Does Not Mean "Self-Repairing System."**
  - The system will not fix the problems itself
    - Everyone involved in the process must be committed to it.
  - The team members need to work with each other to:
    - Achieve the team's iteration goal
    - Continuously improve their ways of working
    - Collaborate with the product owner to groom the scope and understand what is needed

# Why Discipline is Required (continued)

- **The Mechanism of "Inspect and Adapt" Does Not Mean "Self-Repairing System."** (continued)
  - The product owner needs to collaborate with the team.
    - If the product owner becomes complacent with team engagement, the visibility of the team deteriorates.
    - Needs to ensure that the business users and customers are appropriately engaged in the process
      - Prevents risk of misunderstanding between the business and customer needs

# Why Discipline is Required (continued)

- **Sustainable Adaptive Planning Requires an Organization that Respects Change**
  - If a team goes Agile but management's mentality doesn't, then the benefits of Agile are lost
    - Things could become worse than when they started.

# Why Discipline is Required (continued)

- **Sustainable Adaptive Planning Requires an Organization that Respects Change.** (continued)
  - Areas of concern management must consider:
    - Provide long-term vision, direction, and priorities
    - Trust and motivate their teams
    - Focus on business value
    - Encourage teams to deliver quality
    - Ensure continuous flow of work
      - Minimize non-work-related disruptions
      - Facilitate removal of impediments outside the control of the team
      - Support the process of learning, inspecting, and adapting

# Planning at Multiple Levels

## Planning at the Last Responsible Moment

- The longer the details of a plan can be "responsibly deferred," the more flexibility you have to adapt your plan to your situation.
    - Reduces waste created from the work required to create unused plans
- What constitutes being responsible?
    - Deferring commitments that require irreversible scheduling decisions
    - Breaking dependencies
    - Identifying multiple options
- Agile encourages the use of a tiered set of planning horizons.
    - Only plan as far as the project allows you to see.

---

Adaptive planning allows Agile teams to balance frequent delivery, continuous feedback, planning horizon, progressive elaboration, and waiting to plan until the *last responsible moment* as a means of protecting the project from inevitable changes.

This is because Agile focuses on organizing work based on the delivery of features. Specifically, the most valuable features are delivered first. That is in stark contrast to traditional development planning approaches where work is completed through designated phases like: analysis, design, development, deployment, testing, and implementation.

Using adaptive planning, Agile teams identify all features that need to be delivered in a release. They then identify when those release points occur. This approach to value-driven delivery (*see also Value-Driven Delivery*) keeps the team focused on delivering features that will provide the customer with the most value and the quickest return on investment (*see also Return on Investments*) instead of simply completing a task for the sake of being able to say it's complete. This approach to planning also serves to address the common proverbial product development question: "Yes, we built the product—but did we build the *right* product?"

# Planning at Multiple Levels (continued)

- **Planning Horizons**
    - Long Planning Horizons:
        - Used for general planning when situations are uncertain and things are likely to change
        - The more commitment required, the longer the planning horizon should be
    - Short Planning Horizons:
        - Used for detailed, specific plans
        - The more uncertainty surrounding a situation, the shorter the planning horizon required to control that uncertainty

# Planning at Multiple Levels (continued)

- **Rolling Wave Planning**
  - The process of planning for a project like waves unfolding as they approach the shore
    - We can see more clearly what's at a closer proximity.
      - Looking too far ahead distorts our vision.
    - It is important to highlight in the initial plan and the key milestones.
  - Is a multistep process because we cannot provide the details far out in planning
    - Depending upon project length and complexity, we may be able to plan as much as a few weeks or even a few months in advance.
    - Involves the creation of a detailed, well-defined work breakdown structure for the near term
      - Just for highlighting the milestones for the rest of the project.

# Planning at Multiple Levels (continued)

- **Progressive Elaboration**
  - Occurs in the rolling wave planning process
    - As time passes, we elaborate on the work packages, giving them greater detail
    - Refers to the fact that as the weeks and months pass, we have planned to provide the missing details of the work packages …
      - … once they appear on the horizon.
  - The scope of developing projects are progressively elaborated
    - Poses a risk to the schedule and overall cost because the estimation is usually done during the start of the project

# Planning at Multiple Levels (continued)

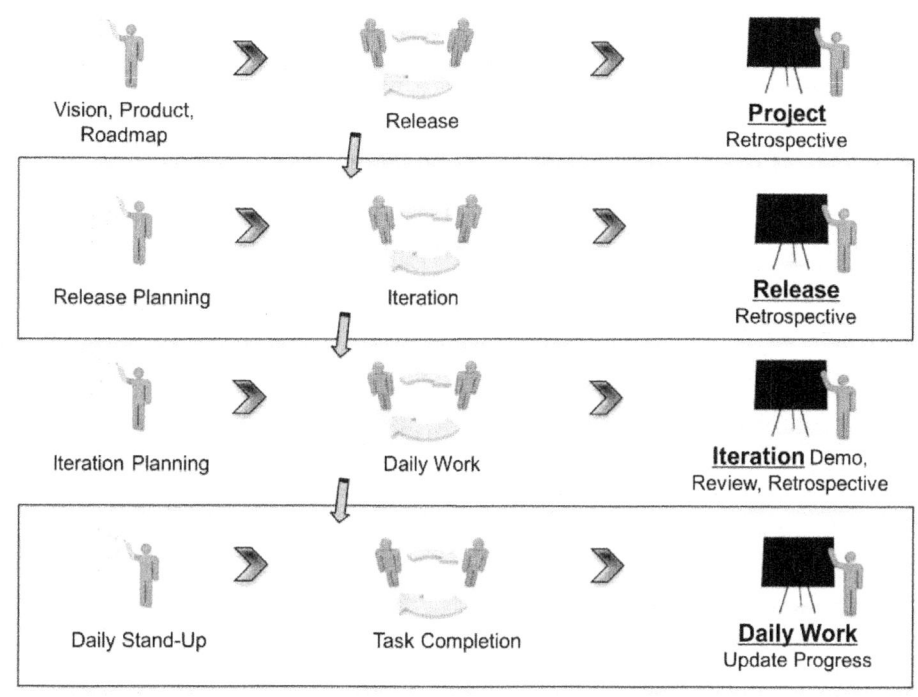

In this illustration we see how Agile goes through multiple levels of planning.

Keeping in mind, that each cycle feeds into the next, as indicated in the center transition point, the first phase is for the business and/or customer to create a Vision and Product Roadmap to take advantage of a market opportunity.

From there, they begin the process initiating Release cycles, and concluding with their Project Retrospective.

Release Planning (initiated at the startup planning level), elaborates further into the project details by defining the iterations that will be required to realize the vision, also concluding with a retrospective.

Iteration planning (initiated at the release planning level) elaborates upon the details of the daily work that needs to take place to realize the vision; and they too conclude with a demo, review and retrospective.

Daily Stand-Up (initiated at the iteration planning level) elaborates upon the tasks that need to be completed to realize the vision; and they wrap up their work by providing daily updates on their progress.

# Planning at Multiple Levels (continued)

- **Comparisons**
  - Rolling wave planning and progressive elaboration are similar concepts.
    - Acknowledge the fact that in many projects what must be done is unknown.
      - The project will unfold as it progresses.
    - The plan is to do more planning when that level of planning is possible.
    - Can see more clearly what is ahead when we learn from the work we do in earlier phases

# Project Decomposition

- **Feasibility Study Projects**
  - When an organization has ideas they would like to pursue but before making a total commitment to them, they study the feasibility of what it might take to accomplish them.
    - Breaking them into separate projects enables budgets to be allocated and provides decision points to pursue.
      - What impact the project might have
    - This is a different approach to that of progressive elaboration or rolling wave planning.

# Planning Strategy

- **Basic Execution Sequence**
  - *Vision*
  - *Release Date*
    - For the next two releases
  - *Minimum Marketable Features*
    - For the current release
    - Start to place features that won't fit in this release into the next release

# Planning Strategy (continued)

- **Basic Execution Sequence** (continued)
  - Features/Stories/Requirements
    - For the current feature and most of the current release
    - Place stories that don't fit into the next release.
  - *Estimate and Prioritize Features*
    - For the current iteration and the following three iterations
  - *Detailed Requirements and Customer Tests*
    - For the features in the current iteration

# Levels of Planning

## 5 Levels of Agile Planning

IV.6

- A misconception about Agile is that it does not do enough planning.
  - In reality, Agile does more planning and risk mitigation than traditional processes.
  - Agile planning is based around short, frequent incremental-planning sessions instead of the traditional exhaustive, monolithic assumption-based approach.
  - The levels of planning can be layered into:
    - Vision
    - Roadmap/Strategy
    - Release
    - Iteration
    - Daily

**Also Discussed in Section Module 4:**

*Planning at the Last Responsible Moment*

Adaptive planning allows Agile teams to balance frequent delivery, continuous feedback, planning horizon, progressive elaboration, and waiting to plan until the last possible responsible moment as a means of protecting the project from inevitable changes.

This is because Agile focuses on organizing work based on the delivery of features. Specifically, the most valuable features are delivered first. That is in stark contrast to traditional development planning approaches where work is completed through designated phases like: analysis, design, development, deployment, testing, and implementation.

Using adaptive planning, Agile teams identify all features that need to be delivered in a release. They then identify when those release points occur. This approach to value-driven delivery (*see also Value-Driven Delivery*) keeps the team focused on delivering features that will provide the customer with the most value and the quickest return on investment (*see also Return on Investments*) instead of simply completing a task for the sake of being able to say it's complete. This approach to planning also serves to address the common proverbial product development question: "Yes, we built the product—but did we build the *right* product?"

# Levels of Planning (continued)

- **5 Levels of Agile Planning**
  Sec. 4
  - Vision
    - Projects and product development efforts ideally start with a vision associated with a business need or direction
      - The vision is framed in the context of a strategy and associated goals
  - Roadmap/Strategy
    - Starts with a vision associated with a business need or direction
      - Strategy is the creation of a unique and valuable position
        - *Involves making choices throughout the value chain*
    - Defines the creation of a unique and valuable position as well as associated goals and objectives
    - The goal is to come up with a strategy that maximizes value retention by incremental and mutually reinforcing execution of the value chain

**Also Discussed in Section Module 2:**

*Who Has What at Stake? – The Business*

Through constant communication and collaboration between the Agile product manager and the customer, a shared understanding of the project scope and deliverables can be accomplished. Additionally, the use of a Vision Statement, a roadmap that reinforces the customer values using the 5Ws, can be used as a guideline to set acceptance criteria and to identify acceptable trade-offs. Adhering to the Agile Principle "Our highest priority is to satisfy the customer through early and continuous delivery of valuable software" sets the stage for the Agile team to organically conduct risk management efforts and be empowered remove constraints in order to continuously delivery valuable software to the customer.

# Levels of Planning (continued)

- **5 Levels of Agile Planning** (continued)
  - Release
    - Represents the large-grained delivery cycle in Agile development
    - Releases typically range between one and six months, but may extend longer in some environments
    - Essential to continuously add value in small increments by utilizing feedback from internal and external customers
  - Iteration
    - Are short, fixed-length subsets of releases where the team's goal is to deliver potentially shippable software
    - Generally in the 1- to 4-week timeframe
    - Once the team has determined the features to deliver in an iteration, they decide what tasks are required to make those features a reality
      - This is the first time the team breakdown has prioritized features into tasks

# Levels of Planning (continued)

## 5 Levels of Agile Planning (continued)

- Daily
  - Each day a short, 15-minute stand-up meeting facilitates the communication of an individual detailed status and any impediments or issues.
    - Keeps the team is focused on completing the highest-priority features.
    - Product is integrated and tested on a daily basis.
    - Burndown charts are used to review progress on a daily basis and to help teams take corrective actions quickly.

As features are completed within each iteration they must be accepted and reviewed by both the team and the product manager as Done-Done. This consensus typically takes place during the daily stand-up when members provide updates on their progress.

# Planning Techniques

- **The 3 Most Common Levels of Planning**
    - Even though Agile planning can consist of five or more levels, Agile teams typically use the last three levels of planning on a regular basis:
        - Release Planning
        - Iteration Planning
        - Daily Planning

# Planning Techniques (continued)

## ■ Release Planning

- Identifies the features that will go into the release, which are chosen from the product backlog and moved into the release backlog.
    - Features are then prioritized and estimated.
    - Based on a prioritized feature list and the number of features that a team can produce, team members establish release points, which will be mapped into iterations.
    - The team performs detailed planning only for the *current iteration* once they have identified the tasks needed to deliver the planned features.
    - The feature list can be modified as the project proceeds, based on a better understanding of the project's problems.
        - Once the feature list has been established, the team prioritizes it based on the relative value delivered by each feature.

---

The release plan identifies which features will be delivered during the project. With contributions from the product manager and development team, the customer can begin identifying features that can be added or removed from the feature list based on the needs of the business, technical feasibility, or the team's capability. From there, the team prioritizes the feature list based on the relative value each feature will deliver to the customer.

Release points are then determined by the team based on the estimated work required to complete the feature list. Next, features are scheduled to be released into production based on the time release points. It is also worth noting that since Agile planning is iterative in nature, the plans are subject to change.

# Planning Techniques (continued)

- **Iteration Planning**
    - Represents the point where the list of features is converted into actual stuff to do
        - Detailed planning takes place in the iteration planning meeting, which can be divided into two parts.
            - First, the team works together to *estimate* what features should be tackled in the iteration.
            - One (of many) estimating techniques used to balance the priorities of the business with the capacity of the team is commitment-based planning.
                - *The team members themselves are making the commitment to complete certain features, so they are more likely to live up to those commitments than when they have commitments thrust upon them.*
            - Also, the team is continuously evaluating their workload as a whole, rather than as a collection of separate items.
                - *Velocity is the term teams use to estimate the amount of work, or story points, they plan to perform in the upcoming iteration.*
                - *A story point is an arbitrary unit of measure, agreed upon by the team, that quantifies the complexity of user stories/requirements – in the feature list.*

# Planning Techniques (continued)

- **Iteration Planning** (continued)
  - Allows team members to incorporate the most current information about design approach, process, risks, assumptions, and constraints
    - Team members select tasks as necessary and appropriate throughout the iteration.
    - Allowing team members to select the tasks that they work on increases the likelihood that they will successfully complete those tasks in an appropriate timeframe.
    - By volunteering for a task, a team member is indicating their interest in successfully completing the task and their belief that the task is well aligned with their skill set.
      - *The process then repeats until the team identifies that they can no longer commit to delivering a feature given the work to which they have previously committed.*

The Backlog is converted into an actual list of items during the Iteration Planning. During this meeting, members of the team select certain features from the list and make a commitment to them. Using this approach makes it more likely for them to follow through on their commitment. It also provides an opportunity for the team to collectively evaluate the amount of work that needs to be completed instead of estimating in isolation. The tendency when evaluating work in isolated bits is to ignore the little pieces that will quickly add up into a very large list of things to do.

With the new level of detail resulting from the Iteration Planning meeting, the team can now begin the process of decomposing Backlog Items (aka user stories, features, requirements) into smaller, individual tasks. In doing so they are also able to incorporate any newly acquired information into the project. For example, they can make adjustments to the project that may have been requested by the customer during the previous iteration or they can formalize a design approach based on realized assumptions and risks.

# Planning Techniques (continued)

- **Daily Planning**
  - Starts with the team identifying the features they wish to deliver in the project during the stand-up meeting.
    - The stand-up meeting is a short meeting—15 minutes max—that allows the team members to coordinate their activities by answering the following questions:
      - Progress – "What did I do yesterday?"
      - Plans – "What am I going to do today?"
      - Problems – "What is getting in my way?"

---

As features are completed within each iteration they must be accepted and reviewed by the team and product owner as Done-Done. This is achieved through daily planning.

Daily planning also serves as part of empirical inspection, in that during the meeting, feature completion is discussed, priorities tracked and impediments are addressed. This meeting is typically known as the daily stand-up. Although the daily stand-up is time-boxed into a 15-minute session, it also provides an opportunity to maintain visibility into the daily project while still allowing the team to remain self-empowered. The brevity of the meeting also embodies the Lean principle of reducing waste, in that team member aren't required to waste time in discussions that they aren't directly involved in.

# Planning Techniques (continued)

- **Daily Planning** (continued)
    - Meetings may be scheduled after the stand-up for more detailed issues.
        - The daily stand-up meeting provides a consistent point to connect in an otherwise chaotic schedule.
    - In general, the daily and iteration planning meetings are the only places where task status is tracked.
        - At every other point, the means of progress measurement is feature completion.

**For the Exam:** If certain team members were not able to get all of their problems resolved during the initial daily stand up meeting, sidebar meetings may be scheduled after the stand-up for more detailed issues.

# Planning Techniques (continued)

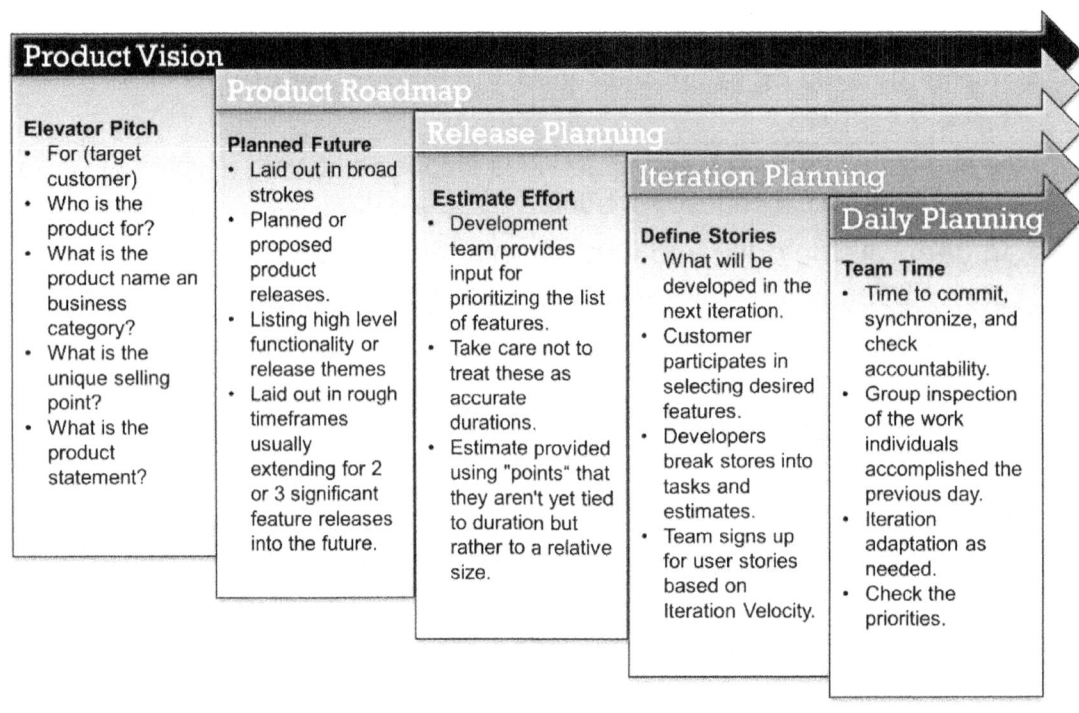

Here is a quick summary of each of the 5 planning phases of Agile, along with the appropriate questions and activities that my take place during each phase.

The Product Vision, you can think of this as an elevator pitch that describes your product.

Followed by the Product Roadmap, this can be thought of as the Planned Future of your product.

Release Planning, this can be thought of as the Estimated Effort required to realize your product.

Iteration Planning, this can be summarized as Defining Stories (Features) of your product.

Lastly, Daily Planning, this can be summarized as the Team Time required that is devoted to realizing the product.

# Planning Techniques (continued)

- **Levels of Agile Planning (For the Exam)**
  - Portfolio
    - Key to value retention is the management of portfolios by inspecting and adapting them in small increments so that feedback from internal and external customers can be utilized.

# Estimating Tools and Techniques

Sec. 9

- **Burndown**
    - At a program/project level, it is the rate at which the whole project is burning the requirements (user stories) from the feature list
        - Without knowing burndown, it's difficult to make longer-term plans or even release plans.
        - The first or second iteration will have to be estimated because the team doesn't have enough data to project their past performance into the future.
            - After 3-4 sprints you should start using an average of your past velocity to plan the future and update the release plan.

 **Also Discussed in Section Module 4:**

*Adaptive Planning in Action – Agile Software Development*

Agile planning usually consists of 5 levels. More often than not, the team will only be engaged in Release Planning, Iteration Planning, and Daily Planning. During the release planning, the team and customer identify features and functionality are going to be delivered for the next several iterations. This is driven by the priorities of the customer (*see also: Customer-Driven Prioritization*) and the capabilities of the team (*see also: Velocity*).

# Estimating Tools and Techniques (continued)

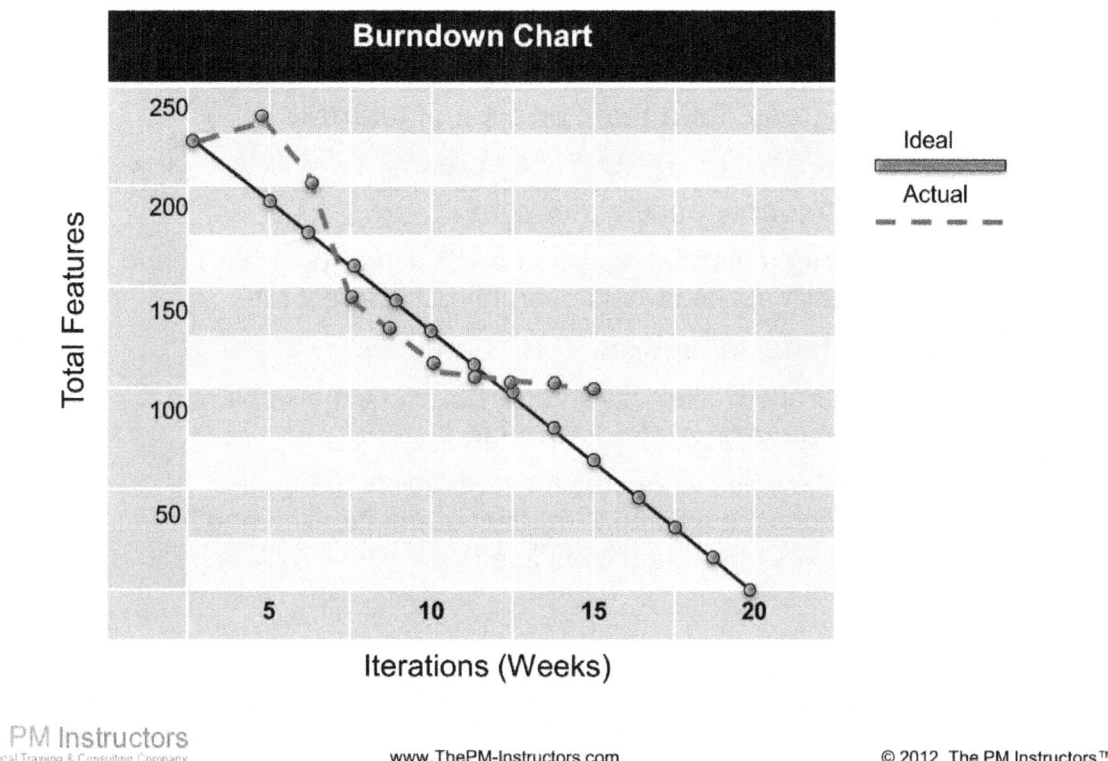

In this illustration we see how a Burndown chart provides a method to track your progress on a daily basis. The axis on the left shows the remaining features required to complete the iteration and the axis on the bottom contains the number of weeks until the end of the iteration.

In this illustration, the solid line shows the ideal scenario if your team performs according to their task estimations, while the dotted line shows their actual performance.

At day 0 (the first day of the iteration), the remaining effort is at its highest because nothing has been completed. The remaining work to be done is calculated by summing the time estimates for task that have yet to be completed. So at the end of the iteration (day 20), the sum should be 0 because there are no tasks left to be completed.

# Estimating Tools and Techniques (continued)

- **Velocity**
  - A term used in Agile software development to illustrate the "rate of progress" for a team or a set of teams
    - The number or features a team/project can convert to a Done-Done
  - Velocity is a team-specific measure
    - A different team estimating the same backlog would likely have a different estimate and would operate at a different rate
  - Allows the team to "track its own" burndown
    - Like the burndown, velocity is represented as the slope of a burndown curve on a burndown chart
    - Illustrates how many features (or story points or hours) team members committed to for the current iteration and how features many have been completed

Velocity is the rate at which the Team is completing user stories from the backlog. By keeping track of their velocity, the team can make achievable commitments in future iterations.

# Estimating Tools and Techniques (continued)

- **Velocity Is Tracked on a Burndown Chart**
  - Depicts the total task hours remaining per iteration
    - Shows where the team stands regarding completion of the tasks that comprise the product backlog items and achieving the goals of the iteration.
    - The outstanding work (or backlog) is often on the vertical axis, with time along the horizontal.
      - The x-axis represents days in the iteration.
      - The y-axis represents effort remaining (usually in ideal engineering hours).

Once a Team knows their burndown rate it helps them identify their capability to meet their commitments. In other words, a team's velocity can be obtained by viewing a burndown chart.

# Estimating Tools and Techniques (continued)

Sec. 3

- **Estimating Velocity**
  - The importance of estimating size according to a given Definition of Done and adhering to that definition is critical.
    - It may be tempting to push a team to project completion faster than its demonstrated, stabilized velocity, but this is a very risky proposition.
      - The increase will likely come at the cost of having to dilute the definition of "done," thereby resulting in lower quality and thus more rework downstream.
      - This rework will eventually interrupt planned work and, in the end, will have the effect of actually lowering the team's velocity.

- **Points**
  - Points are the most common units used by Agile teams to estimate the relative size of stories.

**Note: This Topic was Touched Upon in Module 4:**

*Adaptive Planning in Action – Trust, Commitment, and Collaboration*

A critical factor teams must consider when creating their estimates is the team's velocity. The number of features team members believe they can complete within a given iteration is known as velocity. Velocity is estimated by the team using an estimating technique (i.e. relative sizing, point to scale, affinity estimating, etc.) as an agreed-upon means of measuring the relative size (complexity) of a feature (user story/requirement), then assigning a story "point" to each story. From there, they add up the total number of points assigned to each team member in the iteration to obtain an estimated measure of their velocity. With that information the team can adjust their release plan based on the number of features that will be delivered within each iteration. Although this process isn't an exact science, it prevents the team from over-committing to an iteration by ensuring team members adjust their plan according to the **team's capacity** and resourcing needs, in addition to technical feasibility.

# Estimating Tools and Techniques (continued)

Velocity burndown charts provide a means of measuring a moving average of how many points are being completed per day.

Ideal

Actual

**Velocity**

Features Committed to be Completed

25, 20, 15, 10, 5

Days Remaining in the Iteration: 7, 14, 21

What do you think caused the spike in work around the 17th day?

# ✛ Estimating Tools and Techniques (continued)

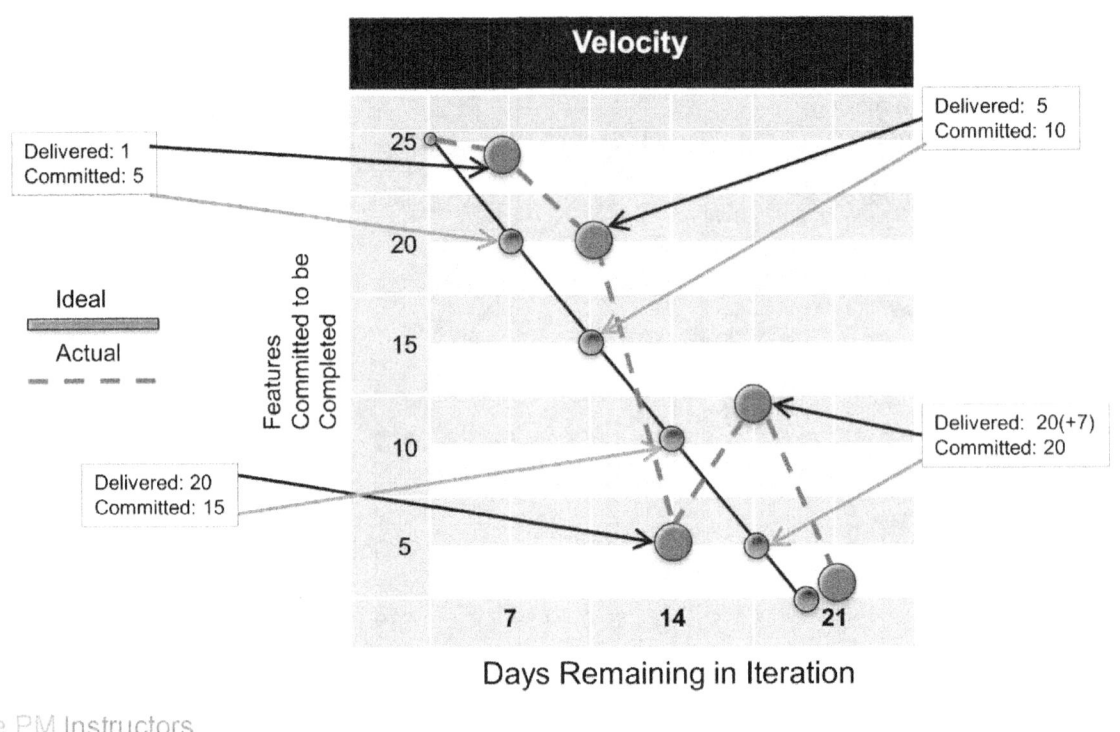

Velocity burndown charts are not nearly as complicated as this one looks. This is illustrating the information they provide. On day 7 of this 21 day iteration the team had estimated that they would complete 20 of the 25 features they had committed to in an iteration planning meeting. Instead, they only delivered 1 feature, or achieved 1 point. They also missed their commitment around day 10, where they had committed to have 10 features completed, but only delivered 5. On day 14 however they find their rhythm and make for lost time by delivering 20 of the stories, whereas they had only committed to having 15 completed by that day. But, around day 17 they experience a spike and fall behind. This example shows one piece of the burndown that isn't properly captured because a spike doesn't necessarily mean the team didn't complete their work, but rather, more work could have unexpectedly been added to their backlog (specifically +7 more features required to complete a task). Differentiated between work that has been completed verses work that has been added is better captured in a burn-up chart. Nonetheless, since this team is made up of high-performers they managed to get back on track and meet their goal.

**Real World Note:** In reality, you wouldn't want a burndown to show this much variation, so you can reference it for more accurate planning and risk management efforts. All the same a burndown chart that uses a perfect downward slope toward the completion date is a not how development actually takes place. Until a team becomes 100% high- performers, toward the beginning of the iteration, you should plan for the amount of ideal work to slope up for several days then gradually trend down to account for the team ramping up on the iteration doing things like meeting, studying and becoming more familiar with the features. Take a moment to think about how you would graph that.

# Estimating Tools and Techniques (continued)

- **Calculating Velocity Scenario**
    - A team reviews a release backlog with the product owner
        - They estimate the relative sizes of features in units of story points. (One feature might be sized at 3 points, another at 1 point, etc.)
        - The release backlog, when estimated, totals 250 story points.
    - After several iterations, the team consistently delivers 20 and 25 story points per 3-week iteration
        - For planning purposes, the velocity is considered to be approximately 21 points per 3-week iteration
        - Given total size of the backlog size of 250 points
            - Using a velocity of 25 points per 3-week iteration
            - It can be determined that it will take this team a total of 10 (3 week) iterations to deliver the entire backlog (250 divided by 25)

*Provides additional details from previous page.*

# Estimating Tools and Techniques (continued)

Sec. 3

- **Relative Sizing**
  - Compares two different pieces of functionality then agrees on which one is smaller (or larger) in size and determines how much smaller (or larger)
    - Rarely do developers disagree on this.
      - If they do, you can be sure that the story is not clear enough or there are major unknowns.
    - One way to estimate using relative sizing is to use T-shirt sizes: small, medium, large, and X-large.
      - Always estimate with more than one developer in the room so that there can be a good debate about confusing points.
    - The skills and experience levels of the developers are not that important. It may even be good to have a wide spectrum of talents.

---

**Note: This Topic was Touched Upon in Module 4:**

*Adaptive Planning in Action – Trust, Commitment, and Collaboration*

A critical factor teams must consider when creating their estimates is the team's velocity. The number of features team members believe they can complete within a given iteration is known as velocity. Velocity is estimated by the team using an estimating technique (i.e. relative sizing, point to scale, affinity estimating, etc.) as an agreed-upon means of measuring the relative size (complexity) of a feature (user story/requirement), then assigning a story "point" to each story. From there, they add up the total number of points assigned to each team member in the iteration to obtain an estimated measure of their velocity. With that information the team can adjust their release plan based on the number of features that will be delivered within each iteration. Although this process isn't an exact science, it prevents the team from over-committing to an iteration by ensuring team members adjust their plan according to the **team's capacity** and resourcing needs, in addition to technical feasibility.

# Estimating Tools and Techniques (continued)

- **Point to Scale**
    - Relates to an abstract point systems
        - It is used to discuss the difficulty of the task without assigning actual hours
    - Common systems of scale are:

        *Constant Sequence Estimations*
        Linear (1,2,3,4...)
        Clothes size (XS, S, M, L, XL)
        *Exponential Sequence Estimations*
        Fibonacci (1,2,3,5,8...)
        Powers-of-2 (1,2,4,8...)

    - Triangulating
        - Estimating a story based on its relationship to one or more other stories

# Estimating Tools and Techniques (continued)

## ■ Affinity Estimates

Sec. 3

- Used to quickly estimate the story points of a large number of user stories based on their similarities

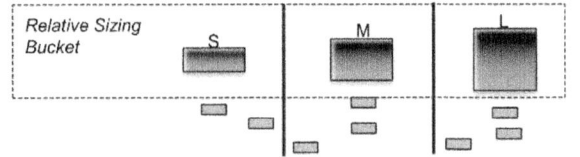

Participants
Product Owner
Delivery Team
Facilitator

▭ Stories

1. Stories are printed on large Post-It cards in large enough print to read from several feet away.
2. Provide a set of reference stories the team has done in the past using good examples of story points: **S, M, L** or **1, 2, 3, 5, 8,** etc.
3. Think of the wall as a spectrum of size from smaller to larger; items stacked vertically on the wall are about the same relative size in effort.
4. Team members are expected to silently size each item relative to other items on the wall, considering the effort involved in implementing it based on the Definition of Done.
5. This is a silent part of the exercise so please refrain from speaking to others except for basic comments like "move out of my way."

---

 **Note: This Topic was Touched Upon in Module 4:**

*Adaptive Planning in Action – Trust, Commitment, and Collaboration*

    A critical factor teams must consider when creating their estimates is the team's velocity. The number of features team members believe they can complete within a given iteration is known as velocity. Velocity is estimated by the team using an estimating technique (i.e. relative sizing, point to scale, affinity estimating, etc.) as an agreed-upon means of measuring the relative size (complexity) of a feature (user story/requirement), then assigning a story "point" to each story. From there, they add up the total number of points assigned to each team member in the iteration to obtain an estimated measure of their velocity. With that information the team can adjust their release plan based on the number of features that will be delivered within each iteration. Although this process isn't an exact science, it prevents the team from over-committing to an iteration by ensuring team members adjust their plan according to the **team's capacity** and resourcing needs, in addition to technical feasibility.

# Estimating Tools and Techniques (continued)

## ■ Top-Down Estimating

- Uses experience from previous project data to draw accurate estimates for new "analogous" projects
    - The comparison may be made directly using "analogous estimating," through an algorithm such as "parametric estimating," or from the memory of estimating experts.

1. If Project A took 1,200 hours of total effort to complete, then it would stand to reason that Project B, if analogous, should also take approximately 1,200 hours of total effort.
2. If the historical records of Project A are extensive and accurate, this approach will be more scientific.
3. The estimation team would need to focus on areas in which the projects vary to adjust estimates.
4. Remember, the key here is accurate project estimating, so if your records are deficient, the pendulum swings to the artistic side of the equation.

# Estimating Tools and Techniques (continued)

## Bottom-Up Estimating

- This approach gets its name because it works up from the bottom of the WBS by approximating the size (duration and cost) and risk of a project (or phase).

  1. Breaking the project down into its smallest work components
  2. Estimating the effort, duration, and cost of each component and aggregating them into a full estimate or the sum of all the project activity estimates

**CAPABILITIES:** Do you have the expertise and resources necessary to produce the product or service (i.e., project management, requirements analysis, training, risk management, quality assurance, etc.)?

---

Also remember to assess your CAPABILITIES: Ask yourself, do you have the expertise and resources necessary to produce the product or service (i.e., project management, requirements analysis, training, risk management, quality assurance, etc.)?

# Estimating Tools and Techniques (continued)

## ■ Bottom-Up Estimating (continued)

- This is a much more analytical approach to estimation and requires a much more accurate set of project documentation, such as:
    - Customer/user requirements
    - Functional/technical specifications
    - A complete WBS or project plan and schedule

# Estimating Tools and Techniques (continued)

## ■ Wideband Delphi

Sec. 3

- Is a consensus-based technique for estimating effort
  - It derives from the Delphi Method, which was developed in the 1940s at the RAND Corporation as a forecasting tool.

1. Facilitator presents each expert with a specification and an estimation form.
2. Facilitator calls a group meeting in which the experts discuss estimation issues with the coordinator and each other.
3. Experts fill out forms anonymously.
4. Facilitator prepares and distributes a summary of the estimates
5. Facilitator calls a group meeting, specifically focusing on having the experts discuss points where their estimates vary widely.
6. Experts fill out forms, again anonymously, and steps 4 to 6 are iterated for as many rounds as appropriate.

 **Note: This Topic was Touched Upon in Module 4:**

*Adaptive Planning in Action – Trust, Commitment, and Collaboration*

A critical factor teams must consider when creating their estimates is the team's velocity. The number of features team members believe they can complete within a given iteration is known as velocity. Velocity is estimated by the team using an estimating technique (i.e. relative sizing, point to scale, affinity estimating, etc.) as an agreed-upon means of measuring the relative size (complexity) of a feature (user story/requirement), then assigning a story "point" to each story. From there, they add up the total number of points assigned to each team member in the iteration to obtain an estimated measure of their velocity. With that information the team can adjust their release plan based on the number of features that will be delivered within each iteration. Although this process isn't an exact science, it prevents the team from over-committing to an iteration by ensuring team members adjust their plan according to the **team's capacity** and resourcing needs, in addition to technical feasibility.

# Estimating Tools and Techniques (continued)

## ■ Planning Poker

- Members of the team independently develop quick estimates. They then compare their estimate and discuss the differences to arrive at a consensus.
    - Participants discreetly estimate each story, concealing it from the other participants until they all show their hands together.
    - This approach serves the purpose of having each person arrive at their own conclusion without being influenced by the thinking of other members.
    - It is important to the process that the participants conceal their assessments from each other and that all participants reveal together.

1. Participants independently make estimates for stories on flash cards
2. Cards are concurrently revealed by holding them up within the group and displaying the relative values of their respective assessment.

---

Planning Poker is another joint-effort technique used to estimate feature sizes. It provides team members with different opinions from their own. Discussion is undertaken of the various opinions raised and those receiving a consensus vote are incorporated into the overall estimating process. As a result, everyone involved has more information about the complexity of the story as a whole, instead of having to estimate by themselves. Planning Poker is also a way to keep the team motivated about the project because this approach to estimating can be more fun and engaging than the other methods.

As you've already seen, there are numerous estimating techniques that can be used by Agile teams. However, the best approach for a project is really going to be determined by the characteristics of the project team.

# Estimating Tools and Techniques (continued)

- **Release Backlog**
  - The release backlog contains all cards that have NOT been scheduled/associated with a particular iteration.

- **Backlog Item**
  - PBIs can be user stories, technical features, defects, or any other item that will require the delivery team's time to deliver.
    - PBIs are typically estimated at the gross and/or plan level.

# Release Planning Concepts

- **Burndown Chart**
  - Provides a historical context of a projects burndown through each iteration
    - The horizontal axis of the burndown chart shows the iterations.
    - The vertical axis shows the amount of work remaining at the start of each iteration.
    - Work remaining can be shown in whatever unit the team prefers—story points, ideal days, team days, and so on.

# Iteration Planning Concepts

- **Iteration**
  - A theme-driven timebox of requests to be worked on and accepted within a product's release
    - It is defined in an Iteration Planning meeting.
    - Completed with an Iteration Demo and Review meeting
      - The terms iteration and sprint are used synonymously.

The terms iteration and sprint are used synonymously, however, sprint is commonly associated with the Scrum methodology.

# Iteration Planning Concepts (continued)

- **Iteration** (continued)
  - Timebox
    - A timebox is a fixed period of time in which a defined deliverable is scheduled.
      - In addition to fixing the start and end points of timeboxes, teams typically also fix the resources available within the timebox.
  - Iteration Units
    - A specified level of functionality in a to-be-completed iteration

- **Scope Verification**
  - Accomplished within the iteration, as the customer gets to review, test, and accept the implemented features
    - Ideally it happens throughout the iteration but it can occur at the end, during the demo of work coding.
    - Features that weren't ready to be accepted move back into the backlog or into the next iteration at the discretion of the customer.

# Daily Planning Concepts

- **Feature**  Sec. 2
  - Feature (software design) is an intended behavior or property of a computer program that is usually documented in the design

- **Persona**
  - Thoroughly describes a fictitious character in detail to represent a specific user within a targeted demographic

- **Task**
  - The decomposition of features into manageable units of a scheduled feature's work completion within the iteration

- **WIP Queue**
  - Work in progress items like specification documents and code waiting to be tested

# Daily Planning Concepts (continued)

- **WIP Limits**
  - Can be viewed as goals that will expose problems in the process and help improve the process by defining a policy based on empirical evidence that suggests a need for change.

- **Impediments**
  - Anything that prevents a team member from performing work as efficiently as possible is an impediment.
    - Each team member has an opportunity to announce impediments during the daily stand-up meeting.
    - The facilitator is charged with ensuring impediments get resolved and is responsible for arranging sidebar meetings when they cannot be resolved on the spot in the daily stand-up meeting.

# Reinforcement Training

## Questions & Exercises

### ■ Time to Test your New Knowledge!
Take the next PMI-ACP practice quiz.

# Exercise 4

Describe the purpose of the following Agile phases and some of the activities/outcomes

| Product Vision | Product Roadmap | Release Planning |
|---|---|---|
| Purpose:<br><br>Activities/Outcomes: | Purpose:<br><br>Activities/Outcomes: | Purpose:<br><br>Activities/Outcomes: |
| **Iteration Planning** | **Daily Planning** | **Daily Work** |
| Purpose:<br><br>Activities/Outcomes: | Purpose:<br><br>Activities/Outcomes: | Purpose:<br><br>Activities/Outcomes: |
| **Demo** | **Review** | **Retrospective** |
| Purpose:<br><br>Activities/Outcomes: | Purpose:<br><br>Activities/Outcomes: | Purpose:<br><br>Activities/Outcomes: |

# Module 4 Quiz

## Exam Practice Questions

1. Which of the following planning events can be identified as the starting point where the team begins identifying the features they wish to deliver in the project during the Stand-up meeting?
   A. Priority Planning
   B. Daily Planning
   C. Feature Planning
   D. Adaptive Planning

2. Top-Down estimating can BEST be described as:
   A. Using the WBS to approximate the size (duration and cost) and risk of a project (or phase)
   B. Using experience from previous project data to draw accurate estimates for new "analogous" projects
   C. Writing points on the bottoms of plastic cups, turning them upside, and assigning stories to them
   D. Writing points on the bottoms of index cards, turning them upside, and assigning stories to them

3. When requirements are described at a very high level and the rest of the planning is driven by priority, it can BEST be described as:
   A. Priority Planning
   B. Customer Value Planning
   C. Feature Planning
   D. Adaptive Planning

4. Which of the following BEST describes the process a team undergoes when they compare two different pieces of functionality and then agree on the size?
   A. Relative Sizing
   B. Relative Complexity Estimating
   C. Relative Poker
   D. Feature Gestimating

5. The project manager of a new software project is in the process of putting together the project plan. While preparing for an upcoming meeting, the project manager asked the customer to start thinking about features he'd like added to the backlog and their order of importance. Which of these meetings is the project manager preparing for?
   A. Iteration Planning Meeting
   B. Customer Sales Meeting
   C. Release Planning Meeting
   D. Visionary Meeting

6. During which meeting is the list of features converted into actual work to be accomplished?
   A. Team To-Do List Meeting
   B. Task List Meeting
   C. Feature Planning Meeting
   D. Iteration Meeting

7. Which of the following BEST describes the rate at which the team is completing user stories from the backlog?
   A. Agile Arson
   B. Velocity
   C. Burndown
   D. Burn-up

8. California Car Emporium is a retail distributor of automobile products that are available to the public. The company has recently decided to take on a modernization program that would bring its legacy systems into the current standards of web-based applications. During California Car Emporium weekly planning meeting, the CIO has requested to see the burndown chart created by the project manager. What information will the CIO learn by looking at the burndown chart?
   A. Number of lines of code written to complete each feature
   B. The total number of new features that have been added to the backlog during the project
   C. The impediments the team is encountering while working
   D. Where the team currently stands in regard to completion of the current iteration's tasks

9. Constant sequence estimations and exponential sequence estimations are examples of:
   A. Sequence Planning
   B. Sequencing
   C. Point to Scale
   D. Poker Pointing

10. Which technique is used to quickly estimate the story points of a large number of user stories based on their similarities?
    A. Affinity Estimates
    B. Comparative Estimate Analysis
    C. Story Estimating
    D. Quantitative Summarizing

11. A misconception about being Agile is that teams are supposed to be able to change their focus at a moment's notice. Which of the following BEST describes the reality of Agile planning:
    A. The customer is only allowed to makes changes up until the iteration has started.
    B. The customer can make changes anytime they need to.
    C. The customer can request changes anytime as long as it increases their ROI.
    D. The business is only allowed to make last minute changes to increase the ROI.

12. All of the following are stages of team development, EXCEPT:
    A. Storming
    B. Forming
    C. Norming
    D. Transforming

13. While traditional managers may believe teams are more financially motivated than intrinsically motivated, Agile project managers under that motivating a team to become high performers is more complex. It may require:
    A. a company policy that include stock options and extra holidays
    B. a company policy so that the team is truly self-organizing and empowered
    C. a company policy that allows the development team to telecommute
    D. a company policy that allows Agile team members to have their own office

14. Which of the following terms would MOST likely be used to describe, "Anything that prevents a team member from performing work as efficiently as possible".
    A. Burndown
    B. Impediment
    C. Risk
    D. Spike

15. A goal that can be used to expose problems in a process and help define policies based on empirical evidence indicating a need for change, can BEST be described as a:
    A. Iteration plan
    B. Roadmap
    C. WIP limit
    D. Vision

16. The intended behavior or property of a computer program that is usually documented in a design specification can BEST be described as:
    A. Features
    B. Tasks
    C. Spikes
    D. Artifacts

17. Which of the following would MOST likely contain information about features that are in progress to be tested?
    A. A WIP queue
    B. Scope verification
    C. A spike list
    D. A spike queue

18. When a customer has the opportunity to review, test, and accept implemented features that were completed during an iteration can BEST be described as?
    A. Tasks
    B. A spike solution
    C. A WIP queue
    D. Scope verification

19. Which of the following BEST describes an artifact that provides a historical context of a projects' burndown through each iteration
    A. Burnup chart
    B. Release burndown chart
    C. Cumulative Flow diagram
    D. Gantt chart

20. Which of the following BEST describes a fictitious character created to represent the different user types within a targeted demographic?
    A. A persona
    B. A feature
    C. A specification
    D. An artifact

# Module 4 Quiz Answers

1. Answer: B

    Explanation: As features are completed within each iteration, they must be accepted and reviewed by both the team and the product manager as Done-Done. This aim is achieved through daily planning.

2. Answer: B

3. Answer: D

    Explanation: When Adaptive Planning is used, requirements are described at a very high level and the rest of the planning is driven by priority. More often than not, the team will only be engaged in Release Planning, Iteration Planning, and Daily Planning.

4. Answer: A

    Explanation: Relative sizing compares two different pieces of functionality then agrees on which one is smaller (or larger) in size and determines how much smaller (or larger).

5. Answer: C

    Explanation: The Release Planning Meeting identifies the features that will go into the release, which are chosen from the product backlog and moved into the release backlog. From there, features are prioritized and estimated.

6. Answer: D

    Explanation: An Iteration Planning Meeting is held at the beginning of each iteration in order to convert the items in the feature list into specific programming tasks.

7. Answer: B

    Explanation: Velocity is the rate at which the team is completing user stories from the backlog. By keeping track of their velocity, the team can make achievable commitments in future iterations. Once a team knows its velocity, they can then provide better estimates of what their burndown rate will be and team members can identify their capability to meet their commitments.

8. Answer: D

    Explanation: A burndown chart shows where the team stands regarding: 1) completion of the tasks that comprise the product backlog and 2) achievement of the iteration's goals. In other words, a team's velocity can be obtained by viewing a burndown chart.

9. Answer: C

    Explanation: Point to scale relates to an abstract point system. It is used to discuss the difficulty of the task without assigning actual hours.

10. Answer: A

11. Answer: A
    Explanation: Although Agile actively embraces change, it also embraces planning. As a result, once an iteration has started changes from anyone outside of the development team are no longer allowed. In fact, it becomes the role of the Agile project manager to protect the team from outside influences that may request changes. If constant change was allowed it would be impossible for the team to meet their iteration commitments. Customer change requests are incorporated in the next iteration.

12. Answer: D
    Explanation: Tuckman's four stages of group development are: Forming, Storming, Norming, and Performing.

13. Answer: B
    Explanation: While all of the other options may be nice perks, creating a company policy that enables an Agile team to truly be self-organizing and empowered is the best answer. The strength of Agile teams come from their ability to function as self-organizing, self-managing and self-empowered units thereby enabling them to deliver on their commitments.

14. Answer: B
    Explanation: Burndown is the rate at which the project is burning the requirements from the feature list. Risk is the potential that a chosen action or inaction will lead to an undesirable outcome. A spike is a small technical investigation to research the answer to a problem.

15. Answer: C
    Explanation: An iteration plan contains the tasks to be accomplished in an upcoming iteration. A roadmap defines the creation of a unique and valuable position as well as associated goals and objectives. The vision is associated with the business need framed in the context of a strategy and associated goals.

16. Answer: A
    Explanation: A task is the decomposition of features into manageable units of a scheduled feature's work completion with an iteration. A spike is a small technical investigation to research the answer to a problem. During the development of software an artifact is one of many kinds of tangible by-product produced.

17. Answer: A
    Explanation: A Work in-process (WIP) queue contains a unfinished items for products in a production process. Scope verification is when a customer has the opportunity to review, test, and accept implemented features that were completed during an iteration. The other options are made up.

18. Answer: D
    Explanation: A task is the decomposition of features into manageable units of a feature's work to be completed within an iteration. A spike is a small technical investigation to research the answer to a problem. A WIP queue contains information about features that are in progress.

19. Answer: B
    Explanation: A Burnup chart shows progress towards a goal. A Cumulative Flow diagram shows the distribution of all work items across various states, over time. A Gantt chart illustrates a project schedule from the start and finish dates. Therefore the Release burndown chart is the correct answer.

20. Answer: A
    Explanation: A persona describes a fictitious character created to represent the different user types within a targeted demographic. A feature defines the intended behavior or property of a computer program that is usually documented in a design specification. A specification is a well-defined set of requirements to be satisfied by a material, product, or service. During the development of software an artifact is one of many kinds of tangible by-product produced.

# Module 4
## Summary

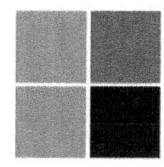

- ✓ Described Adaptive Planning
- ✓ Explained Why Discipline is Required to Make Agile Work
- ✓ Analyzed How to Plan at Multiple Levels
- ✓ Performed Project Decomposition
- ✓ Examined Estimating Tools and Techniques

- ✓ Compared Release Planning, Iteration Planning and Daily Planning Concepts

# Problem Detection Resolution

## Module 5
- PMI-ACP Exam Preparation Course

# Module 5
## Objectives

- ✓ Illustrate How to Resolve Impediments
- ✓ Discuss Why Creating an Open and Safe Environment is Important for Agile Projects
- ✓ Compare Agile Risk and Mitigation Strategies
- ✓ Assess the 5 Core Risk Areas Common to All Projects
- ✓ Explain Risk Management Techniques & Terminology
- ✓ Agile Correlation to PMI Risk Management
- ✓ List Ways to Communicate Status of Risk and Impediments

# Resolve Impediments

- **The Average Employee Is Trying to Do a Good Job**
  - Don't assume laziness or indolence.
    - More likely, the right employee is in the wrong job (a management error) or the wrong employee is in the right job (a hiring error).
  - Removal from the team may be difficult.
    - But it may be necessary for both the employer and employee.
    - At times, the only way to ensure you have the right people on board and in the right seats is to get the wrong people off the bus.
  - Fairness in hiring also means that you expect the same high level of performance from all your employees.
    - If some employees are allowed to underperform it is unfair to colleagues who are striving to excel.
    - In addition to lowering morale, an underperforming employee is an unhappy employee.
      - Nobody wants to feel they are not of value.

In addition to creating a vision for the product, each team must decide how they're going to contribute toward making the vision a reality and create their own set of team goals. With a goal and team vision in place, the product manager must ensure that the team environment promotes an atmosphere where team members are encouraged to speak up about real issues that may be preventing them from achieving their goals. An environment built on trust, open communication, and collaboration allows team members to embrace ownership of problems and encourages them to be eager to find solutions that mitigate risk. This will bring about the best attitude in everyone involved in the project.

# Creating an Open and Safe Environment

- **The Best Way to Deal with On-the-Job Conflicts Is by Dealing with Them**
  - Set the tone for an open, honest, and principled working environment.
  - Don't respond to complaints/requests immediately.
    - If you're interacting in person, thank the employee for the information and promise to investigate.
  - Don't avoid confrontation if needed.
    - Nip problems in the bud and don't overreact.
      - Everyone has an occasional bad day.
      - Anticipate problems before they arise.
  - If conflict arises between employees, suggest that all parties sit down together to discuss, compromise, and resolve.
    - If a resolution is not forthcoming, then avoid openly taking sides.

Being able to openly tackle conflict and address impediments is a must for any team. Organizations and managers cannot expect team members to proactively surface impediments, let alone contribute to a project or explore the possibilities, if they don't feel safe to express what's on their mind. To deal with obstacles, empowered teams must be able to speak honestly in a way that promotes listening to differing perspectives and constructively working towards a solution. Conversely, it also means that when team members raise concerns, it's important for management to close the loop and acknowledge that those concerns are being taken seriously. In other words, simply pandering to the voice of the employee and creating a safe environment is useless if management doesn't communicate back to the team that their message was heard. Doing so, whether the management is able to make the requested changes or not, simply provides an opportunity for them to reset the team's expectations and explain how or if impediments will be addressed.

The way a company treats its employees is the way its employees will treat their clients. That is to say, if it's acceptable for an organization to not keep its promises, it sends the signal that employees don't have to keep their promises to the company, or its clients, either.

# Engage Risk and Mitigation Strategies

## ■ Risk Management Is a Team Responsibility

- The checkpoints and sync-up meetings built into the Agile framework provide an organic means of risk management.
  - Release and iteration planning, daily stand-up, and review/demo meetings provide opportunities to bring up risks and impediments.
  - The product manager and coach facilitate discussions during these meetings

The history of a team's velocity is also an organic means to mitigate risk on a project. If a product managers needs to know the probability of a team being able to complete a given number of features within a specific timeframe, simply looking at their past performance could be a good indicator of what their future performance may be. Obviously, this is only as accurate as the amount of history that has been tracked up to that point.

# Engage Risk and Mitigation Strategies (continued)

- **It Takes Discipline to Make Work Visible and to Be Open to Changes**
  - This approach is the core of Agile risk management.
  - Strategies have to be constantly reevaluated at the end of each iteration.
    - If the team is behind schedule, then the work must be re-scoped and estimated.
    - Lower-priority features are dropped to allow the team to make the date.
  - Traditional Risk Management Is Usually Handled Using Formal Meetings and Documents.
    - The *PMBOK* ® Guide recommends that risk management be conducted incrementally over the life of a project.
      - *The reality is that formal risk management usually only takes places at the beginning of the project and is then neglected as the project progresses.*
    - Make sure risks are made visible and addressed.

Traditional risk management is usually handled using formal meetings and documents. Unfortunately, this is only done at the beginning of the project and neglected toward the end. As a result, Agile advocates using the organic checkpoints built into the Agile SDLC to have more opportunities to deal with risk.

# Engage Risk and Mitigation Strategies (continued)

- **It Takes Discipline to Make Work Visible and to Be Open to Changes** (continued)
  - Involve the entire team in the decision-making process.
    - Reduces the risk of "wishful thinking" estimations
    - Estimates become more accurate once the team has gone through several iterations to better gauge their velocity.
      - This is illustrated in the *PMBOK®* Guide as execution feeding back into planning.

# Engage Risk and Mitigation Strategies (continued)

- **Tom DeMarco and Tim Lister Provide 5 Core Risk Areas Common to All Projects**
    - Intrinsic Schedule Flaw – estimates that are simply wishful thinking or wrong right out of the gate
    - Specification Breakdown – consensus on what to build cannot be reached by the stakeholders
    - Scope Creep – when a project's initial requirement set gets inflated as the project progresses
    - Personal Loss
    - Productivity Variation – actual performance falls short of assumed performance

# 5 Core Risk Areas Common to All Projects

- **Intrinsic Schedule Flaw**
  - Risk: Schedule is wrong from the moment it starts.
    - Mitigation #1: Use the synchronization points in Agile, such as at the end of each iteration, to adjust the scope and priority of the features being worked on.
      - *Lower-priority features are pushed to the bottom of the backlog or moved into the next iteration.*
    - Mitigation #2: Use your velocity history to readjust your schedule and create a more accurate plan.
      - *If for every 1 hour the team works, 0.25 hours of bug fixes are created, what is going to happen if you simply tell the team to start working faster to achieve the goal?*

# 5 Core Risk Areas Common to All Projects (continued)

- **Specification Breakdown**
  - Risk: Confusion between stakeholders and developers and a lack of business direction can result in the team not having any direction as to what they should build.
    - Mitigation #1: Providing access to an Agile customer and product owner who can make decisions about immediate product situations.
  - Risk Identified: Developers can't agree on how to implement the project's functionality.
    - Mitigation #1: Team agrees to work from a set of possible solutions until the best one is selected, also known as the "set-based design" method.
      - *The traditional approach is to use a single choice at each step and refine it until it is ready to be employed, also know as "point-based" design.*

# 5 Core Risk Areas Common to All Projects (continued)

- **Scope Creep**
    - Risk: Extended delivery cycles have an increased likelihood of experiencing "requirement inflation" and change requests.
        - Mitigation #1: Incremental delivery through the use to short iterations allows the customer and team to adjust their processes and incorporate change requests more easily.
            - *It allows for **Customer Prioritization**: The customers can adjust the backlog and priorities as needed to increase product value.*

- **Personnel Loss**
    - Risk: Death marches increase employee turnover on a project.
        - Mitigation #1: When teams are allowed to self-organize and are self-empowered, there is less sense of helplessness and doom, which in turn increases morale.
            - *The active collaboration efforts of Agile also encourage stronger peer support among the team members.*

# 5 Core Risk Areas Common to All Projects (continued)

- **Productivity Variation**
  - Risk: The actual performance of the team and/or product is not meeting the assumptions for performance that were planned.
    - Mitigation #1: Use the synchronization points in Agile, such as at the end of each iteration, to adjust the scope and priority of the features being worked on.
    - Mitigation #2: Use your velocity history to readjust your schedule and create a more accurate plan.

# Risk Management Planning

- **What Is Risk Management?**
  - In the *PMBOK*® Guide, the Project Risk Management Knowledge Area is responsible for:
    - Increasing the probability and impact of positive events, and decreasing the probability and impact of adverse events
      - The primary objective of a risk management plan is to create an agreement as to how risk will be handled.
  - It address six processes:
    - Planning Risk Management
    - Identify Risks
    - Perform Qualitative Risk Analysis
    - Perform Quantitative Risk Analysis
    - Planning Risk Responses
    - Monitor and Controlling Risks

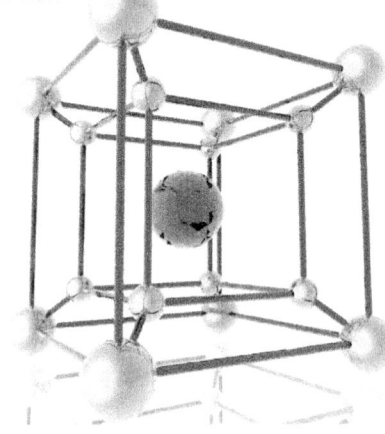

# Risk Management Planning (continued)

- **Informal Risk Management**
  - Agile does not formally address risk management.
    - It is organically built into the framework using the defined synchronization points and highly visible information radiators.
      - If your organization requires formal risk documentation--create it. If not, it's taken care of throughout the Agile planning process.

# Risk Management Techniques & Terminology

- **Risk Burn-Down Graphs**
    - Graphs summarize the risk profile for the entire project and can be used to illustrate new and escalating risks.
        - They are also useful for showing the progress made in early iterations where more work was done on architectural risk reduction rather than purely delivering business functionality.

- **Risk-Adjusted Backlog**
    - To have a smart blend of value-generating business features and risk-reduction actions

# Risk Management Techniques & Terminology (continued)

Sec. 8

- **Constraints**
  - Something that establishes boundaries, restricts limits, or obstructs any aspect of the project

- **Brainstorming**
  - A technique used to stimulate creative thinking and to overcome impasses to problems. Ideas should not be rejected during brainstorming

- **Risk-Based Spike**
  - A small technical investigation whereby an experiment is performed to identify a solution to a problem or to asses the level of technical risk involved in implementing a solution

# Agile Correlation to PMI Risk Management

- Plan Risk Management
  - **Purpose:** To define how to conduct risk management activities for a project
  - **Key outputs:** Risk management plan
  - **Agile equivalent:** The team determines the level of risk on the project, addresses how they plan to handle it, and documents *(or not)* their findings
- Identify Risks
  - **Purpose:** To determine which risks may affect the project and to document their characteristics
  - **Key outputs:** Risk register
  - **Agile equivalent:** This is handled iteratively during the planning meeting and results are recorded in a "spreadsheet" or on the white board. Risks are identified through assumption analysis before the team commits to an iteration or release. Teams that overly handle risk may place these items on a risk board.

# Agile Correlation to PMI Risk Management (continued)

- Perform Qualitative Risk Analysis
  - **Purpose:** To prioritize risks for further analysis or action by assessing and combining their probability of occurrence and impact
  - **Key outputs:** Risk register updates
  - **Agile equivalent:** Organically achieved through team discussions about the probability of risk impact that may occur during a project. Relies on team experience, expert judgment, and intuition to perform analysis.
- Perform Quantitative Risk Analysis
  - **Purpose:** To numerically analyze the effect of identified risks on overall project objectives
  - **Key outputs:** Risk register updates
  - **Agile equivalent:** Not required in Agile, but if performed it should be done during the release and/or iteration planning meetings.

# Agile Correlation to PMI Risk Management (continued)

- Plan Risk Responses
  - **Purpose:** To develop options and actions to enhance opportunities and reduce threats to the project objectives
  - **Key outputs:** Risk register updates, risk-related contract decisions
  - **Agile equivalent:** Organically achieved through team discussions and planning meetings that are conducted to mitigate risks. Is also addressed in retrospectives where the team makes recommendations on how to improve the development process and throughput.
    - Teams that want to overly address risk management can do so using risk boards categorized as:

      Avoid: Don't undertake the pieces that have high risk.
      Accept: Allocate time and money to pay for risk should it occur.
      Transfer: Make the risk the responsibility of someone else.
      Mitigate: Take appropriate actions to reduce the risk or cost of impact.
      Evade: Do none of the above and hope you get lucky!

# Agile Correlation to PMI Risk Management (continued)

- Monitor and Control Risks
  - **Purpose:** To implement risk response plans, track identified risks, monitor residual risks, identify new risks, and evaluate risk process effectiveness throughout the project
  - **Key outputs:** Risk register updates, change requests, organizational process asset updates
  - **Agile equivalent:** Risk reassessments are performed as part of planning meetings and retrospectives; retrospectives also provide the place to conduct risk audits. Burndown charts and task boards serve as highly visible information radiators to assist with monitoring. Evaluation of velocity in review meetings provides a place for technical performance measurement.

# Communicate Status of Risk and Impediments

- **Problems for Risk Communicators Involve How to Reach the Intended Audience**
    - For risk and impediments to be acted upon, you must:
        - Make the risk comprehensible and relatable to other risks
        - Respect the audience's values related to the risk
        - Predict the audience's response to the communication,
    - A goal of risk communication is to improve collective and individual decision-making

# Communicate Status of Risk and Impediments (continued)

- **Seven Cardinal Rules For the Practice of Risk Communication:**
  - Accept and involve the stakeholders as legitimate partners.
  - Plan carefully and evaluate your efforts with a focus on your strengths, weaknesses, opportunities, and threats (SWOT).
  - Listen to the stakeholders' specific concerns.
  - Be honest, frank, and open.
  - Coordinate and collaborate with other credible sources.
  - Speak clearly and with compassion.
  - Meet the needs of the media

# Reinforcement Training

## Questions & Exercises

### Time to Test your New Knowledge!
Take the next PMI-ACP practice quiz.

# Exercise 5

**Describe the tool/technique Agile uses to organically address the following areas of risk management:**

| Performing Quantitative Risk Analysis | Intrinsic Schedule Flaw | Scope Creep |
|---|---|---|
|  |  |  |

| Identifying Risks | Personnel Loss | Plan Risk Management |
|---|---|---|
|  |  |  |

| Productivity Variation | Planning Risk Responses | Monitoring and Controlling Risks |
|---|---|---|
|  |  |  |

| Performing Qualitative Risk Analysis | Specification Breakdown | Other? |
|---|---|---|
|  |  |  |

# Module 5 Quiz

## Exam Practice Questions

1. All of the following actions were identified as ways of dealing with on-the-job conflicts, EXCEPT:
   A. Set the tone for an open, honest, and principled working environment
   B. Don't respond to complaints/requests immediately
   C. If conflict arises between employees, suggest that all parties sit down together to discuss, compromise, and resolve
   D. Avoid direct confrontation

2. All of the following are considered organic means of risk management that are built into Agile, EXCEPT:
   A. Release Planning
   B. Iteration Planning
   C. Daily Stand-Up meetings
   D. Creation of a risk register

3. A project manager on a construction project is in the process of conducting risk management activities. While preparing for a planning meeting to address a possible slip in the schedule, he asks a team member to track down a crucial piece of information that would help him mitigate the risk by helping him to more accurately readjust the schedule. Which of the following pieces of information should the Agile project manager reference?
   A. Velocity history
   B. WBS
   C. Project plan
   D. Risk register

4. Thomas has just been informed by the Team Lead that the team will not be able to release a high-priority feature on schedule. It has dependencies on several other low-priority features that were expected to be done in the next iteration--but the customer has increased their level of complexity. Which of the following responses should the Agile product manager take to mitigate this scheduling risk?
   A. Canceling the iteration and starting from the beginning
   B. Adding more people to the team in order to get the feature completed
   C. Extending the iteration until the features are Done-Done
   D. Adjusting the scope and priorities of the features being worked on

5. A developer on the team is currently working on finalizing the specifications that will be required to complete a feature for the upcoming iteration. However, the customer approached the developer today with a question regarding the performance requirements she is expecting to see in the feature that are drastically higher than what the product manager requested. Obviously, there seems to be some confusion about what needs to take place. Which of the following BEST describes the action that needs to be taken to mitigate this specification breakdown risk?
   A. Tell the product manager to e-mail the customer in order to clarify the specification
   B. Immediately review the contract with the customer to see if her request is within the project scope
   C. Arrange for the product manager to meet face to face with a customer who can make decisions about immediate product situations
   D. Listen to the customer because the customer is always right

6. All of the following are benefits of using set-based design, EXCEPT:
   A. It converges designs more quickly
   B. Decisions are deferred until the "last responsible moment."
   C. It allows multiple design opportunities to be explored at the same time
   D. It incrementally iterates through solutions until the right one is selected

7. A risk manager is leading a multi-phase construction project and beginning the risk management process. Because of the project's complexity and the amount of money invested in it, the project sponsor has stressed the critical nature of managing risks yet getting the project delivered on time. The risk manager has taken this advice seriously and hired an Agile product manager to assist him. Which of the following actions BEST describes the recommendation an Agile product manager would make to the risk manager to minimize risk on a project while remaining focused on the release plan?
    A. Suggest delivering features incrementally through the use to short iterations so that the customer and team have opportunities to adjust their processes and incorporate change requests more easily.
    B. Suggest calculating the number of resources needed to complete all the tasks associated with the project and then padding the result with reserve resources that could be called upon if needed.
    C. Suggest calculating the amount of materials and resources needed to complete all the tasks associated with the project and then padding the results with reserves that could be used if needed.
    D. Require the customer to sign off on every requirement to prevent scope creep and change requests as a means of keeping the project on time and under budget.

8. Given that risk management is organically built into the Agile framework through the use of defined synchronization points and highly visible information radiators, which of the following would not be considered a valuable risk information radiator?
    A. Risk Burn-Down Graph
    B. Risk Adjusted Backlog
    C. Risk Reward Chart
    D. Velocity history

9. Which of the following categories are you LEAST likely to see on an Agile risk board?
    A. Avoid
    B. Transfer
    C. Backup Recovery
    D. Evade

10. Which of the following is LEAST likely to assist a project manager with reaching the business about risk?
    A. Making the risk comprehensible and relatable to other risks
    B. Respecting the audience's values related to the risk
    C. Predicting the audience's response to the communication
    D. Explaining the technical details as to how the risk came into being

11. All of the following are true about a high performing Agile environment, EXCEPT:
    A. It is built on trust
    B. It is built on open communication
    C. It is built on collaboration
    D. It is built on being risk averse

12. All of the following are cardinal rules that should be followed for the practice of risk communication, EXCEPT:
    A. Accept and involve the stakeholders as legitimate partners.
    B. Listen to stakeholders' specific concerns
    C. Only coordinate and collaborate with other team members
    D. Be honest, frank and open

13. Which of the following Agile activities is useless if the information collected during the activity is not communicate back to the team by the management, confirming that the message was heard?
    A. Review meeting
    B. Demo meeting
    C. Retrospective
    D. Release planning meeting

14. Which of the following Agile practices can BEST be used to organically mitigate risk on a project?
    A. Planning poker
    B. Tracking a team's velocity
    C. Use Bottom-up estimating
    D. Affinity estimating

15  Which of the following BEST describes how Agile implements risk management that is traditionally handled during formal meetings and documentation?
    A. Building check points into the Agile SDLC
    B. Creating risk registries
    C. Using Kanban boards to monitor risk
    D. Embedding risk managers onto the team

16  Jason is an Agile project manager that has just received a list of features and delivery schedule from his customer. However, the customer is not sure if the business will want to pursue these features if they do not have the infrastructure to support the new product. As a result, Jason knows that the schedule provided by the customer is inaccurate. Which of the following is LEAST likely to be done as a means to mitigate the risk of intrinsic schedule flaw?
    A. Use a more comprehensive project plan
    B. Use synchronization points at the end of each iteration
    C. Use velocity history to readjust schedule
    D. Use longer iterations

17  Which of the following BEST describes how Agile mitigates the inherent risk of specification breakdown?
    A. By providing access to the marketing manager and product owner that can make immediate decisions about product situations
    B. By providing access to the business analyst that can make immediate decisions about the business case
    C. By providing access to the customer and product owner that can make immediate decisions about product situations
    D. Providing access to the stakeholders so they can make immediate decisions about product vision

18  Which of the following BEST describes how Agile mitigates the risk of scope creep?
    A. Using incremental delivery through the use of short iterations
    B. Using phase-gate delivery through the use of long iterations
    C. Using incremental delivery through the use of long iterations
    D. Using milestones from a WBS incorporated into a project plan

19  Which of the following BEST describes how Agile mitigates the risk of personnel loss?
    A. By allowing teams to be self-organizing to reduce feelings of helplessness
    B. By allowing teams to be to work off hours and reduce their feelings of stress
    C. By allowing teams to be autonomous to reduce feelings of being tied to the company culture
    D. By allowing teams to be independent so they can be managed by their own technical lead

20  All of the following practices could be used by an Agile project manager to mitigate the risk of productivity variations, EXCEPT?
    A. Using more meetings to define more detailed requirements
    B. Using more meeting to collaborate with team members
    C. Using synchronization points at the end of each iteration
    D. Using velocity history to create a more accurate plan

# Module 5 Quiz Answers

1. Answer: D

    Explanation: Being able to openly tackle conflict and address impediments is a must for any team. Organizations and managers cannot expect team members to proactively surface impediments, let alone contribute to a project or explore the possibilities, if they don't feel safe to express what's on their mind.

2. Answer: D

    Explanation: Traditional risk management is usually handled using formal meetings and documents. Unfortunately, such formality is typically only undertaken at the beginning of the project and is neglected toward the end. As a result, Agile advocates using the organics checkpoint that is built in to the Agile SDLC as an opportunity to deal with risk.

3. Answer: A

    Explanation: The velocity history can be used as a means of mitigating the risk of schedule slippage by helping create a more accurate release plan.

4. Answer: D

    Explanation: The Agile product manager should use the synchronization points that are built in to Agile, such as at the end of each iteration, to adjust the scope and priority of the features being worked on. Cancelling the iteration is incorrect because ending the iteration should only be called under the most extreme circumstances. The other options are incorrect because adding more people and time will potentially introduce more confusion to the project and will only hide the dysfunction in the form of technical debt.

5. Answer: C

    Explanation: Provide access to a customer so that the product manager can speak face-to-face with someone who can make decisions about immediate product situations. Answer A is incorrect because e-mail is not a preferred form of communication, especially in a critical situation like this. The other options are incorrect because the Agile Manifestos states, "Customer collaboration over contract negotiation." Therefore C provides the best solution out of all the options.

6. Answer: D

    Explanation: The purpose of set-based design is that is allows multiple design solutions to be explored simultaneously. The benefit to this approach with regard to Agile, Lean, and risk management is that it encourages developers to simultaneously conduct multiple spike solutions to find the best solution to a problem. This is in contrast to a point-based design where only a single solution is explored at a time until one is deemed a viable solution (or not) for a given problem.

7. Answer: A

    Explanation: Answer A is the correct answer because it reduces risk by shortening delivery cycles, thereby reducing the likelihood of experiencing "requirement inflation" and change requests. The other options are incorrect because the padding of extra resources and materials contributes to waste, as defined by Lean. Require the customer to sign off is incorrect because accepting and adapting to change is a core tenant of Agile.

8. Answer: C

    Explanation: All of the options can function as highly visible Agile information radiators except the Risk Reward chart because it doesn't exist.

9. Answer: C

    Explanation: A key word to help distinguish between the options is the word "categories". Backup Recovery is incorrect even though it could be an "action taken" as part of avoiding, transferring, or mitigating risk.

10. Answer: D

    Explanation: The business is rarely concerned with the technical details as to what causes risk. It is more concerned with things like any financial exposure the risk may bring about and what options are available to mitigate or reduce these risks.

11. Answer: D
    Explanation: High performing Agile environments are not risk averse. This is because the better an organization is at risk management, the more risks they are able to take. Since risk management is an integral part of Agile development, it allows high performing Agile teams to take more calculated risks.

12. Answer: C
    Explanation: Only coordinate and collaborate with other team members is in correct because getting input from other domain experts to provider additional insight into risks will increase creditability with stakeholders.

13. Answer: C
    Explanation: The information collected from a retrospective is useless if the management does not communicate back to the team that their message was heard. This type of pandering and lack of follow-through is common within Lessons Learned sessions.

14. Answer: B
    Explanation: The best answer is tracking a teams' velocity. Doing so allows an Agile project manager to compare the teams' performance history to get a better idea of the likelihood of them achieving their commitments, and allowing for time to plan proactively. All of the other options are techniques used for estimating the complexity of work, which can be used as tools to identify risks.

15. Answer: A
    Explanation: Checkpoints are organically built into the Agile SDCL which allows the Agile project manager and team to constantly compare where they are in the project, in comparison to where they need to be. Doing this at the end of each iteration ensures they are always addressing risks with the highest probability of occurrence. Conversely, traditional risk management approaches may create a risk register at the beginning of project but neglect to update it with changes in the project.

16. Answer: D
    Explanation: Short iterations should be used with there is a lot of uncertainty on a project, whereas longer iterations should be used when there is more certainty about a project. In this case, if the customer needs were to change in the middle of a 7 day iteration instead of a 30 day iteration, the Agile project manager and team would be able to work with the customer sooner to readjust the delivery schedule for the the next iteration. Remember, once an iteration has been started it is a bad practice to cancel it or allow the customer to make changes to the iteration plan.

17. Answer: C
    Explanation: The key to mitigating the risk of specification breakdown is to ensure that the customer and product owner are readily available to make immediate decisions. While the other options could also be sources of information to flush out specification details, the customer and product owner are the ones that would have the most information about the needs of the product in relation to the project.

18. Answer: A
    Explanation: Using incremental delivery through short iterations prevents scope creep by ensuring requirements are delivered before they have an opportunity to change. The other options are incorrect because elaborate project plans, phases-gates and milestones do not inherently incorporate short iterations.

19. Answer: A
    Explanation: Allowing a team to function as a self-organizing unit empowers them to take responsibility for their actions and their part in the organization. In turn, this creates higher levels of long lasting intrinsic motivation. Allowing the team to be autonomous for the sake of not having to follow the company culture is not best answer because self-management does not mean going rogue.

20. Answer: A
    Explanation: The key phrase in this list of options is "define more detailed requirements". While the other options encourage more collaboration to find a solution, defining more requirements attempts to solve the problem by increasing documentation—and that's not a good Agile practice.

# Module 5
## Summary

- ✓ Illustrated How to Resolve Impediments
- ✓ Discussed Why Creating an Open and Safe Environment is Important for Agile Projects
- ✓ Compared Agile Risk and Mitigation Strategies
- ✓ Assessed the 5 Core Risk Areas Common to All Projects
- ✓ Explained Risk Management Techniques & Terminology
- ✓ Agile Correlation to PMI Risk Management
- ✓ Listed Ways to Communicate Status of Risk and Impediments

# Continuous Improvement

## Module 6
- PMI-ACP Exam Preparation Course

# Module 6
## Objectives

- ✓ Explain What it Means to Be Lean
- ✓ Examine How Quality Improvement is Achieved
- ✓ Combine Lean/Six Sigma into Agile
- ✓ Propose Ways to Incorporate Lean into Your Organization
- ✓ Illustrate How to Identify Systematic Improvement Opportunities
- ✓ Analyze Kaizen Events
- ✓ Use Method Tailoring to Gracefully Transition into Being Agile

# Lean

- **History**
  - During the mid-1700's the production of goods gradually shifted from a single person to mass production.
    - Referred to as the Industrial Revolution
    - From the beginning of the revolution scientists realized that mass production could cause waste.
  - 1920's – Henry Ford developed the first comprehensive Lean manufacturing strategy to build the Model T automobile.
    - His focus was on improving assembly lines by reducing waste and improving the flow of work.
  - The ideas that would later be called "Lean philosophy" also originated in the early 20$^{th}$ century.

# Lean (continued)

## History (continued)

- Sakichi Toyoda changed the family business from textiles to automobile production.
  - Toyoda sent Taiichi Ohno to America to observe Ford's methods.
  - Ohno's experiences and ideas evolved into the Toyota Production System.
- Kiichiro adopted Sakichi's business philosophy as Toyota's way of doing business.

## Modern Day Lean

- Refers to a set of tools designed to improve flow and reduce waste during a business process or material production.
  - They can be used within Six Sigma efforts or on their own.

---

Lean organizations map workflow to application functionality and vice versa. This provides an opportunity not only for automation but also to remove waste that has been hidden away through inherited business processes. They then identify and develop the features necessary to improve the process, automate it, and ultimately add more value.

# Quality Improvement

- **Six Sigma**
  - Is a set of tools used to control business processes by reducing defects and improving quality.
    - Based on the idea that defects result from deviation
      - Therefore there should be no more than six sigma (standard deviations) between a process and its norm.
      - Involves understanding customer needs, analyzing data, and process improvement.
  - A **Six Sigma Belt** (yellow, green, or black) denotes a particular level of expertise.

# Lean/Six-Sigma (LSS)

## Lean Six Sigma Combines the Two Methodologies

1. Lean methodologies are used to improve processes.
2. Six Sigma tools are applied to reduce deviations and defects.

## Design for Six Sigma (DSS) and Design for Lean Six Sigma (DLSS)

- Methodologies used to design (or re-design) products and processes from scratch using Six Sigma or a combination of Six Sigma and Lean tools.
  - These methodologies focus on getting it right the first time rather than improving it later.

# The Liker Pyramid

- **Overview**
  - One of the most popular descriptions of Lean philosophy for Western audiences is that portrayed by Jeffery Liker in his 2004 book *The Toyota Way*.
    - Organizes the four main principles of Lean as a pyramid.
      - Each part of the pyramid contains one or more key Lean principles.

# The Liker Pyramid (continued)

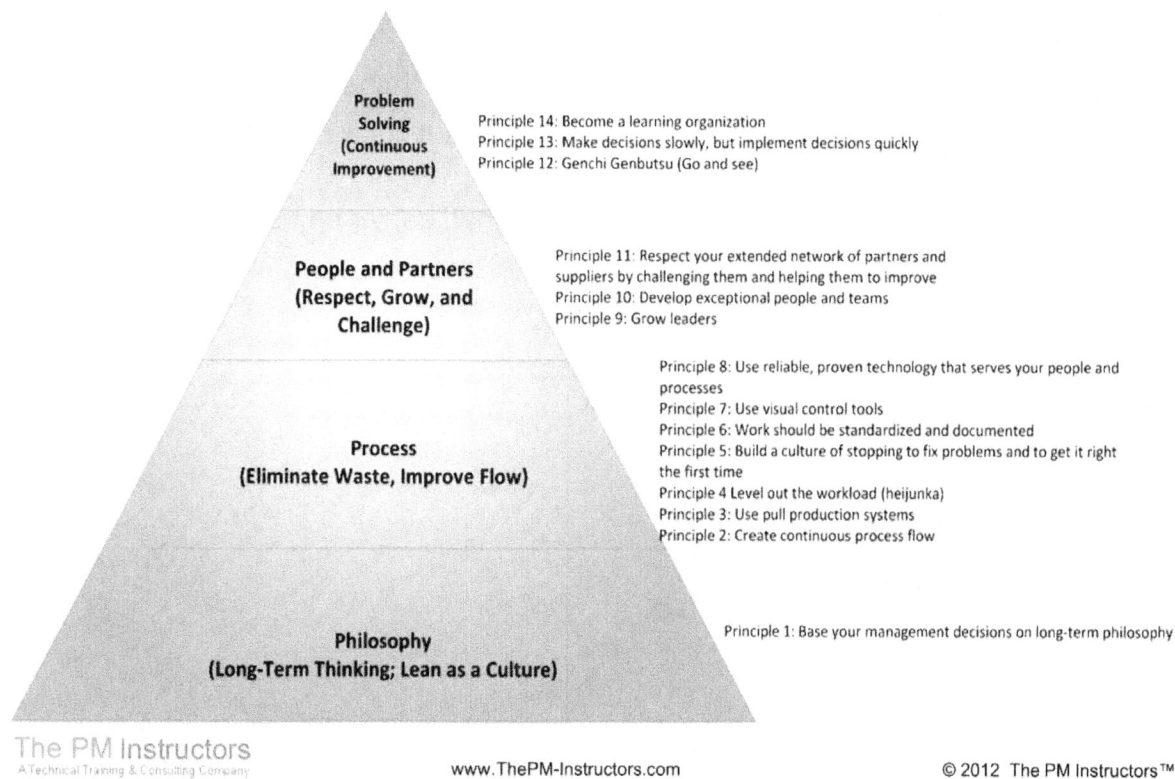

At the base of the pyramid we focus on the Philosophy of Long-Term Lean thinking. Establishing this from the start, will help base your management decisions around long-term Lean best practices.

Next it explains that Process enables to reduce waste and improve flow. Some of the principles reinforced are that of using visual controls, leveling out the workload, using pulls system, etc.

Then it focuses on People and Partners so that you remember to challenge your suppliers to improve the flow to you.

Lastly, if points out the need for constantly Problem Solving so that you are constantly in a mode of continuous improvement.

# Incorporating Lean into Your Organization

- **Building a Lean Foundation**
  - The foundation of the pyramid represents Philosophy
    - Its sole principle is to base your management decisions on long-term philosophy.
    - This ties back to the discussion that we had earlier on Lean being part of the corporate culture.

# Incorporating Lean into Your Organization (continued)

## ■ Building a Lean Foundation (continued)
- The second level is processes where we can eliminate waste and increase value.
  - This involves:
    - Creating continuous flow
    - Using pull production systems, where we make only as much product as is demanded by the customer
    - Leveling out work so that resources are neither overwhelmed nor idle
    - Encouraging members of the organization to get it right the first time and to stop and fix problems
    - Standardizing and documenting work
    - Using visual tools, like lights and signage
    - Using reliable technology

Being a Lean IT organization entails more than just identifying processes and automating them. Organizations that are truly Lean morph their IT architectures into Lean operations, and operations morph into Lean architectures. The result is that the two become indistinguishable from each other. As a result, when an improvement in efficiency is made in to the IT architecture, the ripple of improvement flows across organizational boundaries and is accepted by others as an opportunity for improvement instead of being viewed as "dreaded change."

# Incorporating Lean into Your Organization (continued)

- **Building a Lean Foundation** (continued)
  - The third level represents **People and Partners**.
    - Grow leaders and exceptional people and teams
    - Treat your partners as extensions of your Lean organization
      - Encourage them to improve and challenge them in a respectful manner

Waste can also occur in the way a company deals with its underperforming employees and partners. It can be easy to turn a blind eye to underperformers by simply blaming poor performance on a relaxed company culture or by accepting "That's how it's always been done." But allowing company culture to be an excuse for not expecting the best out of your organization will infiltrate into poor hiring practices, low investment on training, and a lack of need for personal development. On the other hand, Lean organizations understand the value of expecting their employees to be high performers and therefore invest in them. Doing this allows organizations to make the best use of their staff members' ideas, thoughts, and suggestions that lead to improvement.

# Incorporating Lean into Your Organization (continued)

- **Building a Lean Foundation** (continued)
  3.13
  - The top of the pyramid represents Problem Solving
    - Once your Lean system is solidly in place, you can focus on continuously improving your systems.
  - The key principles of continuous improvement are:
    - Always go and see for yourself (genchi genbutsu)
      - Never assume or believe what you are told.
    - Become a learning organization
      - Encourage or require all members to grow and evolve.

# 3 Key Concepts of Lean

- **Waste**
  - It is the opposite of value.
    - Represents anything we do not want or is a result that has no value
      - Eliminating waste lies at the root of most, if not all, Lean processes.
    - In his book *Toyota Production System*, Taiichi Ohno says:
      "In production, 'waste' refers to all elements of production that only increase cost without adding value – for example, excess people, inventory, and equipment."

Creating a constant flow of work, reducing work in progress, and minimizing variation delays and defects are the cornerstones of Lean organizations. The goal is to continuously indentify wasteful activities and remove them. Another hidden form of waste is overburden. This occurs when the results that are expected to be delivered from a process cannot be achieved because the people/processes are not equipped to deal with the workload imposed on them. The customer and Agile project manager must keep these areas of inefficiencies in mind when creating the feature list, and they must filter out as much waste and variation as possible before assigning it to the team.

# 3 Key Concepts of Lean (continued)

- **Complexity**
    - Another factor that can cause waste is complexity. There are four aspects to complexity:
        - **Size** (how many parts are involved in the process)
        - **Volume** (the size of the process)
        - **Density** (the relationship of size to volume)
        - **Time** to complete a product cycle
    - The smaller these parts are, the simpler the system is.
        - Increasing any of these items will increase complexity.
        - This means that in order to make a process lean and efficient, we should make its components simple and straightforward.

Valuable resources are needlessly consumed by waste. For example, assigning a team member to research a new technology that is beyond the technical capabilities of the project team is a form of wasting resources; waste also includes developing solutions that are costly to maintain. To overcome this problem, research projects should be time-boxed into Spike Solutions and either abandoned or adopted at the end of the allocated time.

# 3 Key Concepts of Lean (continued)

## ■ Variation

2.11

- All processes have variation regardless of the level of desirability.
  - Variations in production inevitably causes waste.
  - The key to Lean processing is identifying the cause of variations and resolving them where possible.
- Variations usually arise from three key areas:
  - System Variations
  - Special Cause Variations
  - Structural Variations

# Variance and Trend Analysis (continued)

- **Types of Variation** (continued)
  - **System Variations:** These variations arise from common, random, systemic causes
    - An example is an improperly calibrated measurement device
    - To reduce this type of variation, you need to change the system by identifying the root cause(s) of the variation and addressing that specific problem.

  - **Special Cause Variations:** These variations are caused by an assignable event
    - For example, your sales go down because of a competing product being introduced to the marketplace at a much lower price than your product.
    - To reduce special cause variations, find out what is causing them and examine how it impacts performance.
    - There may be ways that you can minimize the negative effects and boost the positive effects.

# Variance and Trend Analysis (continued)

- **Types of Variation** (continued)
    - **Structural Variation:** These variations happen because of cycles or long-term trends.
        - For example, you may sell a particular product only during a particular holiday. You often cannot address this type of variation directly (for example, you can't cancel Christmas or the 4th of July).
        - However, you may be able to make changes to reduce the impact of the cycle or trend.

Another form of waste in Lean is a result of movement. In manufacturing, this type of waste occurs when you move material or information from one place to another, with no obvious benefit. For example, you may hand carry a package of sealed tools from the production to the assembly line, but that movement does not create any value for the customer. In fact it is lost time because it delays your product or service from getting to your customers.

All the same, another form of waste in Lean can result from excessive movement to an existing structure.

This same concept can be applied to Agile teams in terms of constantly shuffling employees across different teams. To illustrate this point, imagine you have two teams of five people, Team A and Team B. Team A consistently outperforms Team B on delivering projects. In order to improve Team B's performance, the director of the organization suggest swapping two people between Team A onto Team B, in the hopes that the high performance will inspire the underperformers. But given what we know about the stages of Storming, Forming, Norming, and Performing, both teams are going to experience a drop in productivity and there is no guarantee that the swap will be beneficial. On the other hand, an Agile/Lean organization realizes that the best approach to improving the performance of Team B without impacting the productivity of Team A is to train Team B to improve its performance. In other words, teach individual members how to fill in their performance gaps as a team so they can grow and learn to work together effectively as a whole.

# Identifying Opportunities

- **Continuous Improvement**
    - Lean processes must not be one-time events.
        - Your path toward improvement should be a continuous cycle.
        - The most important part of this goal is creating a commitment to constant learning and knowledge management.
        - This can be achieved through organizational problem-solving, a commitment to cyclical Lean efforts and the PDCA cycle.

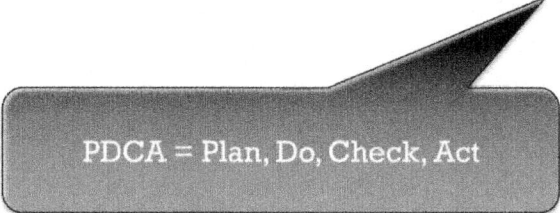

PDCA = Plan, Do, Check, Act

The PDCA cycle is beyond the scope of this course but it would be useful to do some independent study into the concept to obtain a better understanding of Lean.

# Systematic Improvements

## 20 Key Elements of Lean Organizations
- The customer is the starting and ending point.
- Think simplicity.
- Reduce or remove waste.
- Think in terms of process.
- Increase visibility and transparency wherever possible.
- Encourage routine and standardization.
- Make flow as constant and smooth as possible.
- Pull at the customer's rate, rather than pushing product through.
- Get the timing right. Starting work at the optimal time will increase flexibility and reduce waste and risk.
- Be proactive and preventative rather than reactive.

# Systematic Improvements (continued)

## ■ 20 Key Elements of Lean Organizations (continued)

- Keep production and process timelines as short as possible.
- Make continuous improvement a priority for everyone.
- Encourage internal and external players to be partners rather than competitors.
- Create a supply chain that results in value.
- Remember Gemba: Go to where the action is and seek the facts.
- Reduce variation where possible.
- Encourage participation and accountability from all employees.
- When making changes, start with the smallest component and build up.
- Build trust internally and externally by sharing information and acting as a partner.
- Build and distribute knowledge throughout the organization.

# Systematic Improvements (continued)

- **Kaizen**
  - Japanese for "improvement," or "change for the better"
    - Refers to a philosophy that focuses upon continuous improvement of processes
      - Used in:
        - *Manufacturing*
        - *Engineering*
        - *Game development*
        - *Business management*
    - It has also been applied in healthcare, psychotherapy, life-coaching, government, banking, and other industries.

# Systematic Improvements (continued)

- **Kaizen** (continued)
  - When applied in the workplace and used in the business context it refers to activities that continually improve all functions
    - Involves all employees from the CEO to the assembly line workers.
    - Also applies to processes such as purchasing and logistics
      - Cross organizational boundaries into the supply chain.
      - By improving standardized activities and processes kaizen aims to eliminate waste.

A major issue that is encountered during projects is breakdown in communication between the technical team and the customer. Specifically, this communicative roadblock occurs when it comes to using technical terms to resolve problems. For example, a customer may complain that an application doesn't display enough users when a search is done and the developer responds by increasing the number of results returned from 100 rows to 500, only to find out that what the customer really meant is that there weren't enough rows being displayed. However, making the change to return 500 rows increased the system response time from 2 seconds to 10 seconds, and the customer is now upset because not only was the problem not fixed, but the application is now worse. In this common scenario, both the customer and developer were correct in their understanding of the problem, but their technical interpretation of the solution didn't match. This repeated cycle of miscommunication, and the time required to resolve it, all contributes to waste.

Agile attempts to prevent this problem by placing the customer in close proximity to the developer. This form of pairing allows the developer to get immediate feedback from the customer by simply Leaning over and asking, 'Is this what you wanted?' In traditional projects where time gets wasted in dialogs floating back and forth through e-mail, improvement in communication through close contact impresses customers. And that is what creates customer value.

# Systematic Improvements (continued)

## ■ Kaizen Events

- Where an individual or a team uses a specific approach to tear down and rebuild a process or product so that it functions more efficiently, with less waste and more value.
- Kaizen events, also known as Kaikaku, typically take place at five different levels.

**Level 1: Individual**
**Level 2: Mini Point Kaizen**
**Level 3: Kaizen Blitz**
**Level 4: Flow Kaizen**
**Level 5: Supply Chain Kaizen**

# Kaizen Events

## ■ Level 1: Individual

- Individuals should constantly strive to reduce waste and improve efficiency in their own processes at their own workstations.
    - They should keep records of ideas for additional improvement.

## ■ Level 2: Mini Point Kaizen

- At the next level, individuals work with their team (typically about six people) to improve their workspace.
    - They may change a process or change work flows.
    - This level is often done on the fly or through one- or two-day workshops.

# Kaizen Events (continued)

- **Level 3: Kaizen Blitz**
    - This level is also known as a Point Kaizen. It is similar to a Mini Point Kaizen but is longer (usually three to five days) and involves larger work teams and sometimes outside parties.
        - These events typically address bigger issues, such as large workspace changes or cross-departmental process changes.

- **Level 4: Flow Kaizen**
    - At this level, many people from different departments in the organization work to improve cross-functional value streams.
    - They may be led by a Product Manager and/or be assisted by outside consultants.
        - An example would be a plan to change packaging and shipping methods – the marketing, packaging, shipping, and transporting teams would all need to be involved.
    - These events typically take several weeks to three months.

# Kaizen Events (continued)

## Level 5: Supply Chain Kaizen
- These events are very similar to Level 4, except they involve other organizations.
  - In the example above, where the plan is to change packaging and shipping methods, third party transportation companies and the outsourcers who provide packaging materials may be involved.
  - A Product Manager and consultants are almost always present.
  - These types of projects can take months or years.

# Method Tailoring

- **What is it?**  Sec. 2
    - A process of determining the appropriate changes required between contexts creating a systematic approach for the specific project situation
        - Potentially, almost all Agile methods are suitable for method tailoring
        - Situation appropriateness can be considered as a distinguishing characteristic between Agile methods and traditional software development methods
            - The practical implication is that Agile methods allow project teams to adapt working practices according to the needs of individual projects
    - Extreme Programming (XP) makes the need for method adaptation explicit
        - One of the fundamental ideas of XP is that no one process fits every project
            - Practices should be tailored to the needs of individual projects

# Method Tailoring (continued)

- **Theory vs. Practice**
  - The reality of organizations is that they don't come in a very neatly packaged configuration to which we can apply a single project management methodology.
    - For example, the practice of assigning a single Agile project manager will likely be unfeasible for large, complex projects.
    - On such projects, there are typically multiple Agile project managers who need to be represented in any major decisions that impact their domain of ownership.
      - Insisting that the business designate a single person in such projects ignores the reality that no one person in today's complex organizations can be the chief of all answers.

# Method Tailoring (continued)

- **Theory vs. Practice** (continued)
  - To customize the single Agile project manager practice on a project, there is nothing wrong with having multiple Agile project managers.
    - The main driver is that all are in agreement about prioritizing the backlog and performing the other roles that are traditionally performed by a single Agile project manager.
      - It may not be an elegant solution, but it is a practical one that makes it possible for Agile to scale.
  - Successful Agile implementation requires the freedom to selectively adopt, adapt, and apply the Agile practices that are best suited to delivering projects successfully.
    - Insisting that an Agile method (or any method for that matter) must be implemented exactly as it was originally conceived for all projects becomes an obstacle to its adoption in many organizations and projects.

# Method Tailoring (continued)

- **Agile Adoption Strategies**
  - There are two ways organizations adopt Agile:
    - *Wholesale adoption strategy.* This involves the big bang implementation of Agile practices.
    - *Incremental adoption strategy.* This is the "cherry picking" approach where a specific set of Agile practices are introduced gradually.
  - Introducing Agile using the wholesale adoption strategy should be treated like all other types of process improvements that change organizational cultures.
    - It should not be treated simply as a change to an organization's project management approach, software development methodology, or one that only impacts the IT department.
      - It certainly should not be delegated to or driven by a single department (IT).

# Method Tailoring (continued)

- **Agile Adoption Strategies** (continued)
  - Like any effort that attempts to change a culture it should be anticipated as a huge challenge.

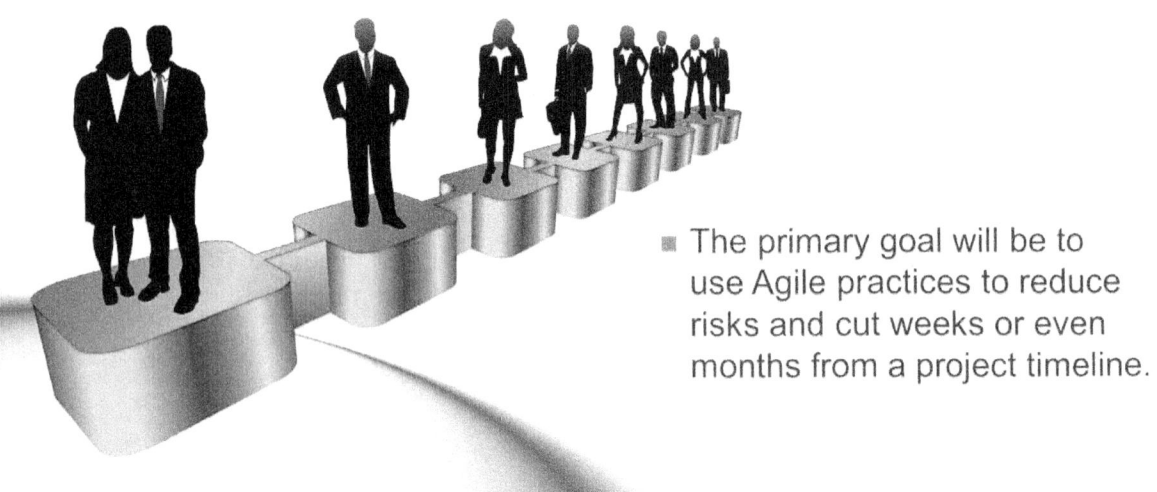

  - The primary goal will be to use Agile practices to reduce risks and cut weeks or even months from a project timeline.

# Incorporating Feedback

- **Understanding the Process and Your Project**
    - In order to improve the process by identifying what's working and what's not working in the current process, you must provide a means to incorporate feedback from:
        - Code that has been delivered
        - Input provided by the team
        - Suggestions from the customers
        - Dialogue with the customers
    - It requires the ability to not let your mind get locked on one area, but rather, being mindful so that you can be aware of what's going on in multiple areas.
        - Use the 5 Whys approach when good and bad situations arise.

Retrospectives provide an opportunity for Agile teams to provide feedback about a project and a chance for the Agile project manager to find ways to remove any impediments that could improve the team's performance. A good technique to incorporate into retrospectives is the Six Sigma tool known as the 5W's.

This approach to incorporating feedback starts by peeling away the layers of symptoms that can lead to the root cause of a problem. It entails repeatedly asking the question "Why"? Five is a good rule of thumb, but it is not requirement. What you'll find is that as you ask one question, it will inevitably lead to another. All the same, you may discover that you will need to ask the question fewer or more times than five before you find the issue related to the problem.

It's common that the same thoughts are shared by team members and will reappear during each retrospective. The key to improvement, however, is that if an issue has been brought up previously, the actions that have been taken or are being taken to remedy the problem must be determined. That is keeping in the spirit of continuous improvement. Conversely, if the same questions keep resurfacing with no resolution attached to the problem, then you need to ask yourself, "Where is the information being gathered from the retrospectives going?"

# Example of Incorporating Feedback

| Kano Questionnaire | |
|---|---|
| **Function form of the question**<br><br>How would you feel if the automatic reminder notification email feature **WAS** available for this release? | ☐ I like it that way<br>☐ It must be that way<br>☐ I am neutral<br>☐ I can live with it that way<br>☐ I dislike it that way |
| **Dysfunction form of the question**<br><br>How would you feel if the automatic reminder notification email feature **WAS NOT** available for this release? | ☐ I like it that way<br>☐ It must be that way<br>☐ I am neutral<br>☐ I can live with it that way<br>☐ I dislike it that way |

To increase customer satisfaction and reduce customer dissatisfaction, companies have to offer attractive quality attributes in new products as well as eliminate possible defects on must-be quality attributes.

There are different types of relationship between quality attributes and customer satisfaction. Product quality elements are classified into:

1. Indifferent quality attribute
2. Reverse quality attribute
3. Must-be quality attribute
4. One-dimensional quality attribute
5. Attractive quality attribute
6. Questionable quality attribute

**Note: You are not required to know the Kano Model/Questionnaire for the exam. The purpose of this example is to provide you with a specific technique that is used to obtain feedback from customers about the value delivered in a product.**

# Example of Incorporating Feedback (continued)

- **Collecting the Voice of the Customer**
    - The customer can answer each part of the question in one of six different ways:
        1. Indifferent quality attribute (I)
        2. Reverse quality attribute (R)
        3. Must-be quality attribute (M)
        4. One-dimensional quality attribute (O)
        5. Attractive quality attribute (A)
        6. Questionable attribute (Q)

Attractive quality attribute: customer satisfaction will occur if full functionality is provided, however, the customer will not be dissatisfied if the functionality is absent.

**Indifferent quality attribute (I), customer** does not care whether the feature is there or not.

**Reverse quality attribute (R),** customer is satisfied when it is not functional and dissatisfied when it is functional

**Must-be quality attribute (M),** customer does not realize the feature is even provided, and does not increase their satisfaction level. However, strong customer dissatisfaction will occur if the feature is not provided.

**One-dimensional quality attribute (O),** the degree of customer satisfaction is proportional to functional fulfillment. In other words, the more functionality provided the higher level of customer satisfaction.

**Attractive quality attribute (A),** customer satisfaction will occur if full functionality is provided, however, the customer will not be dissatisfied if the functionality is absent.

**Questionable attribute (Q),** signifies that the question was phrased incorrectly, or that the person interviewed misunderstood the question or crossed out a wrong answer by mistake.

# Example of Incorporating Feedback (continued)

1.5

### Indentifying the Minimal Marketable Feature

| Feature | I | R | M | O | A | Q | Category |
|---|---|---|---|---|---|---|---|
| Reminder notification feature | 10 | 2 | 2 | 1 | 3 | 0 | Indifferent |
| Voice recognition | 2 | 1 | 5 | 2 | 7 | 5 | Attractive |
| Spell checker | 2 | 2 | 9 | 2 | 1 | 4 | Must-have |
| GPS | 3 | 4 | 3 | 7 | 1 | 3 | One Dimensional |

Distribution of Results from Survey: based on 20 people

The customer completes the survey using the established levels of criteria. Individual attributes are totaled, and the highest ones are placed in the Category section.

For example, in this illustration when it came to understanding how 20 customers felt about a Voice Recognition feature being included in a new product.

2 people were indifferent.

1 person rated it as a reverse quality.

5 people rated it as a must-be quality.

2 people rated it as a one-dimensional quality.

7 people rated it as an attractive quality.

5 people rated it as a questionable quality.

As a result, the feature was categorized as being an Attractive quality to the customer.

# ✚ Reinforcement Training

## Questions & Exercises

### ■ Time to Test your New Knowledge!
Take the next PMI-ACP the practice quiz.

# Exercise 6
**Identify Existing Wasteful Process Elements by Challenging them with New Process Elements in to Order Help the Organization become more Efficient**

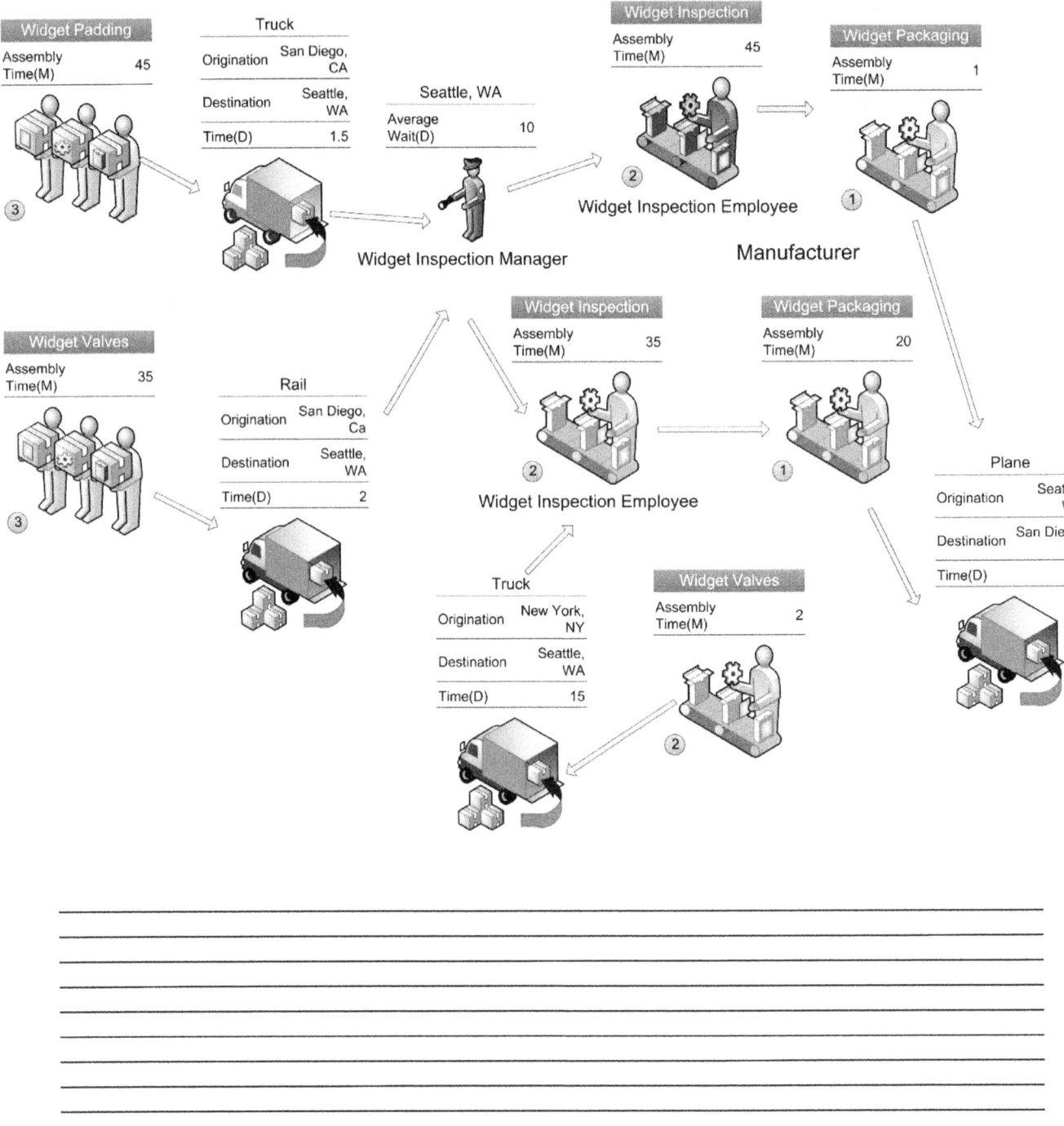

*Image available for view online at: www.pmiacptraining.com/continuous_improvement/exercise5.hm*

# Module 6 Quiz

## Exam Practice Questions

1. Lean has just been used to optimize the workflow at a company. Which of the following BEST describes what would come next?
    - A. Six Sigma quality improvement implementation
    - B. Higher quality and lower production
    - C. Official Three Sigma Waste Reduction Plan
    - D. Creation of a new organizational chart

2. All of the following are forms of waste, EXCEPT:
    - A. Under-Utilized Resources
    - B. Movement
    - C. Transportation
    - D. Error Handling

3. Which of the following is a specific type of Lean waste?
    - A. Breakdown
    - B. Complexity
    - C. Rejects
    - D. Error Handling

4. It has been brought to the attention of the product manager that the defect rate in the widgets his project is responsible for has increased twofold since the introduction of the company's laser controlled optical slicer. To repair the problem, it will cost the company an additional $500,000.00 and will decrease their profit margin by 4%. The product manager decides to adjust the release plan to get back on course, based on the original strategy. The preceding can BEST be described as:
    - A. Earned value rules
    - B. Money already spent
    - C. Waste
    - D. Defined control thresholds

5. The product manager needed to convince the executive team that adding more developers to the project in order to reach the project deadline would provide little benefit. In fact, because of the time required to ramp up the new team members, it would likely cause further delays to the project. To visually explain this to the executives, the product manager used an Ishikawa diagram, which is also known as:
    - A. Influence diagram
    - B. Process flow diagram
    - C. Kaizen diagram
    - D. Cause and effect diagram

6. Speedy Dial Aeronautic Parts manufactures widgets for a large government-funded space exploration program. In order for the company to remain in compliance and maintain good standing with its buyer, all of its parts must be delivered within Three Sigma of the specifications. What is the accuracy level of Three Sigma ($3\sigma$)?
    - A. 99.985%
    - B. 99.73%
    - C. 95.46%
    - D. 68.27%

7. ZipFast Auto Parts recently started working with a new vendor to provide windshield wipers that the company will distribute in the retail stores. Since switching to the new vendor, customers of ZipFast Auto Parts have begun receiving complaints that the new windshield wipers are leaving scratches on drivers' windshield and affecting their ability to drive. When the product manager informs the new vendor of the problem, the vendor adamantly insists that its windshield wipers cannot be the cause because the company's quality control measures require that every product leaving the assembly line is visually inspected and documented by three quality control managers who use a variety of quality assurance tools and techniques. Which aspect of the empirical process control model is the new vendor leveraging?
    A. Inspection
    B. Histogram
    C. Pareto chart
    D. Cause and effect diagram

8. Which of the following quality theories reduces inventory costs by having materials or goods arrive right when they are needed?
    A. Gold Plating
    B. Kaizen Theory
    C. Total Quality Management
    D. Just in Time

9. The Java Architects is a software consulting company that embraces the Agile methodology. As such, the company requires all of its teams to conduct Retrospectives at the end of each iteration. Conducting retrospectives on a regular basis is MOST closely aligned with which of the following management philosophies?
    A. Total Quality Management
    B. Kaizen Theory
    C. Just in Time
    D. Zero Defects

10. A global healthcare provider has recently begun experiencing a high employee attrition rate. The CEO has asked the Human Resources department and managers to compile a report that shows the overall history of employee satisfaction within the company and to compare it to the current employee satisfaction rate. Upon reading the report, the CEO comes across a diagram that reveals an alarming trend: The highest level of dissatisfaction and the largest turnover rate took place immediately following periods during which the work week spiked up to 57 hours prior to the release of a new project. Which of the following diagrams would MOST likely show the various factors that may be connected to potential causes or effects the CEO is seeing?
    A. Histogram
    B. Pareto chart
    C. Ishikawa diagram
    D. Value-stream diagram

11. Which of the following BEST describes modern day Lean?
    A. A set of tools designed to improve flow and reduce waste during business process
    B. A set of tools used to control business processes by reducing defects
    C. A set of software tools used to control business processes by reducing defects
    D. A set of software tools used to control business processes by reducing defects

12. Which of the following BEST describes Six Sigma?
    A. A set of software tools used to control business processes by reducing defects
    B. A set of software tools designed to improve flow and reduce waste during business process
    C. A set of tools used to control business processes by reducing defects
    D. A set of tools designed to improve flow and reduce waste during business process

13. Which of the following would LEAST likely be a Lean principle?
    A. Leveling out work for the production of a product
    B. Creating multiple variations for the production of a product
    C. Creating continuous flow for the production of a product
    D. Using a pull production for the production of a product

14. When an organization truly becomes Lean their IT architectures morphs into Lean operations, and operations morph into Lean IT architectures. What would BEST describe the result of this transformation?
    A. The next step would be to create a new product of the system
    B. The two become indistinguishable from each other
    C. The two entities would be modeled into a Six Sigma system
    D. The next step would be to document the process into requirements

15. Which of the following would LEAST likely be a principle of continuous improvement
    A. Minimize changes to your business process
    B. Encourage members to grow and evolve
    C. Always go and see for yourself
    D. Never assume or believe what you are told

16. All of the following are the cornerstones of Lean organizations, EXCEPT:
    A. Implementing quality control techniques
    B. Minimizing productivity variation
    C. Reducing work in progress,
    D. Creating a constant flow of work

17. In order to improve a process as a means to identify what's working and what's not working in the current process, all of the following are good sources of feedback EXCEPT:
    A. Suggestions from customers in demo meetings
    B. Input provided by the team during retrospectives
    C. Code that has been delivered at the end of an iteration
    D. Annual lessons learned sessions with the customer

18. Retrospectives provide an opportunity for Agile teams to provide feedback about a project and a chance for the Agile project manager to find ways to identify and remove impediments that could improve the team's performance. Given that, which of the following is the BEST technique to incorporate into retrospectives?
    A. The Six Sigma 5W's technique
    B. A Histogram tool
    C. Pareto Velocity Charts
    D. Gantt facilitation tool

19. Which of the following would be the MOST effective way to accomplish Agile adoption when a corporate cultural change is required?
    A. By introducing the change to all aspects of the business
    B. By introducing the change to just the IT department
    C. By controlling the scope of change to just the software development methodology
    D. By controlling the scope of change to just the project management methodology

20. When applying Agile practices to deliver a project, Agile project managers must have the freedom to do all of the following, EXCEPT
    A. Require that all Agile principles be applied
    B. Selectively apply Agile practices
    C. Selectively adapt Agile practices
    D. Require that all Agile practices be applied

# Module 6 Quiz Answers

1. Answer: A

   Explanation: Answer A is the most logical one because after a company has used Lean to improve its business processes, the next step would be to improve the quality of its output. In other words, it wouldn't make much sense to improve the speed at which you are delivering low quality. Three Sigma reduction plan is a fabricated option. Creating a new organizational chart could happen as a result of the new Lean, but there is no indication that the creation of a new organizational chart is required. Therefore, the next logical step would be to move into the quality improvement phase.

2. Answer: D

3. Answer: B

4. Answer: C

   Explanation: When a product requires additional inspection or repair as a result of a defect, waste is created.

5. Answer: D

   Explanation: Ishikawa diagrams are also known as cause and effect diagrams and fishbone diagrams. These diagrams show how an effect (or defect) relates to potential causes and sub-causes.

6. Answer: B

   Explanation: Six Sigma is considered to be the highest level of quality, which is 99.999%; Three Sigma is the next level down, which is 99.73%. Two Sigma is 95.46%, and One Sigma is 68.2%.

7. Answer: A

   Explanation: The vendor is using frequent inspection and adaption from the empirical process control model to adjust processes that are imperfectly defined and to generate unpredictable and unrepeatable outputs.

8. Answer: D

   Explanation: This scenario describes the Just in Time theory, which involves receiving goods or materials just before they are needed. The idea behind this theory is to reduce the cost of inventory. But to implement this strategy, a company must be very efficient with a high focus on quality; otherwise, coordinating and knowing when the goods must arrive will not work.

9. Answer: B

   Explanation: The purpose of retrospectives is to learn what worked well, what didn't, and what could be improved for the benefit of future iterations. Taking these findings and using them to improve processes is a form of continuous improvement, or the application of Kaizen Theory. In contrast, Total Quality Management embeds into employees the mindset that engaging in continuous improvement activities is a good thing, and as a result, employees will be more inclined to participate in continuous improvement activities like Retrospectives. Just in Time is when inventory and goods are obtained just before they are needed; and Zero Defects focuses on achieving zero defects as part of meeting quality requirements.

10. Answer: C

    Explanation: The correct answer is cause and effect diagram, also known as an Ishikawa diagram and a fishbone diagram.

11. Answer: A
    Explanation: Modern day Lean can best be described as a set of tools designed to improve flow and reduce waste during business process. The key word software is what makes the other options wrong because Lean does not have to be implemented using software. Six Sigma focuses on reducing defects through higher standards of quality.

12. Answer: C
    Explanation: The best answer is a set of tools used to control business processes by reducing defects. The key word software is what makes the other option wrong because Six Sigma does not have to be implemented using software. Lean is as a set of tools designed to improve flow and reduce waste during business process.

13. Answer: B
    Explanation: The key word variations is what make this the best answer because Lean emphasizes reducing product variations. The other options are all Lean principles

14. Answer: B
    Explanation: The best answer to this question is that the two become indistinguishable from each other.

15. Answer: A
    Explanation: This can be a tricky one because you may have confused change with variation. Change is associated with continuous improvement and that is a Lean principle. However, minimizing variation is goal of Lean. Lean project manager must always be willing to walk the shop floor and go see things for themselves. So the best answer to this answer question can be obtained through the process of elimination by knowing that the other options are explicit Lean principles.

16. Answer: A
    Explanation: This can be a tricky one because of the key word quality control. Quality control is associated with Six Sigma. However, utilizing Lean principles will invariably improve the quality of production. Nonetheless, the best answer to this answer question can be obtained through a process of elimination by knowing that the other options are explicit Lean principles.

17. Answer: D
    Explanation: Annual lessons learned sessions is not a good option for obtaining feedback in comparison to the other options because annual sessions do not encourage immediate feedback for improvement and one of the problems with "lessons learned sessions" in comparison to retrospectives is that you want immediate feedback that can be acted upon.

18. Answer: A
    Explanation: Using the Six Sigma 5W's technique is a great way to dig deeper into problems during retrospectives. It encourages participants to iteratively question "Why" something happened, up to 5 times.

19. Answer: A
    Explanation: When a corporate cultural change is required it is most effective to introduce the changes to all aspects of the business. Doing so creates less implementation resistance and ensures that everyone in the organization is working toward the same objectives.

20. Answer: D
    Explanation: In order to successfully deliver an Agile project, Agile project managers must have freedom to selectively apply and adapt the Agile *practices* that work before for their project. This encourages method tailoring. However, the *principles* of Agile must be vigorously enforced and not selectively applied as they establish the foundation for all of the practices.

# Module 6
## Summary

- ✓ Explained What it Means to Be Lean
- ✓ Examined How Quality Improvement is Achieved
- ✓ Combined Lean/Six Sigma into Agile
- ✓ Proposed Ways to Incorporate Lean into Your Organization
- ✓ Illustrated How to Identify Systematic Improvements
- ✓ Opportunities Analyzed Kaizen Events
- ✓ Used Method Tailoring to Gracefully Transition into Being Agile

# Full Length Practice Exam

1. Which of the following BEST describes the "list of requirements" in Agile?
   A. Task list
   B. Release Plan
   C. Feature list
   D. Design Stories

2. While looking at the team's burndown chart, the project manager notices that have performed perfectly and are keeping up with their velocity estimation for the past 3 iterations. This time he notices an upward spike around day 5 and 6 of the iteration? What can we assumed happened on day 5 and 6?
   A. Work was added during the of the iteration
   B. Work was removed
   C. A new development resource was added
   D. A new development resource was removed

3. A business analyst discovers a risk in the middle of the iteration. When should he bring up the new risk?
   A. During the next iteration planning meeting
   B. After the next daily standup
   C. By sending an email to all of the stakeholders and team members
   D. By immediately calling a meeting of the team members to discuss it

4. You have two Agile teams located in different countries that are having problems communicating. As a product manager what would be the BEST way to get started at resolving this problem?
   A. Schedule a daily stand-up at a mutual time for both teams to attend
   B. Tell the executives that they need to co-locate the teams
   C. Transfer the remote team to a new project
   D. Only assign work to teams that they can do in alone

5. Only selecting projects that deliver the maximum amount of value to customers by prioritizing which business features to work on based on business value, then managing the projects in a visible portfolio, can BEST be described as:
   A. Lean portfolio management
   B. Project value compositioning
   C. Corporate project valuating
   D. Value Stream Analysis

6. Which of the following BEST describes the technique used when there is a desire to make a collective decision among individuals, in a non-judgmental setting, to discuss a specific agenda item with the goal of coming up with a plan of action?
   A. Charter review
   B. Release plan meeting
   C. Iteration planning meeting
   D. Brainstorming

7. Which of the following is NOT part of the Manifesto for Agile Software Development?
   A. Working software over comprehensive documentation
   B. Teams and interactions over processes and tools
   C. Customer collaboration over contract negotiation
   D. Responding to change over following a plan

8. What input would an Agile product manager measure Earned Value Management (EVM)?
   A. The Net Present Value
   B. The current ROI
   C. The number of iterations completed
   D. The total number of items in the Backlog

9. During the Team Estimation Game, which of the following BEST describes how team members arrange the story cards?
   A. Stories are arranged based on their size. Small stories are placed on the left side of the board and larger stories placed to the right.
   B. Stories are arranged based on their size. Larger stories placed to the right. and small stories are placed on the right side of the board.
   C. Stories are arranged based on their value. Small stories are placed on the left side of the board and larger stories placed to the right.
   D. Stories are arranged based on their value. Larger stories placed to the right. and small stories are placed on the right side of the board.

10. In XP, analysis, coding, design, and testing are performed when?
    A. Simultaneously throughout the iteration
    B. Sequentially
    C. At the end of the iteration
    D. At the beginning of each iteration

11. Which of the following BEST describes the advantage of using Kanban?
    A. Increasing the accuracy of a story estimation
    B. Measuring risk
    C. Monitoring risk in a work flow
    D. Helping identify waste in a process

12. When would be the least appropriate time to seek assistance from a Domain expert?
    A. When building the domain model
    B. When use cases and workflows are vague
    C. When identifying business rules
    D. When in need of a business definition

13. Which of the following is MOST likely to need a strategic report that provides the status of all projects taking place and what areas within each project need attention?
    A. The product manager
    B. The steering committee
    C. The product manager
    D. The Customer

14. Which of the following is the least beneficial way to use a spike solution?
    A. Making it quick and disposable
    B. To create a small program that performs a demonstration
    C. To obtain concrete data instead of speculation
    D. Making it large and reusable

15. What is MOST likely to be the communication commonality between the team on the product manager?
    A. Pair programming
    B. Code review
    C. Story estimating
    D. Product Backlog

16. Which of the following is the BEST means of sharing information between the team and the stakeholders?
    A. The most highly visible information radiators
    B. Emails
    C. Telephone calls
    D. Weekly meeting

17. A burndown chart is an example of:
    A. An information radiator
    B. A chart that graphs the work lost from operating in firefighter mode
    C. Risk estimation
    D. High velocity information

18. Which of the following is NOT a good example of using Lean-Agile in software development?
    A. Automating the build
    B. Just in Time
    C. Cumulative flow diagrams (CFD)
    D. Technical debt

19. Which of the following is NOT something that would be used on an XP team:
    A. a manual test coverage plan
    B. pair programing
    C. stand up meetings
    D. continuous integration

20. A project would use incremental delivery to:
    A. Decrease employee turn over
    B. Retain continuity on the project
    C. Get a quicker return on their investment
    D. Increase Kanban output

21. The smallest set of functionality that must be realized in order for the customer to perceive value can BEST be described as:
    A. Functionality return on investment
    B. Rate of return on investment
    C. A minimal marketable feature
    D. A threshold feature

22. After a story is completed during an iteration, when can it be discarded?
    A. As soon as the project ends
    B. As soon as it is done
    C. As soon as the iteration ends
    D. As soon as the work has been started

23. The Agile methodology is MOST closely aligned with:
    A. The Pareto Rule of 20%
    B. The hygiene theory
    C. Waterfall
    D. Townhall meetings

24. Which of the following provides the BEST example of the Participatory Decision-Model?
    A. Sending an email
    B. Team member showing up for meetings
    C. Developers checking code into the repository
    D. Product manager and customer coming up with ideas through the entire life of the project

25. During a daily stand-up meeting, several team members get distracted explaining the implementation details of tasks they are reporting on. What is the best course of action that should be taken to resolve this?
    A. Wait for the coach to intervene and manage the problem
    B. Allow the self-empowered team to resolve the situation by reminding everyone of the purpose of the stand-up meeting
    C. Do nothing, and let them solve the problem
    D. Make it a team discussion so everyone can contribute

26. Which of the following BEST describes how using a "spike story" reduces architectural risk?
    A. By removing uncertainty about technology
    B. By decreasing the teams estimation time
    C. By increasing team velocity
    D. It does not have an impact

27. On an Agile project, which of the following is NOT the responsibility of the customer?
    A. Writing acceptance test and criteria
    B. Defining business value currencies for the project
    C. Helping define data rules
    D. Adding new items to the iteration backlog

28. What are the 6 features (INVEST) that make up a well written story?
    A. Independent , Negotiable, Valuable, Estimable, Small, Testable
    B. Independent , Negotiable, Velocitized, Estimable, Small, Testable
    C. Incremental, Negotiable, Valuable, Estimable, Small, Testable
    D. Independent , Negotiable, Valuable, Easy, Small, Testable

29. The benefit in providing a persona is:
    A. that it allows the team to think of use cases that may have been overlooked.
    B. that it provides a name to attach the story to.
    C. that it makes the estimation process accurate.
    D. adds excitement to the development process.

30. Which of the following BEST describes the benefit of Continuous Integration?
    A. Make sure that the product is technologically shippable at any moment
    B. Increase team cooperation
    C. Increase team collaboration
    D. Maintains the Takt of the team

31. A story card is likely to contain:
    A. Developer assignments
    B. Implementation details
    C. The end-result that the customer values and successful completion criteria.
    D. Velocity required to complete

32. Which of the following BEST describes the benefit of using the Agile methodology in comparison to Waterfall?
    A. It is easier
    B. Risk is reduced because the length of the development time is shorter
    C. It does not require planning
    D. Better code is written

33. You are a new product manager introduced to a new organization that is starting Agile. What would be the BEST way to get them started?
    A. Ask someone to be the Agile Coach
    B. Start holding daily stand up immediately
    C. Have them start pair programming
    D. Introduce them to the Agile manifesto

34. What is technical debt?
    A. The amount of work that must be repaid toward bug fixes at the end of project due to taking shortcuts during development
    B. Lack of funds to complete a project
    C. Lack of value to complete project
    A. Lack of value found in a project that must be deposited to make ready for incremental delivery

35. Software tailoring can BEST be described as:
    A. Combining multiple Agile methods
    B. Cutting the length of the development cycles
    C. Cutting the size of the project
    D. Tuning a process to meet the needs of a specific project

36. Which of the following BEST describes a benefit seeing a demo performed at the end of an iteration:
    A. Keep the team focused on delivering value
    B. Sell the product to new customers
    C. Test the speed of the software
    D. Compare technical risks

37. How should the team estimate for nonfunctional requirements in the Backlog?
    A. Place them at the very beginning of the project backlog
    B. Save them until the very end of the project backlog
    C. Estimate them just like any other user story or product backlog item
    D. Estimate them using the non-functional velocity measurement

38. Which of the sequences below BEST describes what information is shared with stakeholder after Release Planning?
    A. Feasibility and chartering, scope, benefits, key dependencies, constraints, risks, and the release schedule
    B. Feasibility and chartering, iteration plan, retrospectives, key dependencies, constraints, risks, and the release schedule
    C. Team velocity, scope, benefits, retrospectives, dependencies, constraints, risks, and the release schedule
    D. Feasibility and chartering, scope, benefits, scrum of scrums, constraints, risks, and the release schedule

39. On an Agile project, who is responsible for making sure the project is producing value?
    A. Agile Coach
    B. product manager
    C. the business
    D. the Team

40. Alpha Team has a velocity of 13 points, and received 3 new ultra-high processor computers for their project as part of the contract. Delta Team has a velocity of 8 points and are still using their standard computers. A product manager new to Agile has joined the company and insists that Delta Team performs as well as the Alpha Team. How should Delta Team explain the difference in performance and set his expectation?
    A. Tell the product manager that the velocity of two separate teams cannot be compared
    B. Tell the product manager that Delta Team needs ultra-high processor computers also
    C. Tell the product manager Delta Team needs to management from him
    D. Tell the product manager to reduce the number of items in Delta Teams backlog

41. A high performance team would be expected to solve problems because they have been:
    A. Working with the Agile coach longer
    B. Self-empowered and self-organized
    C. Project management experience
    D. At the company longer

42. Which of the following BEST describes two similarities between XP and Scrum?
    A. They both place a high value on pair programming and automated build scripts
    B. They both place a high value respect and courage
    C. They both place a high value on commitment and courage
    D. They both place a high value on simplicity and openness

43. When should a product manager place a member on a fractional assignment?
    A. it should be done whenever possible
    B. when someone on the team has free-time
    C. when multiple projects end on the same iteration
    D. it should be avoided whenever possible

44. When would be the BEST time for the team to come together to discuss what worked well on a project and how they can improve value?
    A. During the iteration planning
    B. Over a team lunch
    C. During the retrospective meeting
    D. During stand-up meetings

45. Which of the following BEST describes the process used to analyze and "optimize the whole" during the flow of information in order to remove waste from a process and bring a service to a consumer?
    A. Value Stream Mapping
    B. Continuous Integration
    C. Story Decomposition
    D. Business Analysis

46. You are the product manager on a new team. After several weeks you begin to notice that although the team works well together on most days, they have an equal amount of days where there is a lot of conflict. What action should you take?
    A. Inform the team that conflict is a natural part of being a high performance team, and that they should strive to increase the amount of positive integrations to negative conflicting ones.
    B. Do nothing since they are only in conflict 50% of the time and perform well the other 50%. If the problem continues, find the people causing the conflict and move them to a new team.
    C. Immediately find the people causing the conflict and move them to a new team.
    D. Resolve the conflicts yourself so the team can stay focused on completing their work.

47. What would be the first step the team would take to start estimating their first set of stories?
    A. Sort the stories based on ideal time
    B. Divide the stories up by the teams velocity
    C. Agree upon a unit of measure for the story
    D. Sort the stories based on complexity

48. What is the BEST example of intrinsic value?
    A. What others are willing to pay
    B. The value of melting down a gold coin
    C. The legally defined value
    D. Value which arises because of an agreement

49. After the release planning session, which of the following can a stakeholder expect to have a better idea of about a project?
    A. Acceptance test criteria
    B. Members of the team
    C. Return on investment of the project
    D. Takt time of the project

50. On an Agile project, when would a stakeholder most likely use the opportunity to express dissatisfaction with the performance of the software that was delivered?
    A. During the review meeting
    B. During the go-no-go meeting
    C. During the daily stand-up
    D. During the iteration planning meeting

51. Release and iteration planning, pair programming and pair rotation, daily standup meetings and cross-functional teams are examples of:
    A. Knowledge sharing
    B. Risk-mitigation
    C. Go-no-go sessions
    D. Continuous improvement

52. If collaboration is sharing with the team, then cooperation can BEST be described as:
    A. Is working together to achieve a goal
    B. The smooth flow of work-in-progress from one team member to another
    C. The act of sharing knowledge, learning and building consensus.
    D. An activity that requires leadership

53. Using a tiered set of planning horizons allows project teams to:
    A. Plan at the latest responsible moment
    B. Create multiple cost estimates
    C. Create multiple versions of the product backlog
    D. Create a tiered burndown chart

54. An Agile team can BEST be described as:
    A. A well-organized, delivery team that is managed by a product manager
    B. Highly skilled, experienced professionals that refuse to work with documentation
    C. Cross-functional, collaborative and knows how to resolve conflict
    D. Cross-functional, collaborative and knows how to avoid conflict through planning

55. The three legs that make up the empirical process control are:
    A. Visibility, communication, refactoring
    B. Visibility, inspection, refactoring
    C. Visibility, inspection, adaptation
    D. Insight, inspection, adaptation

56. Which of the following BEST describes refactoring:
    A. Optimizing code with private modifiers
    B. Modifying existing code to use the factory design patterns
    C. Making changes to code without changing the external behavior
    D. Implementing code using just in time (JIT)

57. Which of the following is NOT a benefit of pair programming?
    A. Physically increases brain functions
    B. Enables developers to spend more time in flow
    C. Reduces focusing on a problem
    D. Encourages collaboration

58. A product manager would use velocity on a team to:
    A. Ensure the team is not over committing on estimates
    B. Estimate how much work a potential developer can perform
    C. Ensure the customer is not asking for too much
    D. Ensure the cpu speed of the all of the development computers are the same

59. A team has a known velocity of 14. Given the following, which stories should they pick?
    A. A = 2,
    B. B = 4,
    C. C = 3,
    D. D = 5,
    E. E = 7

    A. A, B, C, D
    B. A, B, C, E
    C. B, C, D
    D. A, B, C, D, E

60. A high-level initial estimate of the requirements maintained by the product manager throughout the entire project describes which of the following?
    A. A Sprint list
    B. A Backlog
    C. An Iteration
    D. A Timebox

61. The intersection of a trend line for work remaining (or backlog) and the horizontal axis indicating the most probable completion of work at the point in time would be found in which graphical chart?
    A. Velocity graph
    B. Burn-up chart
    C. Execution chart
    D. Burndown chart

62. A product manager sits through a demonstration meeting for his product, and realizes that if changed the release schedule of a newly identified feature he could immediately increase the business value of the project without increasing the cost of implementation. By realizing this value and making this last minute adjustment which of the following BEST describes what he did to the project?
    A. Increase the ROI of the project
    B. Change the requirements specification
    C. Improved the quality of a feature in the product
    D. Increase risk of project failure

63. During this Team meeting everyone provides a status update to the other team members. It is a 10-5 minute 'semi-real-time' status meeting that allows participants to become aware of potential challenges as well as coordinate efforts to resolve difficult and/or time-consuming issues. This BEST describes:
    A. Collaboration meeting
    B. Brown Bag meetings
    C. Brevity meetings
    D. Daily Stand-ups

64. A team that focuses on delivering increments of functionality and removal of defects while making orderly process toward completing a release with potentially shippable functionality can BEST be described as:
    A. Business case development
    B. Incremental delivery
    C. Value driven development
    D. Iteration planning

65. Which of the following BEST describes the approach that Agile is based on?
    A. Empirical process control
    B. Feedback theory
    C. Automation theory
    D. Control engineering theory

66. Which of the following is NOT something an Agile Coach provides?
    A. Leadership
    B. Guidance
    C. Coaching
    D. Acrimony

67. When a well-defined set of inputs produce the same outputs every time within a defined process can be described as:
    A. Continuous improvement
    B. Anti-chaos theory
    C. No-chaos theory
    D. Defined process control

68. Which of the following does NOT contribute to the implementation of empirical process control?
    A. visibility
    B. inspection
    C. adaptation
    D. rework

69. Agile addresses the complexity of developing software through utilizing which of the following control requirements?
    A. Refactoring, repeatability and adaptation
    B. Visibility, repeatability and adaptation
    C. Visibility, inspection and adaptation
    D. Visibility, repeatability and continuous improvement

70. 5. How many roles exist in Scrum?
    A. 3
    B. 4
    C. 5
    D. 6

71. Who is responsible for the success of each iteration?
    A. The product manager
    B. The team
    C. The Agile coach
    D. The business

72. Who is responsible for making sure everyone is following the Agile rules?
    A. The team
    B. The product manager
    C. The Agile coach
    D. The business

73. Who is responsible for managing the ROI on an Agile project?
    A. The team
    B. The product manager
    C. The Agile coach
    D. The business

74. On an Agile project, how are items in the feature list organized?
    A. By placing the requirements with the highest level of risk at the bottom
    B. By placing the requirements within Team capabilities at the top
    C. By placing the requirements with the highest probability of highest ROI toward the top
    D. By placing the requirements on index cards and dropping them off a table

75. On a Agile project, how long is an iteration?
    A. undetermined
    B. Twice as long as an iteration
    C. Half of an iteration
    D. 5 business days

76. Which of the following BEST describes the maximum amount of time that should be spent in an Iteration Planning Meeting?
    A. An average of 4 hours
    B. No more than 6 hours
    C. A timeboxed 8 hours
    D. As long as it takes to complete the planning

77. An Agile team is discussing the priority levels of the feature list with the product manager. During this discussion they address things like the content, meaning and intentions of the feature list, then select how much of the feature list they can deliver on during the iteration. Given this, which of the following BEST describes where in the Agile development process the team is at?
   A. End of the previous iteration
   B. The beginning of the iteration
   C. In an iteration Demo Meeting
   D. In the first 4 hours of the Iteration Planning Meeting

78. On an Agile project, what's the difference between a feature list and a backlog?
   A. There is no difference
   B. The feature list contains the tasks required to complete the upcoming iterations, whereas the backlog contains all of the requirements to be delivered during the project.
   C. The backlog contains the tasks required to complete the upcoming iteration, whereas the feature list contains all of the non- functional requirements to be delivered during the project.
   D. The feature list contains the functional requirements to be completed the upcoming iteration, whereas the backlog contains all of the functional requirements to be delivered during the project.

79. Where would a developer MOST likely be expected to provide answers to the following questions: "What have you done on this project since yesterday", "What do you plan on doing on the project between now and tomorrow", and "What impediments are you currently facing that are preventing you from meeting your commitments?"
   A. The Daily stand-up
   B. ATBS report
   C. A TPS report
   D. A performance evaluation plan

80. An Agile Team is preparing to hold an informal, 4 hour meeting to show the product manager and interested stakeholders what was completed at the end of their iteration. What can this event BEST be described as?
   A. A wrap-up
   B. A planning Meeting
   C. A review meeting
   D. An iteration completion meeting

81. Immediately after an iteration review, but prior to the next planning meeting, which of the following activities is an Agile Facilitator MOST likely to do?
   A. Work with the product manager to update the backlog
   B. Work with the Team to reprioritize the backlog
   C. Work with the Customer to reprioritize the backlog
   D. Work with the Team by conducting a retrospective

82. Which Agile activity BEST constitutes the empirical inspection and adaptation practices?
   A. The retrospective
   B. The iteration planning meeting
   C. The charter meeting
   D. The empirical meeting

83. Who is responsible for updating the backlog?
   A. The stakeholders
   B. The stakeholders and the product manager
   C. The product manager and the Team
   D. The team

84. Which of the following are you LEAST likely to see on a backlog?
    A. Task description
    B. Hours of work remaining
    C. Status
    D. A vision statement that explains how the product will benefit the team

85. Which of the following would you LEAST likely discuss during a Iteration Planning meeting
    A. What will be developed in the next iteration
    B. Prioritization of features
    C. Dividing stories into tasks and estimates
    D. Group inspection of the work individuals accomplished the previous day

86. Jason is the Agile Coach on his project. Prior to the company switching to Agile, Jason was a product manager. During the Daily stand-up Jason often assigns tasks to the Team members, tells them how to solve the impediments, and requires them to solve breakdowns in customer communication themselves. He prides himself in being a hands-on Agile Coach but in reality which of following skills does he need to improve in order to be truly effective as an Agile Coach?
    A. Facilitation
    B. Time management
    C. Leadership skills
    D. All skills listed

87. The Fizzy Wizzy Fun Factory is holding the annual Go-Carting event on the same day that Susan's Team is scheduled to deliver set of crucial features TO their client. As the Agile Coach, she informs the CEO of the conflict and asks if the Team can be excused from the event. The Team has already agreed that they would rather reach their team goal, and honor their commitment instead of attending the Go-Carting event. Which of the following BEST describes how Susan should handle the event?
    A. Politely tell the CEO that the Team cannot attend the event, and leave it at that
    B. Ask the Team to each personally send an email pleading their case to the CEO
    C. Inform her Team that they should attend the event as requested by the CEO, and adjust the Sprint Backlog to reflect the schedule change
    D. Require the team to stay later the night before to complete their tasks

88. In order for Agile to work, what must the team have?
    A. Laptops and pairing stations
    B. Access to whiteboards and sticky pads
    C. Experienced developers and executive buy-in
    D. A visceral understanding of collective commitment and self-organization

89. On Scrum projects, which of the following BEST explains the benefit of bringing Sashimi to the team?
    A. It is the ultimate sign of appreciation for their hard work
    B. It signifies the team's dedication to hard work
    C. It enables them to reduce complexity to manageable levels
    D. It allows them prioritize their Product Backlog

90. All of the following are responsibilities of the Agile Coach, EXCEPT:
    A. Removing barriers between the development team and the product manager and customers so that the customer can drive development
    B. Showing the product manager how to use Agile to maximize project ROI
    C. Managing the team during the Daily Standup meeting
    D. Facilitating the Retrospective meetings

91. All of the following are questions addressed in the iteration planning process, EXCEPT:
    A. What can those funding the project expect to have changed once the project is finished?
    B. What progress will have been made by the end of each iteration?
    C. Why should those being asked to fund the project believe that the project is a valuable investment, and why should they believe that those proposing the project can deliver those predicted benefits?
    D. Which action items will be assigned to team members after each retrospective?

92. Which of the following BEST describes the minimum amount of planning necessary to start an Agile project?
    A. A vision and feature list
    B. A project plan and a feature list
    C. An ROI goal and a feature list
    D. Stakeholders and a vision

93. All of the following are true about the feature list, EXCEPT:
    A. It defines the functional and non-functional requirements that the system should meet to deliver the vision
    B. It should be prioritized and estimated
    C. It can be changed once the iteration has started
    D. It is dynamic and lives as long as the project does

94. Prior to starting an Agile project, in order to create estimates for the requirements in the feature list, which of the following is MOST important?
    A. The exact composition of the requirement
    B. The exact interaction of the requirement
    C. The mood of the people doing the work
    D. The size of the requirement relative to the others

95. During an Agile project, when you are creating estimates for requirements based on the feature list, which should influence your estimates the LEAST?
    A. Time required to create unit tests
    B. Time required for code reviews
    C. Time required for refactoring
    D. The preliminary estimates provided to stakeholder before the initial iteration planning meeting

96. What is the first artifact needed to manage an Agile project?
    A. A feature list
    B. A Project Charter
    C. A Project Plan
    D. A detailed Requirements Document

97. Which of the following would an Agile project NOT provide a report on?
    A. Exceptions that place during the project plan
    B. Response to exceptions the took place during the project plan
    C. The impact the exception had on the product plan
    D. How closely the project is moving in accordance with the initial project plan

98. Which of the following LEAST describe the Agile development process?
    A. self-organizing
    B. emergent
    C. rigid
    D. empirical

99. Which of the following reports would LEAST likely be used on an Agile project?
    A. A feature list report created at the start of previous iteration
    B. The feature list report created at the start of a new iteration
    C. A Changes report created to show the difference between the previous iteration feature list and the new iteration feature list
    D. A Gantt Chart

100. Which of the following pieces of information are you LEAST likely to see in a Change report?
    A. Changes that took place during a iteration
    B. Inspections that took place during a iteration
    C. Adaptations that took place during a iteration
    D. Program Evaluation Technique Reviews that took place during a iteration

101. You are the Agile coach on a team where the company has recently started to use Agile as their development methodology. During lunch, David, the Director of Engineering, comes to your office and says that he would like to set up in meeting in an hour with you and the Team to review the work that has been done. Unfortunately, the team is in the middle of an iteration but that does not matter to David. He wants information about what the team is working on now. Which of the following responses would be BEST?
    A. Immediately summon the team to attend the meeting
    B. Refuse to hold the meeting because it goes against the rules of Agile
    C. Offer to provide a Change report instead, and request that the review meeting be conducted at the end of the iteration
    D. Agree to hold the meeting but only at the end of the day because it is more convenient for the Team

102. Which of the following BEST describes Just in Time (JIT)
    A. A production strategy that strives to improve business return on investment by reducing in-process inventory carrying costs
    B. A production strategy that strives to improve risk management by reducing in-process inventory carrying costs
    C. A production strategy that strives to improve release planning by reducing in-process inventory carrying costs
    D. A production strategy that strives to improve business return on investment by reducing in-process failover

103. Which of the following BEST describes the Agile process:
    A. It only works when everything is visible, and everyone can inspect the progress to make recommended adaptations
    B. It only works when everyone attends the meetings, follows the direction of the Agile Coach and strong leadership is provided by the product manager
    C. It only works when everyone attends the meetings, follows the direction of the product manager and strong leadership is provided by the Agile Coach
    D. It only works when everything is flexible, and everyone can change the Sprint Backlog to make recommended adaptations

104. Which of the following LEAST describes a self-organizing team?
    A. It is unmanaged
    B. It must assume responsibility for planning its own work
    C. It must have a plan detailed enough to be meaningful and specific
    D. It must enable team members to remain synchronized

105. When more than one team is working on an Agile project it is referred to as?
    A. A Scaled Project
    B. An Ultra Agile
    C. An XScrum
    D. A Scaling Mechanism

106. All of the following are important steps when building a scaled project, EXCEPT:
    A. Build the infrastructure for scaling prior to scaling
    B. Deliver business value while building the scalable infrastructure
    C. Optimize the capabilities of the initial team
    D. Include one member from the newly created additional team to the initial scaling team

107. Which of the following is LEAST important to obtain while attending the daily stand-up:
    A. Commitments being made and checked on
    B. Identifying what each team member is working on
    C. Input from users that are non-stakeholders
    D. Work performed the previous day

108. The following image represents what in the Net Present Value (NPV) calculation?

$$(1+i)^{-t}$$

   A. The amount by which the future net cash flow will be discounted.
   B. The amount by which the present net cash flow will be discounted.
   C. The amount by which the future net cash flow will be incremented over a release.
   D. The sum of the current net cash flow will be discounted.

109. In Agile development, when a developer estimates a story point by gauging the amount of effort required to complete a task based on the amount of time she will have to focus exclusively on the task, with no interruptions, it is called:
    A. Alternative Time
    B. Velocity
    C. Ideal Time
    D. Timebox

110. When features are written so as to minimize the technical dependencies between them, the product manager has the greatest amount of flexibility to do what with them?
    A. Constrain
    B. Prioritize
    C. Assign to developers
    D. Weigh

111. The product manager is leading the Team to decide which features they should include in the Sprint Backlog first. They decide to select the most important features by identifying which features will bring the most benefits if implemented, as well as the penalty incurred if not implemented, on a relative scale of 1 to 9. This can BEST be described as:
    A. Darwinism estimation
    B. Value base computation estimate
    C. Relative prioritization
    D. Must-have prioritization

112. What is the difference between NPV and IRR?
   A. NPV is a measure of how much money a project can be expected to return in today's present value, whereas IRR is a measure of how quickly the money invested in the project will increase in value.
   B. There is no difference.
   C. IRR is a measure of how much money a project can be expected to return in today's present value, whereas NPV is a measure of how quickly the money invested in the project will increase in value.
   D. NPV is a measure of how much money a project can be expected to return in future value, and IRR is a measure of how quickly the money invested in the project will decrease in value.

113. In XP, how long is an iteration?
   A. 30 consecutive days
   B. 30 business days
   C. 1 - 3 weeks
   D. 5 Sprints

114. When a Team takes the opportunity to gather for a meeting and reflect on situations they encountered during a project, in an effort to better align their processes with their changing situations, what Agile tool are they said to be using?
   A. A retrospective
   B. A contingency review
   C. A lessons learned management session
   D. Brainstorming

115. The smallest set of functionality that must be realized in order for the customer to perceive value, BEST describes?
   A. minimum marketable feature
   B. story decomposition
   C. feature decomposition
   D. business case analysis

116. A product manager that creates a series of detailed planning horizons as a means to show that certain commitments to the project will be met is BEST described as:
   A. "done done" planning
   B. feature horizoning
   C. requirement analysis
   D. stakeholder management

117. Which of the following would NOT provide useful information in creating a Persona?
   A. A picture of the persona
   B. An age for the persona
   C. A name for the persona
   D. All of them are useful

118. John is the Product Manager working for the Dizzy Izzy Widget Company. On Monday morning he gathers the Team members in the room, hands out index cards, and asks each of them to start brainstorming possible catastrophes that might impact the project. Which of the following options BEST describes what John is trying to accomplish by doing this?
   A. scare the team into meeting their deadline
   B. create alternate development plans
   C. pragmatic planning
   D. create a risk census

119. During the planning game customers are responsible for:
    A. providing refreshments
    B. performing feasibility studies
    C. prioritizing
    D. requirements analysis

120. Which of the following is NOT considered during risk planning:
    A. Mitigation activities
    B. Transition indicators
    C. Dooms day scenarios
    D. Risk exposure

# Answers

1. Answer: C - Feature list

   Explanation: The backlog is the list of work the team must address during the next sprint. Features are broken down into tasks, which, as a best practice, should normally be between four and sixteen hours of work. See also: Source: Schwaber, Ken. Agile Project Management with Scrum. Pg. 7, par. 1

2. Answer: A - Work was added during the of the iteration

   Explanation: In this example, around day 5 and 6, some unpleasant surprises were discovered and led to an increase in remaining hours. When a burndown graph goes up even though the team is performing as expected, one can assume additional work was added to the project.

3. Answer: D - By immediately calling a meeting of the team members to discuss it

   Explanation: Risk needs to be address as soon as possible. An added benefit to working in an Agile open environment with close communication is that informal meetings can be called to resolve problems immediately.

4. Answer: A - Schedule a daily stand-up at a mutual time for both teams to attend

   Explanation: Coordinating schedules so that remote team can participate in meetings like daily standups alleviates many of the communications of remote teams. Although collocation is the recommended approach for Agile teams, virtual teams is a reality of the modern world that must be dealt with.

5. Answer: A - Lean portfolio management

   Explanation: "...delivers value to customer more quickly by prioritizing which business features to work on based on business value and then managing the project in a visible portfolio. We call this Lean portfolio management."

   Source: Alan Shalloway, Guy Beaver, James R. Trott. Lean-Agile Software Development. Pg. 59, par. 3

6. Answer: D - Brainstorming

   Explanation: Brainstorming is a technique that is used when there is a desire to make a collective decision. Specifically, it allows multiple individuals to discuss a specific agenda item with the goal of coming up with a plan of action. During the process, all of the individuals are encouraged to suggest ideas which then may be considered and discussed by the group as a whole. Depending on the team structure, all individual suggestions get recorded, or only the ones that the team decides on will be kept track of. Brainstorming sessions can also be used as a non-judgmental team building activity where participants are encouraged to offer ideas for discussion without fear of reproach.

7. Answer: B - Teams and interactions over processes and tools

   Explanation: The Agile Manifesto states, "Individuals and interactions over processes and tools", not teams

8. Answer: C - The number of iterations completed

   Explanation: You need four measurements to calculate AgileEVM metrics:

   The number of Iterations completed

   The total story points completed

   The total Actual Cost

   The total story points added to or removed from the release plan

9. Answer: A - Stories are arranged based on their size.

   Explanation: The team starts with a stack of cards containing stories or features. As the game progresses, story cards are physically arranged in a linear order based on their size. Small stories are placed on the left side of the board and larger stories placed to the right. For stories that have the same or similar size, they are stacked together in a group.

10. Answer: A - Simultaneously throughout the iteration

    Explanation: "Using simultaneous phases, an XP team produces deployable software every week. In each iteration, the team analyzes and, designs, codes and deploys a subset of features."

    Source: Shore, James & Warden, Shane. The Art of Agile Development. Pg. 18, par. 7

11. Answer: D - Helping identify waste in a process

    Explanation: Kanban helps identify waste by managing flow.

    Source: Alan Shalloway, Guy Beaver, James R. Trott. Lean-Agile Software Development. Pg. 100, par. 1

12. Answer: B - When use cases and workflows are vague

    Explanation: "Domain experts are ideal resources when building a domain model and identifying business rules, but workflow and usage issues are better derived from actual users."

    Source: Cohn, Mike. User Stories Applied. Pg. 58 para. 4

13. Answer: B - The steering committee

    Explanation: "What they [steering committee] need is a quick way to see the status of each project and spot what needs attention" Source: Cockburn, Alistar. Agile Software Development. Pg. 280 para. 3

14. Answer: C - To obtain concrete data instead of speculation

    Explanation: Ideally, spike solutions are small programs that demonstrate functionality that are created on the spur of the moment, and do not need to be reusable.

    Source: Shore, James & Warden, Shane. The Art of Agile Development. Pg. 336 - 337

15. Answer: D - Product Backlog

    Explanation: Code reviews, story estimating and pair programming are all activities where development teams share a common communication. The feature list is the only one that the average product manager would readily be able to discuss with the team.

16. Answer: A - The most highly visible information radiators

    Explanation: An Information radiator is a display posted in a place where people can see it as they work or walk by. It shows readers information they care about without having to ask anyone a question. This means more communication with fewer interruptions."

    Alistair Cockburn

17. Answer: A - An information radiator

    Explanation: An information radiator is a large, highly visible display used by software development teams to track progress.

18. Answer: D - Technical debt

    Explanation: Technical debt occurs on a project when we knowingly--usually because of pressure--do something the "quick & dirty" way, with the intent to "do it right" later.

    Source: Shore, James & Warden, Shane. The Art of Agile Development. Pg. 41, par. 4

19. Answer: A - a manual test coverage plan

    Explanation: Automation is a key component to XP, and automated test coverage plans are strongly encouraged.

    Source: Shore, James & Warden, Shane. The Art of Agile Development. Pg. 286, par. 5

20. Answer: C - Get a quicker return on their investment

    Explanation: By delivering functionality as early as possible, projects can begin getting ROI from the software faster than if we waited until the originally scoped software was complete to release it.

    Source: Schwaber, Ken. Agile Project Management with Scrum. Pg. 148 – 149

21. Answer: C - A minimal marketable feature

    Explanation: The smallest set of functionality that must be realized in order for the customer to perceive value is the correct answer. This is characterized by the three attributes: minimum, marketable, and feature.

22. Answer: B - As soon as it is done

    Explanation: Story cards are only used for the purpose of planning and are not meant to become a repository. Cards can be thrown away after they have been translated into acceptance test scripts or as defined as done.

23. Answer: A - The Pareto Rule of 20%

    Explanation: "By de-scoping early, we focus on the Pareto Rule of 20% of the work providing 80% of the value." Source: Alan Shalloway, Guy Beaver, James R. Trott. Lean-Agile Software Development. Pg. 132, par. 5

24. Answer: D - Product manager and customer coming up with ideas…

    Explanation: Participation activities can be motivated from product manager perspective or a customer perspective. From the product manager viewpoint, participation can build support for activities. It can also be used to keep the customer informed about the teams activities, and facilitate useful information exchange about the project status.

25. Answer: B - Allow the self-empowered team to resolve the situation…

    Explanation: The daily stand-up meeting is not another meeting to waste people's time with sidebar discussions. Communication among the entire team is the purpose of the stand-up meeting. A self-empowered team must be responsible for facilitating these guidelines, and not expected to be managed for them.

26. Answer: A - By removing uncertainty about technology

    Explanation: Spike stories assist in reducing the risk of a technical problem and can increase the reliability of a User Story estimate. When a technical unknown threatens to hold up, quickly developing a solution to the problem can reduce the technical risk.

    Source: Shore, James & Warden, Shane. The Art of Agile Development. Pg. 268, par. 6

27. Answer: D - Adding new items to the iteration backlog

    Explanation: The customer is not allowed to change iteration backlog once an iteration has started.

    Source: Schwaber, Ken. Agile Project Management with Scrum. Pg. 12, par. 1

28. Answer: C - Incremental, Negotiable, Valuable, Estimable, Small, Testable

    Explanation: A well written story is Incremental, Negotiable, Valuable, Estimable, Small and Testable.

29. Answer: A - that it allows the team to think of use cases that may have been overlooked.

    Explanation: It encourages the team to go into detailed conversations about finding additional ways actual users would use the system.

30. Answer: A - Make sure that the product is technologically shippable at any moment

    Explanation: "The point is to be technologically ready to release even if you're not functionally ready to release."

    Source: Shore, James & Warden, Shane. The Art of Agile Development. Pg. 183, par. 8

31. Answer: C - The end-result that the customer values and successful completion criteria.

    Explanation: 1. "They describe an end-result that the customer values, not implementation details."

    2. "Stories have clear completion criteria." Source: Shore, James & Warden, Shane. The Art of Agile Development. Pg. 265, par. 7

32. Answer: B - Risk is reduced because the length of the development time is shorter

    Explanation: Risk scales with scope and project duration. The Waterfall approach to delivery risks the complete loss of investment, whereas Agile projects aim to deliver incremental value as early as possible. As a result, Agile reduces risk by maximizing the probability of getting some ROI.

33. Answer: D - Introduce them to the Agile manifesto

    Explanation: In order for the Team to embrace Agile they must first acquire a solid understanding of what it's designed to accomplish, and that's laid out in the Agile Manifesto. "The practices are an expression of underlying Agile principles. Unless you understand those principles intimately--that is, unless you've already mastered the art of Agile development--you're probably not going to choose the right principles."

    Source: Shore, James & Warden, Shane. The Art of Agile Development. Pg. 10, par. 2

34. Answer: A - The amount of work that must be repaid toward bug fixes at the end of project...

    Explanation: James Shore provides this great explanation of technical debt: "When a team is working under pressure, they take shortcuts that compromise design quality. It's like taking out a high-interest loan. The team gets a short-term boost in speed, but from that point forward, changes are more expensive: they're paying interest on the loan. The only way to stop paying interest is to pay back the loan's principle and fix the design shortcuts."

    Source: Shore, James & Warden, Shane. The Art of Agile Development. Pg. 41, par. 4

35. Answer: D - Tuning a process to meet the needs of a specific project

    Explanation: "Software tailoring refers to the activity of tuning a standardized process to meet the needs of a specific project."

36. Answer: A - Keep the team focused on delivering value

    Explanation: Seeing their hard work keeps the Team focused on delivering value and allows the stakeholders an opportunity to see the work. It is a great benefit of the Iteration. Source: Shore, James & Warden, Shane. The Art of Agile Development. Pg. 138, par. 7

37. Answer: C - Estimate them just like any other user story or product backlog item

    Explanation: Estimate them just like another other time consuming task.

38. Answer: A - Feasibility and chartering, scope, benefits, key dependencies, constraints, risks...

    Explanation: "The project team shares the information gathered during the feasibility and chartering exercises, including scope, benefits, key dependencies, constraints, risks, and the release schedule."

    Source: Smith, Greg & Sidy, Ahmed. Becoming Agile in an Imperfect World. Pg. 201 para. 2

39. Answer: B - product manager

    Explanation: "The product manager represents the voice of the customer and is accountable for ensuring that the Team delivers value to the business."

    Scrum (development) - From Wikipedia, the free encyclopedia

40. Answer: A - Tell the product manager that the velocity of two separate teams cannot be compared

    Explanation: The product manager should be made aware that in Agile, different teams will have different levels of expertise, experience and team objectives. As a result, this will make each teams velocity unique. Therefore, attempting to compare velocities between different teams is like trying to compare two different units of measure.

41. Answer: B - Self-empowered and self-organized

    Explanation: A high performance Agile team is a committed team that has the right people, has been effectively empowered, has established trust and works at a sustainable pace to deliver quality software of a quantity that reflects a consistent high velocity factoring in influences such as capacity and customer support." Building High Performance Teams: AgileBok.org

42. Answer: B - They both place a high value respect and courage

    Scrum Values

    Respect

    Commitment

    Focus

    Courage

    Openness


    XP Values

    Simplicity

    Communication

    Feedback

    Respect

    Courage

43. Answer: D - it should be avoided whenever possible

    Explanation: "I have some good news. You can instantly improve productivity by reassigning people to only one project at a time. Fractional assignment is dreadfully counterproductive: fractional workers don't bond with their teams, they often aren't around to hear conversations and answer questions. and they must task switch, which incurs a significant hidden penalty." See also: Source: Shore, James & Warden, Shane. The Art of Agile Development. Pg. 40, par. 5

44. Answer: C - During the retrospective meeting

    Explanation: Retrospectives are used to look back at the previous iteration, discuss what went well, what didn't and find ways to increase value delivered on project. Source: Slinger, Michele & Broderick, Stacia. The Software Managers Bridge to Agility. Pg. 166 para. 4

45. Answer: A - Value Stream Mapping

    Explanation: Value stream mapping is a Lean technique used to "optimize the whole" by identifying waste. Source: Alan Shalloway, Guy Beaver, James R. Trott. Lean-Agile Software Development. Pg. 18, par. 2

46. Answer: A - Inform the team that conflict is a natural part of being a high performance team...

    Explanation: On high performance Agile teams conflict is natural and unavoidable. One of the best things to do is try to increase the number of positive interaction in comparison to the negatives ones, but a ratio of at least three to one. Source: Adkins, Lyssa. Coaching Agile Team. Pg. 222 para. 4

47. Answer: C - Agree upon a unit of measure for the story

    Explanation: Stories allow individual teams to define what unit of measure they will use to quantify story points. Therefore, the first thing they need to do is decide on the measurement of a story point. Source: Cohn, Mike. User Stories Applied. Pg. 87 para. 1

48. Answer: B - The value of melting down a gold coin

    Explanation: Intrinsic Value: The value of melting down a gold coin.

    Extrinsic Value: The value which arises out of an agreement.

    Market Value: What others are willing to pay.

    Book Value: The legally defined value.

49. Answer: C - Return on investment of the project

    Explanation: One of the outputs of the release planning session is being able to estimate the value and cost of features required for a project. With this information stakeholders will be able to get a better idea of their return on investment. Source: Alan Shalloway, Guy Beaver, James R. Trott. Lean-Agile Software Development. Pg. 126 - 128

50. Answer: A - During the review meeting

    Explanation: A Review meeting signifies a formal end to an iteration and focuses the team into completing functionality, which they can demo to the stakeholders. During the demo, if performance is of important value to the the stakeholder, the review meeting would be an ideal time to perform a demonstration of that feature.

    Source: Smith, Greg & Sidy, Ahmed. Becoming Agile in an Imperfect World. Pg. 269 para. 2

51. Answer: A - Knowledge sharing

    Explanation: "In Agile processes, knowledge sharing is encouraged by several practices: release and iteration planning, pair programming and pair rotation, on-site customers in case of XP, daily Scrum meeting, cross-functional teams, and project retrospectives in Scrum." Knowledge Sharing Support in Agile Processes - in AgileBOK.org

52. Answer: B - The smooth flow of work-in-progress from one team member to another

    Explanation: "Cooperation features the smooth flow of work-in-progress from one team member to another and between the team and the wider organization." Source: Adkins, Lyssa. Coaching Agile Team. Pg. 231 para. 2

53. Answer: A - Plan at the latest responsible moment

    Explanation: "To plan at the latest responsible moment, use a tiered set of planning horizons." Source: Shore, James & Warden, Shane. The Art of Agile Development. Pg. 216, par. 5. See also: Planning at the Last Responsible Moment

54. Answer: C - Cross-functional, collaborative and knows how to resolve conflict
    Explanation: Cross-functional, collaborative and knows how to resolve conflict is the best description of an Agile team from the list.

55. Answer: C - Visibility, inspection, adaptation

   Explanation: Visibility, inspection, adaptation. Source: Schwaber, Ken. Agile Project Management with Scrum. Pg. 3 – 4. See also: Empirical process (process control model) - From Wikipedia, the free encyclopedia

56. Answer: C - Making changes to code without changing the external behavior

   Explanation: "Disciplined technique for restructuring an existing body of code, altering its internal structure without changing its external behavior"

   Fowler, Martin (1999). Refactoring. Improving the Design of Existing Code. Addison-Wesley

   See also: Code refactoring - From Wikipedia, the free encyclopedia

57. Answer: A - Physically increases brain functions

   Explanation: Sitting next to someone will not cause your brain to grow (hopefully). All of the other options are true.

58. Answer: B - Estimate how much work a potential developer can perform

   Explanation: "The main idea behind velocity is to provide a lightweight methodology of measuring the pace at which a team is working and to assist in estimating the time needed to produce additional value in a software. Measuring velocity also helps in providing additional information about a team's performance over time."

   Velocity - From Wikipedia, the free encyclopedia

59. Answer: A - A, B, C, D

   Explanation: The team should pick the same number of story points that would equal their known velocity. Going over would place them at risk of not meeting their deadline, and selecting too few would create waste.

60. Answer: B - A Backlog

   Explanation: A Backlog list is a high-level, dynamic list of requirements for the system or product being developed. It is maintained throughout the life of a product by the product manager. It aggregates backlog items such initial estimates of requirements, prioritization, and complexity factor. The Product Backlog is the "What" that will be built, sorted by importance. Source: Schwaber, Ken. Agile Project Management with Scrum. Pg. 10, par. 1. Learning Scrum - The Product Backlog - Mountain Goat Software

61. Answer: D - Burndown chart

   Explanation: A burndown chart provides a graphical representation of the amount of work left to do versus time.
   Source: Schwaber, Ken. Agile Project Management with Scrum. Pg. 11, par. 3
   See also: Burn down chart - From Wikipedia, the free encyclopedia

62. Answer: A - Increase the ROI of the project

   Explanation: One of the benefit to the Agile methodology is that it allows product managers to adjust their Return On Investment (ROI) based on current state of their requirements, or on information they may not have been aware of at the start of the project.

   The other answers are not the best choices because of change to the release schedule doesn't imply a change to the requirement specification requirement specification, quality of the project or level of risk incurred by making the change. Source: Schwaber, Ken. Agile Project Management with Scrum. Pg. 8-9, par. 4 See also: Return On Investment (ROI) - From Investopedia

63. Answer: D - Daily Stand-ups

   Explanation: The daily standup is not the place for problem-solving or issue resolution meeting. When issues are raised they are taken offline and dealt with by relevant team members immediately after the standup. During the daily standup, each team member provides answers to the following three questions: What did you do yesterday? What will you do today? Are there any impediments in your way? Source: Shore, James & Warden, Shane. The Art of Agile Development. Pg. 131, par. 4. See also: Patterns for Daily Standup Meetings - From Martin Fowler. See also: The Daily Scrum Meeting - From Mountain Goat Software

64. Answer: B - Incremental delivery

   Explanation: Incremental delivery allows teams to complete the features most important to the business. It also allows them to reduce risk by demonstrating working features to customers early in the projects to receive feedback. Source: Schwaber, Ken. Agile Project Management with Scrum. Pg. 42, par. 3. See also: Incremental Delivery Through Continuous Design - MSDN Magazine

65. Answer: A - Empirical process control

   Explanation: A key principle of being Agile is its recognition of the frequent changes that increase the complexity of software development. As such, it adopts an empirical approach that accepts that the "problem of change" by focusing on maximizing the team's ability to deliver quickly respond to change. Source: Schwaber, Ken. Agile Project Management with Scrum. Pg. 2, par. 5. See also: Agile Project Management with Scrum By Ken Schwaber (Google Books)

66. Answer: D - Acrimony

   Explanation: The best Agile Coaches are team players who receive their satisfaction from facilitating other's, and view their teams success as their own. That's because the Agile Coach is not the team leader but rather the team facilitator and buffer from outside influences. Source: Schwaber, Ken. Agile Project Management with Scrum. Pg. 25 – 26

67. Answer: D - Defined process control

   Explanation: "The defined process control model requires that every piece of work be completely understood. Given a well-defined set of inputs, the same outputs are generated every time."

   Defined process - From Wikipedia, the free encyclopedia

   See also: Source: Schwaber, Ken. Agile Project Management with Scrum. Pg. 2, par. 5

68. Answer: D - rework

   Explanation: "The three legs that hold up every implementation of empirical process control: visibility, inspection, and adaptation." Source: Schwaber, Ken. Agile Project Management with Scrum. Pg. 3, par. 1

69. Answer: C - Visibility, inspection and adaptation

   Explanation: "The three legs that hold up every implementation of empirical process control: visibility, inspection, and adaptation." Source: Schwaber, Ken. Agile Project Management with Scrum. Pg. 5, par. 2

70. Answer: A - 3

   Explanation: The 3 roles are Product Owner (product manager), Scrum Master (Agile Coach) and Team

   The Product Owner represents the voice of the customer and is accountable for ensuring that the Team delivers value to the business. The Team is responsible for delivering the product.

   Scrum is facilitated by a Scrum Master, also known as an Agile Coach, who is accountable for removing impediments to the ability of the team to deliver the sprint goal/deliverables." See also: Source: Schwaber, Ken. Agile Project Management with Scrum. Pg. 6, par. 4

71. Answer: B – The team

    Explanation: Once the Team commits to completing a set of features for an iteration, it is their responsibility to achieve the goal. Source: Schwaber, Ken. Agile Project Management with Scrum. Pg. 7, par. 1

72. Answer: C - The Agile coach

    Explanation: "The Agile Coach is the enforcer of rules." See also: Source: Schwaber, Ken. Agile Project Management with Scrum. Pg. 7, par. 1

73. Answer: B - The product manager

    Explanation: The product manager (Product Owner) represents the voice of the customer and is accountable for ensuring that the Team delivers value to the business. Source: Schwaber, Ken. Agile Project Management with Scrum. Pg. 7, par. 1

74. Answer: C - By placing the requirements with the highest probability of highest ROI toward the top

    Explanation: The feature list is prioritized so that items most like to generate value are placed toward the top, then further divided into releases. Source: Schwaber, Ken. Agile Project Management with Scrum. Pg. 8, par. 1

75. Answer: A - undetermined

    Explanation: Setting the length of an iteration can be quite confusing because there is no set rule. XP advocates 1 week iterations while Scrum uses 30 consecutive days. The length of your iteration should be determined by the amount of uncertainty on the project--and then timeboxed. In other words, the more uncertainty there is, the shorter the iterations should be. This allows you to opportunities to get feedback from your customers, users and stakeholders to correct any misunderstandings. All the same, timeboxing iterations is crucial so that you do not spend all of your time trying to plan for the unknown. See also: http://jamesshore.com/Agile-Book/iteration_planning.html; Schwaber, Ken. Agile Project Management with Scrum. Pg. 8, par. 2

76. Answer: C - A timeboxed 8 hours

    Explanation: The key word in this question is timeboxed. Ideally, iteration planning meetings are timeboxed into eight hours, however, teams may go longer or short. The important thing is that you have a specific time to the meetings least you get stuck in planning mode. Source: Schwaber, Ken. Agile Project Management with Scrum. Pg. 8, par. 2

77. Answer: D - In the first 4 hours of the Iteration Planning Meeting

    Explanation: During the first four hours of the iteration planning meeting, the product manager and Team selects as much of the feature list can be delivered for the upcoming iteration. Review meeting is incorrect because the purpose of that meeting is to review/demonstrate what the team developed during the previous iteration. The other options are incorrect because they reference specific points in the project which can not be determined based on the question. Source: Schwaber, Ken. Agile Project Management with Scrum. Pg. 8, par. 3

78. Answer: B - The feature list contains the tasks required to complete the upcoming iterations,...

    Explanation: The Customer creates a list of features they would like delivered in their product. This list of features is typically called a backlog. The list of features, or backlog items, are then prioritized according to the needs of the customer and order in which the team agrees to work on them. The benefit to this approach is that it allows the customer to reprioritize as needed, while ensuring the team is always working on the highest priority items.

79. Answer: A - The Daily stand-up

   Explanation: Each day during the iteration a project status meeting occurs. This is called a daily standup. The guidelines for this meeting are to provide feedback on: What have you done since yesterday? What are you planning to do today? Any impediments?

80. Answer: C - A review meeting

   Explanation: The review meeting is an opportunity for the team to:

   1. Review work that was completed and not completed

   2. Show completed work to the stakeholders using a demonstration

   Source: Schwaber, Ken. Agile Project Management with Scrum. Pg. 8, par. 1

81. Answer: D - Work with the Team by conducting a retrospective

   Explanation: "The sprint retrospective meeting is held at the end of every Sprint after the sprint review meeting." See also: Source: Schwaber, Ken. Agile Project Management with Scrum. Pg. 9, par. 1

82. Answer: A - The retrospective

   Explanation: The retrospective is a time to reflect on what worked, what didn't work and how processes can be improved. These activities are more closely aligned with inspection and adaptation. The iteration planning meeting is a good answer but not the best answer because that activity would be better aligned with the visibility leg of the empirical process. The other two options are made up.

83. Answer: D - the team

   Explanation: Only the Team is allowed to make changes to the Backlog. Source: Schwaber, Ken. Agile Project Management with Scrum. Pg. 12, par. 1

84. Answer: D - A vision statement that explains how the product will benefit the team

   Explanation: The vision is defined during the initial planning of the project. Source: Schwaber, Ken. Agile Project Management with Scrum. Pg. 68, par. 2

85. Answer: D - Group inspection of the work individuals accomplished the previous day

   Explanation: Group inspection of the work individuals accomplished the previous day is something that would be discussed during the Daily Planning meeting. The Iteration Planning meeting is geared more toward group discussions about defining and prioritizing the work that will be done for the next iteration.

86. Answer: A - Facilitation

   Explanation: The Agile Coach role does not represent one of authority, but rather one of a leader and facilitator. Source: Schwaber, Ken. Agile Project Management with Scrum. Pg. 30, par. 5

87. Answer: C - Inform her Team that they should attend the event as requested by the CEO,…

   Explanation: While the Agile Coachs job is to protect them from impediments, it is also the Agile Coach's responsibility to operate within the culture of the company. Source: Schwaber, Ken. Agile Project Management with Scrum. Pg. 32-33

88. Answer: D - A visceral understanding of collective commitment and self-organization

   Explanation: In order for Scrum to truly be effective, the Team must truly embrace the values and practices of Agile to where they no longer function as individuals, but rather as one.

   Source: Schwaber, Ken. Agile Project Management with Scrum. Pg. 48 par.5

89. Answer: C - It enables them to reduce complexity to manageable levels

    Explanation: Like Sashimi, project functionality should be neatly sliced into easily manageable pieces for each team member to work on. YUM! Source: Schwaber, Ken. Agile Project Management with Scrum. Pg. 55 par.2

90. Answer: C - Managing the team during the Daily Standup meeting

    Explanation: The Agile Coach does not manage, rather, they lead and facilitate. Source: Schwaber, Ken. Agile Project Management with Scrum. Pg. 53

91. Answer: D - Which action items will be assigned to team members after each retrospective

    Explanation: Retrospectives are dynamic and driven by the event of the previous Sprint, so being able to assign tasks in the Sprint planning is not possible. Source: Schwaber, Ken. Agile Project Management with Scrum. Pg. 67

92. Answer: A - A vision and feature list

    Explanation: If a customer can provide a vision that describes what features their product should have, then they have enough information to start an Agile project. In fact, all they really need is feature list to start an Agile project. All of the other options can play a part in the project but they are not required to get an Agile project started. Remember, in Agile…"Less is More".

93. Answer: C - It can be changed once the iteration has started

    Explanation: The feature list is frozen until the end of the iteration. Source: Schwaber, Ken. Agile Project Management with Scrum. Pg. 136 par. 9

94. Answer: D - The size of the requirement relative to the others

    Explanation: It would be too early to nail down the exactly complexity of each requirement at the start of the project, so the starting point should be to just identify the size of each requirement relative to each other. Source: Schwaber, Ken. Agile Project Management with Scrum. Pg. 70 par. 3

95. Answer: D - The preliminary estimates provided to stakeholder…

    Explanation: Estimates are not contracts. As information is acquired adjustments may need to be made to ensure that the team is always working on items that will deliver the most value (ROI) to the customer. Source: Schwaber, Ken. Agile Project Management with Scrum. Pg. 72-73

96. Answer: A - A feature list

    Explanation: All that is required to start an Agile project is a simple feature list. As such, it should be the first artifact created to get the project moving. The other artifacts may be used on Agile projects as well, but the goal is to keep our Agile toolbox light and avoid as much Big Design Up Front (BDUF) as possible.

97. Answer: D - How closely the project is moving in accordance with the initial project plan

    Explanation: How closely a project is moving according to a plan is information typically captured in periodic management reports. Scrum, however, focuses on reporting about exceptions to the plan and how those exceptions could impact the project. Source: Schwaber, Ken. Agile Project Management with Scrum. Pg. 86 par. 1

98. Answer: C - rigid

    Explanation: Rigid is the total opposite of Agile. Source: Schwaber, Ken. Agile Project Management with Scrum. Pg. 86 par. 3

99. Answer: D - A Gantt Chart

    Explanation: A Gantt chart is a traditional reporting tools designed to show how well a project is going according to initial plan. Since Agile actively embraces change, Agile reports are geared more toward tracking the changes and exceptions that impact the project plan.

100. Answer: D - Program Evaluation Technique Reviews that took place during a iteration

Explanation: Change reports summarize the changes, inspections and adaptations that took during a Sprint. Source: Schwaber, Ken. Agile Project Management with Scrum. Pg. 87 par. 1

101. Answer: C - Offer to provide a Change report instead, and request that the review meeting…

Explanation: An Agile Coach is responsible for protecting the team and making sure they are not interrupted. All the same, the Agile coach does not want to lose the support of the management team by not keeping them apprised of the development. A nice trade of to meet these needs is providing an interim-reporting mechanism. Source: Schwaber, Ken. Agile Project Management with Scrum. Pg. 95 par. 2

102. Answer: A - A production strategy that strives to improve business return on investment by reducing in-process inventory carrying costs

Explanation: Just in Time (JIT) is a production strategy that strives to improve business return on investment by reducing in-process inventory carrying costs. Risk management and release planning are not directly tied to JIT. In-process failover is a made up term.

103. Answer: A - It only works when everything is visible, and everyone can inspect the progress…

Explanation: This falls under the empirical process control: visible, inspection and adaptation.

Source: Schwaber, Ken. Agile Project Management with Scrum. Pg. 98 par. 2

104. Answer: A - It is unmanaged

Explanation: Self-organized teams create a plan that is used for them to work against, and manage themselves. Source: Schwaber, Ken. Agile Project Management with Scrum. Pg. 99 par. 1

105. Answer: A - A Scaled Project

Explanation: All of the other answers are made up. Source: Schwaber, Ken. Agile Project Management with Scrum. Pg. 119 par. 1

106. Answer: D - Include one member from the newly created additional…

Explanation: Source: Schwaber, Ken. Agile Project Management with Scrum. Pg. 122 par. 1

107. Answer: C - Input from users that are non-stakeholders

Explanation: Collecting input from non-stakeholders is the least important piece of information to collect from a daily stand-up. The purpose of the daily stand-up is to provide the team with an opportunity to share their status with one another and make necessary adaptations. Source: Schwaber, Ken. Agile Project Management with Scrum. Pg. 136 par. 2

108. Answer: A - The amount by which the future net cash flow will be discounted.

Explanation: The amount by which the future net cash flow will be discounted.

NPV the difference between the present value of cash outflows and cash inflows. By finding Net Present Value (NPV), a person can decide whether a financial investment is worth the cost. A positive value indicates a profit, whereas a negative value indicates a loss. Source: Martin C. Robert. Agile Estimating and Planning. Pg. 103, par. 1

109. Answer: C - Ideal Time

Explanation: Ideal time is an estimation that considers the time it would take to complete a task without interruptions. Source: Shore, James & Warden, Shane. The Art of Agile Development. Pg. 263, par. 2

110. Answer: B - Prioritize

Explanation: One of the ways an Agile team demonstrates a commitment to business values is by delivering features that produce the greatest returns for an organization. To do this, the product manager is expected to prioritize and combine features based on their highest return on investment. Accomplishing this requires that features are written with the least amount of dependencies between them. Source: Martin C. Robert. Agile Estimating and Planning. Pg. 25, par. 2

111. Answer: C - Relative prioritization

Explanation: Relative prioritization attempts to determine which features a product should satisfy, given the time and resources available, by weighing them on a relative scale. For example, a product manager and team will collaboratively decide the most important features by identifying which will bring the most benefits if implemented as well as the penalty incurred if not implemented, on a relative scale of 1 to 9. Source: Martin C. Robert. Agile Estimating and Planning. Pg. 117, par. 2

112. Answer: A - NPV is a measure of how much money a project can be expected to return...

Explanation: NPV (Net Present Value) is a measure of how much money a project can be expected to return in today's present value, whereas IRR (Return on Investment) is a measure of how quickly the money invested in the project will increase in value. Source: Martin C. Robert. Agile Estimating and Planning. Pg. 104, par. 2

113. Answer: C - 1 - 3 weeks

Explanation: While the length of an iteration can be of any length (as determined by the team), XP iterations are typically between 1-3 weeks. Sprints are normally 30 calendar days. Source: Shore, James & Warden, Shane. The Art of Agile Development. Pg. 42, par. 8

114. Answer: A - A retrospective

Explanation: Organizations often can't see their problems because they have worked around them and made them a regular part of the business culture for so long. To overcome this issue, retrospective meetings are held at the end of each iteration. A retrospective meeting can start by asking the participants questions about how they felt the last iteration went, what worked, what didn't, and more importantly, to use the 12 Agile principles as the guidelines for solutions.

115. Answer: A - minimum marketable feature

Explanation: The minimal marketable feature (MMF) is the smallest set of functionality that must be realized in order for the customer to perceive value. It can be characterized by the three attributes: minimum, marketable, and feature. A feature being something is perceived by the user as having significant value; where value may include revenue generation, cost savings, competitive differentiation, brand-name projection, or enhanced customer loyalty. "Marketable" meaning that it provides significant value to the customer. Source: Shore, James & Warden, Shane. The Art of Agile Development. Pg. 211, par. 1

116. Answer: D - stakeholder management

Explanation: The best answer here is stakeholder management. When there are high levels of uncertainty on your project, yet commitments still need to be made about deliverables, it is best to create multiple levels of horizontal planning to manage your stakeholder expectations. For example, if you have stakeholders that require solid commitments, the longer your detailed horizon planning should be. On the other hand, when there are high levels of uncertainty, the shorter your horizon planning will be. Source: Shore, James & Warden, Shane. The Art of Agile Development. Pg. 216 par. 4

117. Answer: D - All of them are useful

Explanation: When choosing a persona it is important to make sure the Team has enough market and demographic research available to truly represent the product's target audience. Even going so far as to associate a picture, with a solid persona definition, will allow everyone on the team to feel like they intimately know the persona instead of just referring to them as "the user". Source: Cohn, Mike. User Stories Applied. Pg. 38-39

118. Answer: D - create a risk census

Explanation: Answer A is incorrect because using scare tactics is not the way to motivate a team to meet their deadline. While B and C could be considered options this question does not does not mention anything that would infer that either of these answer are related to the problem of managing the impact of a catastrophe. Conversely, D is the BEST answer because the team is working together to build a risk census to deal with possible catastrophes. See also Shore, James & Warden, Shane. The Art of Agile Development. Pg. 228 par. 4

119. Answer: C - prioritizing

Explanation: Prioritizing the list of features is always the customer's main priority. The team is responsible for executing the work to get the features implemented. Feasibility studies would have taken place in the early stages of the project. And there is no official rule for who is responsible for providing refreshments—that can be decided be a game of Rock, Paper, and Scissors. So the answer is C. On the exam also look for the keywords customer and some version of "priority" in the answer if available. See also: Shore, James & Warden, Shane. The Art of Agile Development. Pg. 223, par. 1

120. Answer: C - Dooms day scenarios

Explanation: All of the options are valid during risk planning with the exception of C. Source: Shore, James & Warden, Shane. The Art of Agile Development. Pg. 230

# Exercise Answers

## Exercise 1 Answers

**Match the Description with the Role:**

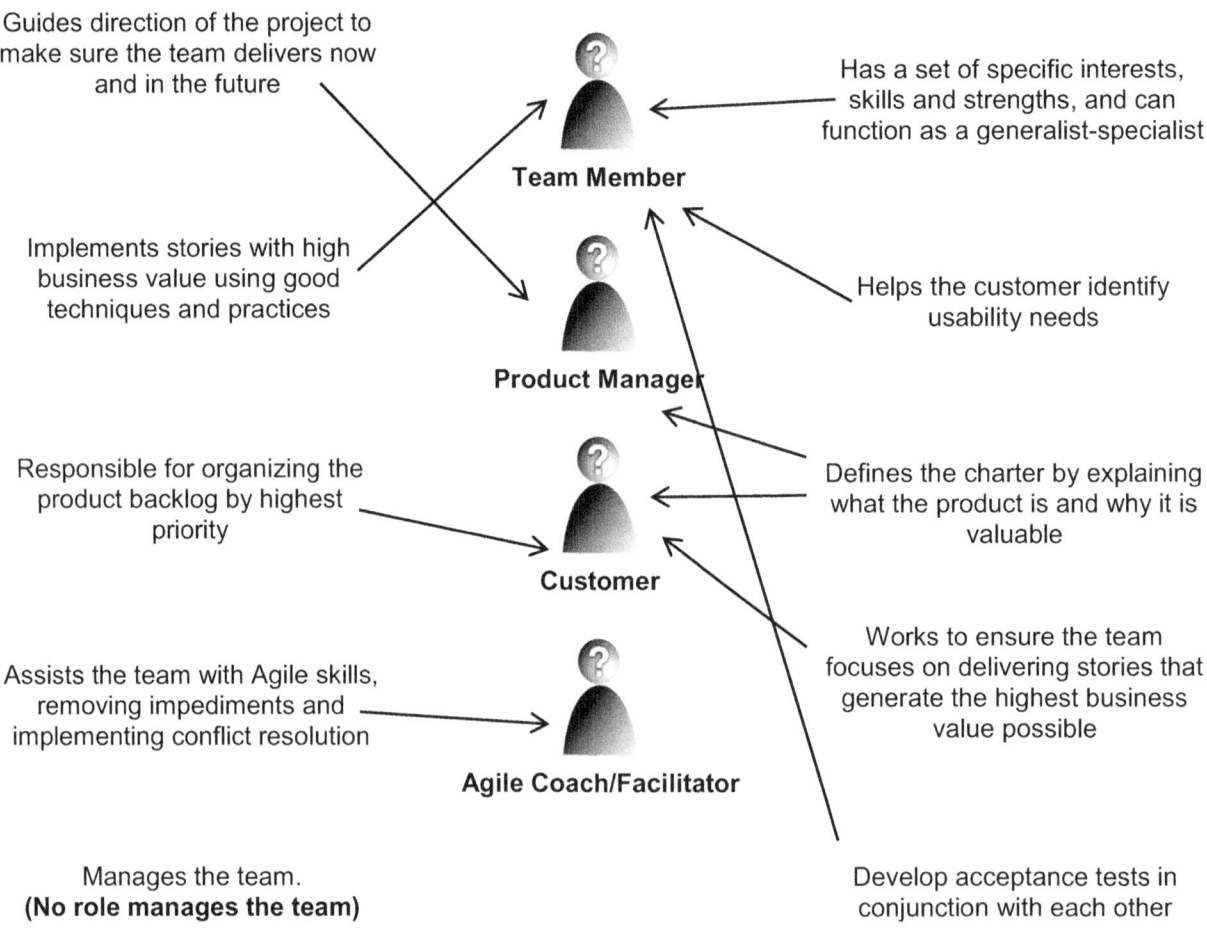

# Exercise 2 Answers

Identify the Top 3 High-Quality Project Deliverables You Would Recommend to Stakeholders to Get the Highest ROI and Explain Your Answers.

|    | Requirement | Priority | ROI% | Risk |
|----|-------------|----------|------|------|
| 1  | Add Content and Content metadata | 3 | 9.0 | Med |
| 2  | Administrator defines User Role |  | 14.0 | High |
| 3  | Administrator edits Roles assigned to CPS user (add/remove) |  | 16.0 | High |
| 4  | Administrator edits the actions that a Role allows |  | 15.0 | High |
| 5  | Assign a pricing Policy to an Asset | 1 | 10.0 | Low |
| 6  | Assign a Subscription Policy to a Channel or Channels | 2 | 16.5 | Med |
| 7  | Create a discount Coupon |  | 11.0 | High |
| 8  | Create a one-time-use Coupon |  | 12.0 | High |
| 9  | Create a Subscription Policy |  | 6.0 | Low |
| 10 | Create pricing Policy |  | 1.8 | Med |
| 11 | Link related Assets |  | 4.0 | Low |
| 12 | Load Content media files and images |  | 5.0 | Low |
| 13 | Use one-time-use Coupon |  | 13.0 | High |
| 14 | User logs into CPS Administrative System |  | 2.0 | Low |
| 15 | User logs out of the CPS Administrative System |  | 3.0 | Low |

Prioritizing based exclusively on ROI and risk should direct you to look for the features that have the highest ROI and lowest risk. While other features listed may have had higher ROI's then the indicated answers, they also have higher risk--and risk erodes value. Conversely, items with lower risk have lower ROI. In reality this type of prioritization would require many additional factors such as the probability of the risk and even a company's risk tolerance. For the exam just remember that you want to prioritize based on what the customer has indicated as being valuable to them.

# Exercise 3 Answers

**Match the Description with the Role:**

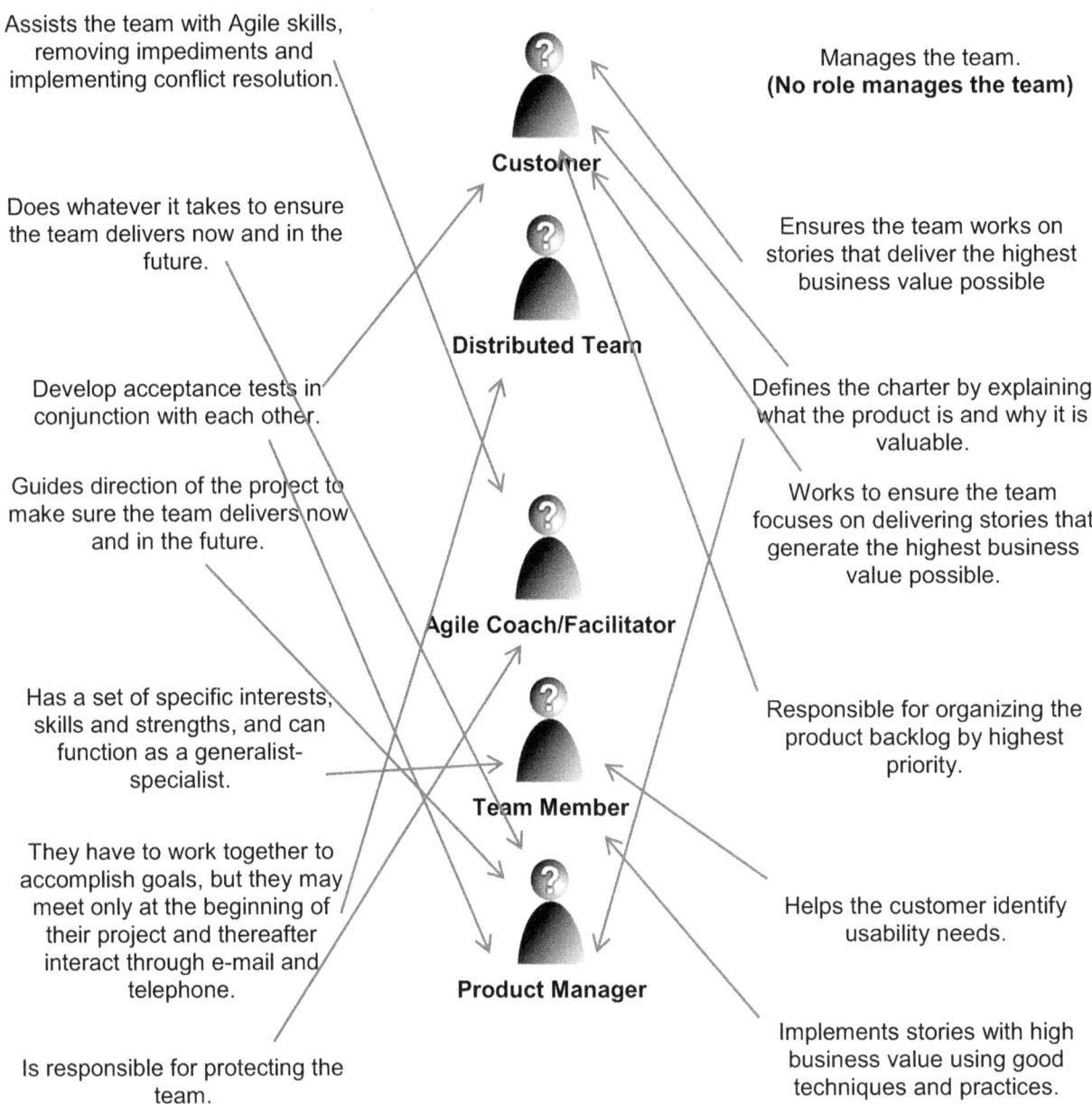

# Exercise 4 Answers

Describe the Purpose of the Following Agile Phases and Some of the Activities/Outcomes

| Product Vision | Product Roadmap | Release Planning |
|---|---|---|
| **Purpose:** Associated with a business need or direction<br><br>**Activities/Outcomes:** The vision is framed in the context of a strategy and associated goals. | **Purpose:** Defines the creation of a unique and valuable position as well as associated goals and objectives<br><br>**Activities/Outcomes:** The goal is to come up with a strategy that maximizes value retention by incremental and mutually reinforcing execution of the value chain | **Purpose:** Represents the large-grained delivery cycle in Agile development<br><br>**Activities/Outcomes:** Development team provides input for prioritizing the list of features. |
| **Iteration Planning** | **Daily Planning** | **Daily Work** |
| **Purpose:** A subsets of releases where the team's goal is to deliver potentially shippable software<br><br>**Activities/Outcomes:** Team signs up for user stories based on Iteration Velocity. | **Purpose:** Keeps the team is focused on completing the highest-priority features.<br><br>**Activities/Outcomes:** Group inspection of the work individuals accomplished the previous day. | **Purpose:** Product is integrated and tested on a daily basis.<br><br>**Activities/Outcomes:** Features marked as Done-Done; updates to Velocity burndown |
| **Demo** | **Review** | **Retrospective** |
| **Purpose:** Provides an opportunity for scope verification<br><br>**Activities/Outcomes:** Keeps the team motivated and stakeholders engaged by allowing everyone to see their progress. | **Purpose:** This provides the same purpose as the demo and the two are often combined.<br><br>**Activities/Outcomes:** This entails the same activities as the demo and the two are often combined. | **Purpose:** Can be used to engage stakeholders by asking them questions and identifying areas of improvement for the project.<br><br>**Activities/Outcomes:** Act on feedback from retrospectives. |

These can all have more than the single answer provided. The important thing to comprehend for the exam is the purpose(s) of the phase and expected outcome(s). Upon understanding this it will also make it easier to remember their sequences, and when/why certain phases may move out of sequence based on the needs of the project.

# Exercise 5

Describe the Tool/Technique Agile uses to Organically Address the Following Areas of Risk Management:

| Performing Quantitative Risk Analysis | Intrinsic Schedule Flaw | Scope Creep |
|---|---|---|
| Not required in Agile, but if performed it should be done during the release and/or iteration planning meetings. | Use the synchronization points in Agile, such as at the end of each iteration, to adjust the scope and priority of the features being worked on. | Incremental delivery through the use to short iterations allows the customer and team to adjust their processes and incorporate change requests more easily. |
| **Identifying Risks** | **Personnel Loss** | **Plan Risk Management** |
| This is handled iteratively during the planning meeting and results are recorded in a "spreadsheet" or on the white board. Risks are identified through assumption analysis before the team commits to an iteration or release. Teams that overly handle risk may place these items on a risk board. | When teams are allowed to self-organize and are self-empowered, there is less sense of helplessness and doom, which in turn increases morale. | The team determines the level of risk on the project, addresses how they plan to handle it, and documents (or not) their findings. |
| **Productivity Variation** | **Planning Risk Responses** | **Monitoring and Controlling Risks** |
| Use the synchronization points in Agile, such as at the end of each iteration, to adjust the scope and priority of the features being worked on. | Organically achieved through team discussions and planning meetings that are conducted to mitigate risks. Is also addressed in retrospectives where the team makes recommendations on how to improve the development process and throughput. | Risk reassessments are performed as part of planning meetings and retrospectives; retrospectives also provide the place to conduct risk audits. Burndown charts and task boards serve as highly visible information radiators to assist with monitoring. Evaluation of velocity in review meetings provides a place for technical performance measurement. |
| **Performing Qualitative Risk Analysis** | **Specification Breakdown** | **Other?** |
| Organically achieved through team discussions about the probability of risk impact that may occur during a project. Relies on team experience, expert judgment, and intuition to perform analysis. | Providing access to an Agile customer and product owner who can make decisions about immediate product situations. | |

# Exercise 6 Answers
Identify Existing Wasteful Process Elements by Challenging them with New Process Elements in Order Help the Organization become more Efficient

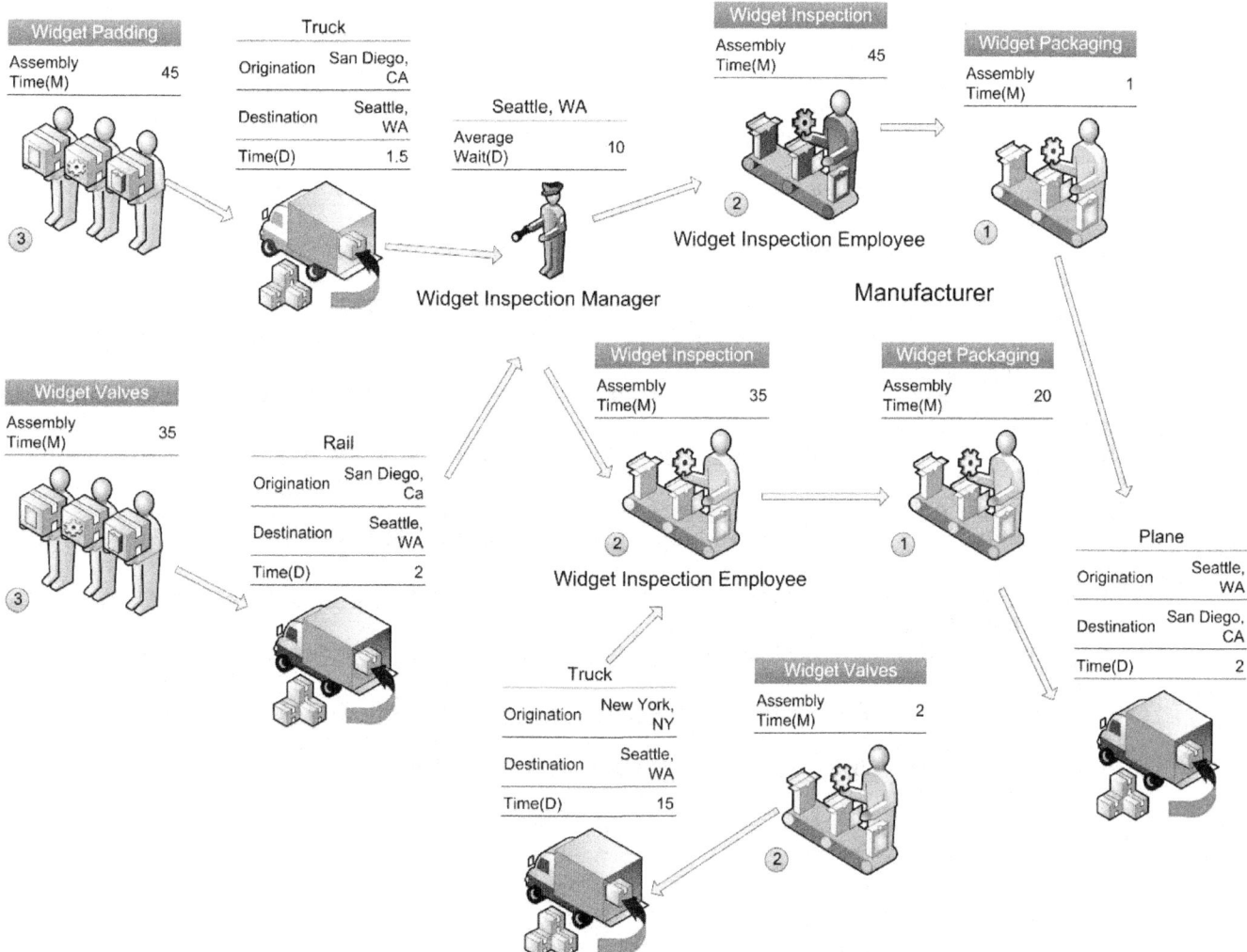

While there aren't enough details behind the rational for the current processes—giving way to numerous possible answers—the following indicators should have raised concerns about potential waste, and used as drivers for identifying opportunities of improvement:

1. Process 3: There is a duplication of Widget transportation from the same location to the same destination. (Duplication of work/transportation)
2. The 10 day inventory required by the widget inspector and the 45 day duplication of inspection by the widget employee. (Extended Inventory and multiple hand-offs)
3. Widgets originating from New York bypass the Widget Inspection Manager. (Variation in process)
4. Process 1: There is duplication of Widget packaging.
5. The product is being sent back to the origination San Diego, Ca. Maybe the entire process should be done in San Diego?

Image available for view online at: www.pmiacptraining.com/continuous_improvement/exercise5.hm

# Reference List

1. Ambler, Scott. <u>Agile Modeling</u>. New York, NY: Wiley Computer Publishing. 2002.
2. Adkins, Lyssa. <u>Coaching Agile Teams</u>. Upper Saddle River, NJ: Addison-Wesly. 2010.
3. Cockburn, Alistair. <u>Agile Software Development. $2^{nd}$ Edt</u>. Upper Saddle River, NJ: Addison-Wesly. 2007.
4. Cohn, Mike. <u>Agile Estimating and Planning</u>. Upper Saddle River, NJ: Prentice Hall Professional Technical Reference. 2006.
5. Cohn, Mike. <u>User Stories Applied</u>. Upper Saddle River, NJ: Addison-Wesly. 2008.
6. Hunt, Andrew and Thomas, David. <u>The Pragmatic Programmer</u>. Upper Saddle River, NJ: Addison-Wesly. 1999.
7. Jacobsen, Lisa. Alleman, Glen, B. and Deschenes, Stephane. <u>Managing Agile Projects</u>. First Edt. Ed. Aguanno, Kevin. Lakefield, Ontario: Multi-Media Publications, Inc.
8. Larman, Craig and Vodde, Bas. <u>Scaling Lean & Agile Development</u>. Upper Saddle River, NJ: Addison-Wesly. 2009.
9. Little, John. <u>The Warrior Within</u>. Chicago, IL: Contemporary Books. 1996.
10. Mangano, Vanina and Smith, Al. Jr. <u>PMP Exam Preparation Courseware</u>. San Diego, CA: Never Limited, Publishing. 2012.
11. Mangano, Vanina and Smith, Al. Jr. <u>PM-RMP Exam Preparation Courseware</u>. San Diego, CA: Never Limited, Publishing. 2010.
12. Mangano, Vanina. <u>PM-SP Exam Preparation Courseware</u>. San Diego, CA: Never Limited, Publishing. 2011.
13. Schwaber, Ken. <u>Agile Project Management with Scrum.</u> Redmond, WA: Microsoft Press. 2003.
14. Shore, James and Warden, Shane. <u>The Art of Agile Development.</u> Sebastopol, CA: O'Reilly Media. 2007.
15. Shalloway, Alan. Beaver, Guy and Trott, James. R. <u>Lean-Agile Software Development</u>. Boston, MA: Pearson Education, Inc. 2009.
16. Sliger, Michele and Broderick, Stacia. <u>The Software project manager's Bridge to Agility</u>. Upper Saddle River, NJ: Addison-Wesly. 2008.
17. Smith, Greg and Sidky, Ahmed. <u>Becoming Agile in an Imperfect World</u>. Greenwich, CT: Manning Publications Co. 2009.
18. Pyzdek, Thomas. <u>The Six Sigma Handbook</u>. New York, NY: McGraw-Hill. 2003

**We'd like to hear from you!**

Please send us your comments and suggestions to help us improve this courseware by registering your copy of this material. By doing so you'll also receive an additional access to the latest updates to the online version of this book and practice question. To register go to pmiacptraining.com/courseware_voc.html and use registration code: AMSA0R0812

# Visit www.OnlineSkillBuilder.com

# for additional practice exams, training material or earn Agile Project Management PDU's

CPSIA information can be obtained at www.ICGtesting.com
Printed in the USA
LVOW03s0043040915

452807LV00002B/20/P